Southern Strategies

Southern Strategies

Narrative Negotiation
in an Evangelical Region

Michael Odom

© 2024 University of South Carolina

Published by the University of South Carolina Press
Columbia, South Carolina 29208

uscpress.com

Printed in the United States of America

Library of Congress Cataloging-in-Publication Data
can be found at https://lccn.loc.gov/2023049645

ISBN: 978-1-64336-465-0 (hardcover)
ISBN: 978-1-64336-466-7 (ebook)

In memory of Gordon

CONTENTS

Acknowledgments ix

Introduction *Southern Strategies* 1

Part One Narrative Resistance

Chapter 1. Evangelical Authoritarianism
in W. J. Cash's *The Mind of the South* 13

Chapter 2. Deconversion and Redemption
in Lillian Smith's *Killers of the Dream* 35

Part Two Narrative Satire

Chapter 3. Evangelical Sales Culture
in Flannery O'Connor's *Wise Blood* 61

Chapter 4. Diagnostic Satire in Walker Percy's Fiction 77

Part Three Narrative Negotiation

Chapter 5. Descent and Vision in Dennis Covington's
Salvation on Sand Mountain 101

Chapter 6. Evangelical Whispers in Doris Betts's
The Sharp Teeth of Love 117

Coda *Narrative Reckoning* 133

Notes 143
Bibliography 159
Index 169

ACKNOWLEDGMENTS

This project took place over the course of a decade, involving many important people who helped me along the way. First, I want to thank Robert Brinkmeyer, whose mentorship not only demanded but also modeled scholarly excellence. I'm indebted to your influence and legacy. Thank you to Qiana Whitted for providing guidance and research opportunities at a critical time. Thank you to Catherine Keyser for encouraging confidence and challenging me to make my work more cohesive. I am grateful to Bruce Gentry and the Flannery O'Connor estate for the opportunity to work in the archives at the Ina Dillard Russell Library of Georgia College & State University. Thank you to Todd Hagstette for support and opportunities to hone my research and writing. Thank you to Conor Picken for being a great friend, advocate, and academic brother from whom I've learned so much. Last, I want to thank Aurora Bell for her interest and advocacy in my project; it's thrilling to finally release this book into the academic world, and your help made that possible.

Chapter 3 was adapted from the article "How to Win Friends and Convert People: Onnie Jay Holy and the Sales Culture of American Evangelicalism," originally published in the *Flannery O'Connor Review*, Volume 11 (2013). Used by permission from the *Flannery O'Connor Review*.

Chapter 5 was adapted from the article "Dennis Covington's Salvation on Sand Mountain: Descent and Vision in the Southern Memoir," originally published in *Southern Literary Journal*, vol. 46, no. 1 (Fall 2013). Used by permission from the University of North Carolina Press.

Special thanks to the Research Foundation of The City University of New York for subventionary funding on this project.

Introduction

Southern Strategies

The American South has long served as a site for identitarian fantasies. Throughout the twentieth century, the South functioned as the nation's region, a distinct "other" for critics to either discredit for terminal ignorance and racism or romanticize as a remnant of manners and traditional values. Fortunately, the new Southern studies subverts these essentializing tendencies with progressive perspectives on race and class that disentangle language and expand traditional boundaries. By highlighting the complexities of the region, the new Southern studies demystifies the South by expanding and contracting its borders, debunking myths of exceptionalism, and exposing how its documented inequities belong to the entire nation's legacy. Despite these advances, there remains a notable dearth in religious studies as a critical node for exploring the American South. In his influential study, *Finding Purple America: The South and the Future of American Cultural Studies,* Jon Smith concedes this point by lamenting how scholars in both American and Southern studies remain unfamiliar with the tenor of theological arguments that form the basis of contemporary conservative ideology. This scarcity is perplexing when considering that apart from race, religion constitutes the most vital signifier for interpreting Southern culture and history. Such disregard misses an opportunity to understand the social forces that shaped centuries of white supremacy rooted in a theological history.

This book aims to fill that void by studying evangelical Protestantism as a cultural conduit for exploring and understanding the American South. American culture was shaped in the mold of evangelical Protestantism: Its rugged individualism, anti-intellectualism, and general suspicion of institutions are hallmarks of evangelical influence. Evangelicalism marshals conformity through its talent to adapt and harness culture to its own ends. The Southern region embodies a microcosm of evangelical hegemony unrivaled in the rest of the United States.

Without question, evangelicalism has left an indelible mark on the Southern literary tradition. By tracing the primary role evangelical religion has played in shaping white Southern identity and its sociopolitical landscape, the subsequent chapters flesh out the tensions of white Southern writers who engage in narrative strategies to navigate the terrain of evangelical communities.

Evangelical comes from the Greek word *evangel* ("good news" or "Gospel"), which became associated with the revivals that swept across the nation during the eighteenth and nineteenth centuries. The term encompasses a consensus affirming the following practices: conversionism (identified as the "new birth" or "born-again" religious experience), biblicism (marked by a belief in the Bible as divinely inspired and authoritative), christocentrism (centered upon the person and work of Jesus Christ), and activism (commitment to sharing one's faith and living a spirit-filled life).[1] Richard Hofstadter marks the Great Awakening (ca. 1730–1740) as the beginning of the American evangelical movement that would largely define the nation's religious identity as democratic and anti-intellectual: "The awakeners were not the first to disparage the virtues of mind, but they quickened anti-intellectualism; and they gave to American anti-intellectualism its first brief moment of militant success. With the Awakenings, the Puritan age in American religion came to an end and the evangelical age began. Subsequent revivals repeated in an ever larger theater the merits and defects of the revivals of the eighteenth century."[2] The movement of evangelicalism into the South in the eighteenth century would prove transformational to a frontier region less educated and more inclined to emotional and ecstatic experiences.

Indeed, the zenith of American revivalism occurred in the South when, on 6 August 1801 in Cane Ridge, Kentucky, an extraordinary camp meeting ensued for a week that resulted in as many as twenty-five thousand people converting to Christianity, accompanied by ecstatic experiences that simultaneously blended and dissolved denominational differences in the region. Maryland-born Presbyterian minister Barton Stone, who would eventually lead the formation of Restoration movements such as the Disciples of Christ and the Church of Christ, came to Cane Ridge in the spring of 1801 to pursue the religious excitement of a New Birth movement led by other Presbyterian ministers like James McGready, who were also abandoning the doctrines of Calvinism of which they believed were providing hindrances to sinners seeking salvation. Cane Ridge marked white Southern identity as evangelical in its rugged individualism (excluding the social dimension) and emphasis on experience (rather than intellect). Such frontier revivals with circuit-riding preachers in the early 1800s became known

Introduction 3

as the Second Great Awakening, spreading a populist zeal and evangelical hegemony that lasted through the end of the century. From that moment forward, the Baptist and Methodist denominations, which embodied the evangelical spirit most, would dominate the region to the present day.[3]

The South's identity as a distinct region would continue to be based largely on its vision of itself as a bulwark of Christian morality. In addition to religion, the South's politics can also be understood as a manifestation that grew out of the region's revivalism in the nineteenth century. Revivalism stressed the centrality of individuals making life-altering decisions with the coaxing of demagogues who mastered the art of rhetoric and emotional manipulation. Religious historian Mark Noll asserts that the "great men and women of American evangelicalism have been those who knew best how to persuade." The voluntarism shared by evangelicalism and American democracy has been key among Southern religious culture to elicit assent in political persuasion. Religion and morality became indistinguishable in the South since, as Hill explains, they were one in the same: "To speak of morality and ethics in the setting of the American South is to draw attention to its churches. The most visibly religious region of the country looked to its ubiquitous churches and their pervasive evangelical Christian worldview for directives on how to practice godly living."[4]

Despite its dominant influence upon society and cultural institutions during the nineteenth century, American evangelicalism split over the issue of slavery. While northern evangelicals wrestled with modernist thought and industrialization resulting in many divisions and sociopolitical reforms, Southern evangelicals entrenched themselves in a closed society—a proud isolation enabling premodern thought and white supremacy to flourish. As northern evangelicals increasingly advanced reforms, emancipation became the most pressing issue of social justice; their assaults on slavery induced Southern evangelicals to codify a doctrine known as "the spirituality of the church," asserting that the church permitted no involvement with the state, thus foreclosing participation in social reform. As Frances Fitzgerald explains, Southern evangelicals were just as puritanical as their northern counterparts, but they focused almost exclusively on the individual's relationship with Christ to the exclusion of a social ethic: "Paradoxically, this intensely individualistic, asocial religion created an extraordinary degree of social cohesion among white southerners. It helped, of course, that the South was in many ways a homogeneous region—largely rural, largely agricultural, and largely composed of small communities, where relationships were face-to-face." By the middle of the nineteenth century, Southern Baptists and Methodists split from their general denominations over slavery, building schools and colleges to establish an evangelical consensus over the entire region. "By 1840," Fitzgerald concludes, "there was a South."[5]

Southern evangelical churches became, in the words of historian Charles Reagan Wilson, "the most effective morale-building agencies" during the Lost Cause period of 1865–1920. By sanctifying the virtues of Southern culture, churches consolidated support for states' rights in the face of centralized government. Wilson highlights how evangelicals aligned with the Democratic Party to create a civil religion of the Lost Cause movement wherein ministers sacralized the virtues of Southern culture in an attempt to consolidate support for the Democratic Party. Wilson's treatment of this period reveals how the "Solid South" sustained the greatest homogeneity of outlook and attitude in the region's history—made possible because of the religious authorization of its transcendent cause and status.[6]

In spite of the considerable changes occurring in the nation during the twentieth century, the South continued to display a remarkable conformity that can be attributed to the region's evangelical commitments. Such homogeneity would be tested during the 1920s, a disorienting period for evangelicals who became increasingly aware they were ideological strangers in their own land. The intertwining of culture and religion was no longer a given in the rest of the country, as the 1925 Scopes "Monkey Trial" in Dayton, Tennessee, cast Southern evangelicals as a national laughingstock. John Scopes was accused of violating the Butler Act, which prohibited the teaching of evolution in public schools because it violated the biblical account of creation. Garnering the attention of the national media (H. L. Mencken chief among them), legal scholars (Clarence Darrow) and prominent politicians (three-time presidential candidate William Jennings Bryan), the trial proved devastating for evangelicals in the court of public opinion. Consequently, evangelicals began retreating from the American public and political spheres to shore up their own and protect from the encroachment of modernist thought. As historian Randall Balmer notes, white evangelicals constructed an entire subculture comprised of "an interlocking network of congregations, denominations, Bible camps, Bible institutes, colleges, seminaries, missionary societies, and publishing houses"; because they deemed broader American culture corrupt, "the subculture provided a safe space, a refuge from the dangers of an increasingly secular society."[7]

Throughout the twentieth century, Southern white people embraced evangelicalism in the aftermath of humiliating cultural, political, and legal defeats to restore and repair their identity as moral people. Despite national trends of

Introduction   5

increasing secularization, evangelical hegemony continued to thrive in Southern culture. Writing in 1935, historian Edwin McNeill Poteat expanded the Solid South to include the region's singular religious orientation, noting that the "hold of orthodox Protestantism upon Southerners of the twentieth century is a likely explanation of why the section, in the face of earth-shaking changes in industry, transportation, and education, has kept its identity as the most conservative portion of the United States." Even during the height of the civil rights era, Southern historian Francis Simkins claimed that "faith in the Biblical heritage is a factor second only to White Supremacy as a means of conserving the ways of the South."[8]

While evangelicals were routed in the American culture wars of censorship, evolution, and prohibition in the early part of the twentieth century, the arena of politics after World War II afforded a broader coalition and punitive capacity in which to wield power. Evangelical engagement with American culture shifted dramatically, according to Kristin Kobes Du Mez, during the postwar era when "a potent mix of patriarchal 'gender traditionalism,' militarism, and Christian nationalism coalesced to form the basis of a revitalized evangelical identity"[9] During the Eisenhower era, evangelicals acquired powerful new allies in opposition to the social reforms of the New Deal and "godless Communism." With the additions of "In God We Trust" to currency and "one Nation, under God" to the pledge of allegiance, the civil religion of the 1950s cultivated a hospitable environment for evangelicals to mainstream their methods and identity. Evangelical appropriation of technology and media hype escalated in the crusades of North Carolina native Billy Graham, with his innovative preaching techniques and barrages of publicity and marketing. Evangelical parachurch organizations, unfettered by denominational boundaries, were empowered to engage political culture in profound ways; these organizations, what John Turner calls "religion gone free enterprise," would possess a unique vitality among the military, college students, and younger families by harnessing marketplace practices and creative technological usage. Evangelicals moved toward the center of American society in a virtual "baptism of American culture."[10]

Seeing the religious impetus behind the success of the civil rights movement, white Southerners sublimated their moral and cultural failures into evangelical churches that sanctioned counternarratives, revisionist histories, and opposition to racial progress. The Supreme Court's landmark *Brown v. Board of Education* (1954) ruling to desegregate public schools turned education into a political battleground for Southern white people. Most Southern private schools, also known as "segregation academies," were formed by evangelicals in the 1960s when the federal government began enforcing the desegregation of public schools in the Southern region that defied the Supreme Court's decision. Consequently, another Supreme Court decision, *Green v. Connally* (1972), removed tax-exempt status from private schools and colleges that discriminated against students on the basis of race. When Bob Jones University, a South Carolina evangelical college, had its tax-exempt status removed in 1975, Southern evangelicals began to feel a sense of embattlement. The threat of the federal government forcing desegregation culminated in the formation of the modern Christian right.[11]

Seizing an opportunity to reshape the political landscape, the Republican Party began employing a "southern strategy" for increasing political support of white voters by appealing to racism against Black people. Commencing as early as Richard Nixon's 1968 presidential campaign, the "Southern Strategy" involved slowing down desegregation, creating alternatives to public education, and appointing conservative judges; rhetorically couched in the language of states' rights, school choice, and vouchers, this strategy spawned a mass exodus of Southern white people to the Republican Party that accelerated over the next three decades, encompassing the most dramatic shift in political allegiance in the twentieth century. Ronald Reagan's election in 1980 revealed the permanent realignment of white evangelicals to the Republican Party, making the Southern Strategy complete. By the end of the twentieth century, the cultural hegemony established by evangelicals in the South began to circulate to the rest of the country. While early Southern scholars ranging from C. Vann Woodward to the Nashville Agrarians argued that with further assimilation the South would enrich the rest of American society with its virtues, later scholars such as Peter Applebome and John Egerton observed how the South's vices were, in fact, exported to the rest of the nation.[12]

Evangelicals now comprise the base of the modern Republican Party and remain the greatest organizing force among white conservatives. Evangelicals coalesce around right-leaning conservative politics, sensing a comprehensive and theological worldview that acknowledges innate sinfulness and the primacy of individual responsibility. Politics supply a public arena in which a sense of absolute rightness about the world, akin to religious orthodoxy, might be realized in an evangelical engagement with broader secular culture. Evangelicals revolt against intellectualism in American culture with a general suspicion of the mind and hostility to institutions hospitable to expertise, elevating emotional power and rhetorical manipulation above rationality—a legacy that continues in the current political and cultural landscape of conspiracy theories and seething

Introduction 7

resentments. Understanding the connection between evangelical religion and white identity helps illuminate paradoxes that plague cultural critics who wonder how a thrice-married, compulsively dishonest, philandering, reality television star and real estate mogul from New York could inspire a narcissistic personality cult among a subculture marked by outspoken faith, traditional family values, and obedience to Scripture.

My study investigates questions of culture and identity, and the degree to which Southern culture and whiteness have been shaped by evangelical religion. In this sense, I examine the theological underpinnings of white Southern identity as well as the authoritarian streak that animates conservative politics in the American South. The interplay between evangelicalism and Southern culture, along with the negotiation between individuals and evangelical community, creates fascinating tensions, which have been dramatized and given expression in great works of Southern literature. I have chosen pivotal authors in Southern letters who write about evangelical religion with an earnestness that matches the significance of their subject matter. These writers empirically perceived how evangelical religion was essential for making meaning and shaping Southern culture; moreover, their narrative strategies illuminate the complicated and often misrepresented history of poor Southern white people—those "deplorables" who are caricatured and dismissed with elitist scorn.

Writing critically about Southern religion can be polarizing. For skeptics and unbelievers, the Southern evangelical landscape evinces a minefield of social and professional consequences. For this reason, I find it beneficial to study different strategies employed by Southern writers who critically engage evangelical culture. This project is divided into three sections according to both genre and strategy employed by the particular Southern writers under discussion; each section includes two chapters. Because the narrative strategies of resistance, satire, and negotiation depend upon genre, my study of both fiction and nonfiction explores the array of strategies used to write about the evangelical South. Each genre offers distinct benefits in how Southern writers engage evangelical culture.

While the South is home to other religions, my study focuses exclusively on white evangelical culture found among Southern Baptists, Methodists, Pentecostals, and parachurch ministries that flourish in the region. Consequently, I do not treat other religious communities in the South, though there is some discussion of Anglo-Catholic communities as they relate to writers who grew up or embraced these respective denominations. Ultimately, this study aims to present a range of responses within a culture of evangelical hegemony where writers construct motifs to depict the South as a site of struggle for identity. With this in mind, I focus on texts that critically engage with such struggles to navigate religious communities as well as the religious crises that initiate a reexamination of entrenched beliefs and values.

In part one, I examine the narrative strategy of resistance by highlighting authors whose writings boldly confront not only the racist culture of the South but also the religious institutions that enabled white supremacy to flourish. The 1940s produced several landmark memoirs by Southern intellectuals who sought to transcend and critique Southern conformity fostered by evangelical community as well as the psychic violence that resulted from such an environment. These memoirs come to terms with a crisis of faith centered on race. While moments of racial awareness often center pivotal childhood experiences, these stories are recounted by an adult who has fled the South and metaphorically returned through the writing of the memoir. The literal and figurative separation enables these writers to write about not only race but also religion in a forthright manner.

My choice of authors, W. J. Cash and Lillian Smith, reflects a strikingly similar account of growing up in the evangelical South as emerging writers and intellectuals. Both writers embody the strategy of resistance by using narrative nonfiction and memoir to critique an authoritarian culture of white supremacy. In addition to the strategy of resistance, I explore the concept of deconversion narratives: the divesting of religious faith, triggered by intellectual and moral objections to evangelical religion. Both writers' own personal experiences with religious faith and doubt, as well as the costs and emotional toll of their opposition, prove significant in their discursive interventions. As we shall see, their resistance posed actual risks to their safety and well-being. The rhetorical strategies employed in these works of creative nonfiction pose challenges, particularly when writers attempt to find new language and discourse for a new system of belief and ethics. Such struggles with language and values strike me as central to the literary works treated in my study.

Part two examines satirical depictions of evangelicalism with an aim to display a more oblique approach to writing about Southern religion. Both Flannery O'Connor and Walker Percy, two pillars of Southern religious fiction, satirize the officialdom of late capitalist American consumption and the antithetical imperative of evangelical Christianity subsumed within the same culture. Both writers employ dialogical parody through their use of language and protagonists who

Introduction 9

struggle with opposing ideologies. In both O'Connor and Percy, we see parody of secular intellectuals and positivists, salesmen and swindlers, evangelists and backwoods prophets. These conflicting frameworks decenter readers, revealing compromise and incoherence in both ideologies.

O'Connor famously remarked that while the South may not be Christ-centered, it is most certainly Christ-haunted; she was keenly aware of how the region constructs its worldview in theological terms. Both writers embody an insider-outsider status as Catholics who grew up, lived, and wrote about the evangelical Protestant South. Despite sharing many essential convictions and doctrines with evangelicals, Catholics have historically been perceived suspiciously in the South. This outsider status informed how each writer saw and wrote about an evangelical region that served as home. The detached comical tone of fictional satire presents a strategy that proves critical yet disarming: The earnest faith of both writers affords them credibility as well as a receptive audience. Both O'Connor and Percy present a Southern culture that is saturated with a self-assured evangelicalism; despite sharing many theological convictions with evangelicals, they did not refrain from satirizing the obvious distortions in the South.

These writers of narrative satire reveal an adaptable, thriving Southern evangelical culture that successfully mainstreamed its ideology within postwar American capital and consumption—a compromise warranting satirical scrutiny in their fiction. These chapters provide analysis of O'Connor and Percy novels with the aim to trace the mainstream emergence of evangelical culture in the postwar American 1950s and 1960s, and the subsequent political coalitions that would spawn in the 1970s and 1980s, which exert considerable influence today. Historical context provides a view of the South as a region that comfortably combines conspicuous consumption, patriotism, and evangelical fervor. Correspondence in both authors' letters, essays, and interviews demonstrate a far more critical assessment of the evangelical South that has been neglected by scholars.

After covering nonfiction in part one and fiction in part two, part three explores both genres in two works of 1990s Southern literature that illustrate a more compassionate and creative approach to writing about evangelical religion. Drawing from nonfiction and fiction, I examine the participatory orientation of works premised on immersion and experience as a mode of writing the self into the religious culture of the South. Dennis Covington and Doris Betts depict conversion and deconversion narratives where struggles between faith and doubt are mirrored by recalling past events and illustrated through geographic mobility. Both writers embody the narrative strategy of negotiation by complicating categories and blurring boundaries.

A key feature of part three is to contrast the strategies of these latter works with former approaches; consequently, I discuss examples from memoir (contrasted with part one) and fiction (contrasted with part two) that reveal a propensity to engage evangelical religion with more curiosity and compassion. It should be noted that the contrast resides in how the religious South is depicted, not in the region's abiding religious proliferation. In all these texts, an evangelical South is as much a given as a hot summer. By depicting evangelical culture more sympathetically and embracing redeemable qualities, these latter works redefine spirituality and reconfigure approaches to matters of the body and spirit with the aim of providing a sense of community, vision, and selfhood.

Part One

Narrative Resistance

Chapter 1

Evangelical Authoritarianism in W. J. Cash's *The Mind of the South*

The Mind of the South expresses the anxiety of a Southern intellectual coping with the pressures of living in a community of conservative conformity. Upon its fifty-year anniversary, Louis Rubin extolled W. J. Cash's tour de force as a "virtuoso performance, a one-man show, written out of [an] author's impassioned identification with and revulsion at the South, and both its existence and the form it assumes are a testimony to the powerful hold of the South's community identity upon so many of its citizenry." Perhaps Rubin's commendation can also be understood as an act of solidarity, acknowledging Cash's masterpiece as a dramatization of an old Southern custom: the love-hate relationship Southern intellectuals have with their own culture.[1]

Cash initially published his critique as a 1929 essay in the *American Mercury,* leveling a harsh depiction of Southerners that validated H. L. Mencken's infamous attacks upon the South as a terminally ignorant region. Cash employed biblical metaphors to dramatize the high stakes of independent thought among a culture of evangelical conformity. Regarded as "an enemy of the people," Cash contends that a thinker in the South, by default, will "repudiate the whole Southern scheme of things, to go outside God's ordered drama and contrive with Satan for the overthrow of Heaven."[2] With such hyperbolic imagery, the essay was immediately successful, leading to a publishing contract with Alfred Knopf for a book-length study that would not be completed until 1941.

During this twelve-year period, a profound shift occurred in Cash's understanding and treatment of the Southern mind. This pivot was illuminated in Robert Brinkmeyer's *The Fourth Ghost* (2009), a study that features Cash as one of many Southern writers during the 1930s and 1940s haunted by the specter of European Fascism and its parallels with the conspicuously authoritarian culture present in the American South. Working as a journalist in the frightening milieu of the 1930s, Cash observed these parallels, noting how ideology marshals cultural conformity in authoritarian societies. As Brinkmeyer points out, the 1929 essay depicts Southerners as imprisoned by their own ignorance, while the 1941 book depicts Southerners as "prisoners of authoritarian forces."[3] Cash came to realize that authoritarian ideology was a more compelling causal explanation for Southern conformity when considering how the poor economic conditions of the South rarely led to class consciousness and discontent among lower- to middle-class white people. With the indoctrinated, white Southern "man at the center" now serving as the subject of his book, Cash posited the ideological construction of a "Proto-Dorian bond" of white supremacy by the wealthy class to palliate poorer white people to ignore their own economic inequality and embrace a virtual caste system. Moreover, Cash's study demonstrates how evangelical religious culture serves as the primary ideological underpinning for the South's authoritarian cultural establishment—a phenomenon unmatched in other regions of the United States.

Hannah Arendt's 1951 masterpiece, *The Origins of Totalitarianism,* remains a standard in political theory for understanding how ideology ensures mass conformity. Arendt states that ideological consistency persuades masses through simplistic and holistic senses of comprehension rather than facts. In an arresting passage, Arendt argues how persuasion is achieved by constructing a world of consistency, an initial step for securing authoritarian power: "Before they seize power and establish a world according to their doctrines, totalitarian movements conjure up a lying world of consistency which is more adequate to the needs of the human mind than reality itself; in which, through sheer imagination, uprooted masses can feel at home and are spared the never-ending shocks which real life and real experiences deal to human beings and their expectations." Arendt's description of ideological consistency as a means of asserting mass conformity fits the description of Southern culture, where evangelical religion has played a primary role in communicating a transcendent ideology to ground Southern politics with a sense of moral superiority as well as a higher calling.[4]

Anne Goodwyn Jones discusses the primacy of ideology at work in *The Mind of the South,* noting how the text "can be read as a systematic and careful study of the ways ideology works to maintain the power of the ruling class." According to Jones, Cash not only exposes the ways in which ideology constitutes how Southerners conceptualize reality, but he also uses *The Mind of the South* as a form of ideology itself. The effect, Jones writes, is to make the reader aware of ideology by showing historical representation as a form of invented narrative, thus tearing down the boundaries between history and fiction. Instead, Jones concludes that Cash "sought a rearticulation of the relation between 'fact' and 'fiction'—a new ideology, with more progressive effects than the old, grounded in a more congruent relation between reality and representation." By exposing the faulty separations of fact and fiction, Cash's aim was to combat the Southerner's capacity to "deny reality and live in fantasy." This ideological framework proves helpful in understanding Cash's depiction of Southern minds manipulated by religious ideology.[5]

Cash recognized the human agency of narrative to construct history by framing ideas and events into a coherent ideology. Narrative comprises a conscious construction of language to inscribe experience within a localized context and its underlying values. According to Kent Puckett, narrative "results from the effort to make real or imagined events and objects meaningful in relation to one another."[6] In narrative theory, representation is central to understanding what H. Porter Abbott refers to as "the difference between story (the event or sequence of events) and discourse (how the story is conveyed)."[7] Since history itself becomes accessible only through narrative, human agency and intervention, Linda Myrsiades asserts, are "made possible by the self-reflexivity of narration, which actively forms the subject position." Myrsiades refers to this discursive intervention as narrative resistance, a strategy that alters "the official singular story of domination [by] inscribing the local and the subjective into the process of time, liberating the local from oppressive uses of the past, and opening up interventions to create a future."[8]

An excellent example can be found in Laura Beard's *Acts of Narrative Resistance: Women's Autobiographical Writings in the Americas* (2009), which studies how female autobiographies resist and subvert established orders of patriarchy and racism. Drawing parallels between authors' lives and their respective narratives, Beard reveals how the genre affords realism, credibility, and urgency in an effort to overcome hegemonic structures. Narrative resistance is also codified by postcolonial scholars to highlight the use of native language and rhetorical strategies to subvert absorption into colonial culture.[9] In similar fashion, my approach in this first section arranges biographical details of Southern writers into a framework of religious experience to highlight their personal struggles in navigating evangelical hegemony. Foregrounding religious upbringings serves to authorize these authors' discursive interventions to not only resist but liberate themselves and others from oppressive ideology. While the writers of my first section are white, their strategies nevertheless resist white supremacy sanctioned by evangelical communities in the South. Through the self-reflexivity of narrative nonfiction, their strategies of resistance seek to reproduce social reality.

Resisting authoritarian ideology requires discursive intervention; therefore, Cash inscribed himself in the subject position to construct a different narrative with a different ideology. Cash's act of narrative resistance identifies evangelical Christianity as both an institution and ideology that marshals conformity in the political, cultural, and social spheres of the South. Exposing the harmony with which religion functions alongside conservative politics as a cultural dominant, Cash advances a narrative depiction of white Southerners as imprisoned to an authoritarian evangelical culture, in which their psyches split into public and private identities. Because Cash's book is more of an imaginative study based largely upon his own experiences as a white Southerner in the Carolina Piedmont rather than an intellectual history of the South, I begin by examining key moments in the writer's brief but tumultuous life to highlight the persistent struggle and resistance Cash endured with evangelical religion as a son, student, scholar, and Southerner.

Cash's formative years were permeated by evangelical religion. The conservative Carolina Piedmont provided him with firsthand experience of the religious authoritarianism of the South. Cash was born in the cotton-mill town of Gaffney, South Carolina, on 2 May 1900. Christened as Joseph Wilbur—the former name after his grandfather and the latter after a preacher his parents admired—it seemed that evangelical religion made its mark on Cash from the start. Cash would eventually reverse his initials to "W. J." as to signify his independence from his father who had the same initials. If there were any traces of religious doubts during Cash's childhood or adolescence, he did not indicate such to his parents. Biographer Bruce Clayton recounts how Cash surprised his parents at a very young age by announcing that he wanted to come forward to be baptized; being devoted Baptists, his parents objected on account that he was too young to make such a decision, that he had yet to reach the age of accountability when a person is old enough to accept Christ for personal salvation. The urgency to commit at such an early age was understandable, for as Cash later wrote in his correspondence with Mencken, the terrors of judgment were preached to him regularly as a child: "The keening of the five-o'clock whistles in the morning drilled me in sorrow. And for years, under the influence of the Baptist preacher's too graphic account of the Second Coming, I watched the West take fire from the sunset with a sort of ecstatic dread." His father, John, purchased him a student Bible when he was seven years old, a volume that was kept by Cash's side for the duration of his life; the King James Version was "rehearsed and reread" by Southerners of Cash's generation and "constituted a ponderable influence and made an incalculable impression upon the style and imagination of that generation." Wilbur grew particularly attached to the worldly wisdom of Ecclesiastes, a book that remained a favorite throughout his life. The first chapter encapsulates what would become the trajectory of Cash's own life: "Because in much wisdom there is much grief, and increasing knowledge results in increasing pain" (Ecclesiastes 1:18).[10]

At the age of twelve, Cash was moved to Boiling Springs, North Carolina, as his father accepted a partnership in a general store with Wilbur's grandfather. The town sat in the county seat of Cleveland and boasted a new academy, Boiling Springs High School, chartered by Baptists, where the young man received his formal education. As biographer Joseph L. Morrison documents, "Boiling Springs was an unexceptional and homogenous Piedmont country village. The town charter, granted the year before the Cashes moved there, reflected the conventional puritanism, prohibiting, among other things, the sale of cigarettes and the appearance of carnival shows lest the high-schoolers be exposed to undue temptation." Both of his parents, Morrison recounts, "remained anxious for the state of his soul while they waited for Wilbur to join the church as a little boy, but his parents had preferred to wait until he matured enough to consider his action, and now he kept them in suspense until he finally took his decision for baptism in high school." Cash's evangelical upbringing was appropriately sealed when the Boiling Springs High School commencement address of his 1917 graduating class was delivered by Reverend Walter Nathan Johnson; the Southern Baptist preacher assured the community that these young students knew the Scriptures which contained timeless truths to prepared them for their adult lives.[11]

Cash's father insisted that his son attend Wofford College, at the time a provincial Methodist school in Spartanburg, South Carolina. Despite Cash's protestations that he wanted to go to a real college rather than a "preacher's school," he attended for one year. His father relented the following year, allowing Cash to transfer to Valparaiso College in Indiana, which proved too cold for the young scholar. Eventually, Cash and his father settled upon Wake Forest, a Baptist college closer to home in North Carolina. Cash maintained that his father was unrelenting about him attending a religious school. Wake Forest was supported by the Southern Baptist State Convention's cooperative program whereupon a percentage of tithes and offerings given to the state's churches would be sent to the college to help train the next generation of Christian leadership. Wake Forest, it seems, provided just the right combination of intellectualism (afforded by some of its professors) and evangelicalism (among the general student population and the sectarian associations) for Cash to develop independently as a thinker while being constantly reminded of the pervasive religiosity that shaped Southern culture; it would be the perfect climate for the budding intellectual's deconversion experience. Despite Cash's exposure to evangelical religion, Morrison keenly observes how this Baptist college would be the place where the writer would "unlearn and discard the excess intellectual baggage of his boyhood. It was there that he began to probe and analyze the mind of the South."[12]

Among Cash's collegiate reading, Mencken proved inspirational. Mencken's most notorious essay about the South, "Sahara of the Bozart," published in *Prejudices* (1920) captivated Cash by ridiculing the South's religiosity and closed-minded ignorance. Mencken's catalogue of "boobery" highlighted in the Southern region summarized the values that Cash's father held most dear. After reading the explosive polemic, Cash became, in the words of Clayton, an "unabashed Menckenite." Clayton summarizes the essay's profound impact upon Cash's intellectual development and unlearning: "What many others in Dixie took as South-baiting in Mencken's tirades about the low state of 'Kulture' in the South, [Cash] took as bracing realism. Mencken's diatribes against fundamentalism, Ku Kluxery, bigotry, and southern narrowness pushed Cash toward intellectual liberation." Cash not only heeded the master's ideology, but he also imitated Mencken's prose style to such an extent that critics dubbed him "cotton-patch Mencken."[13] Fred Hobson's summary of Cash's writing prior to 1935 illustrates just how much the young reporter idolized and imitated Mencken, "It was as if the young newspaperman had read Mencken so often and had quoted him so frequently that the same words, the same rhythm, even at times the exact phrases reverberated in his mind; thus, when he sat down to write, in the years before 1935, he wrote pure Mencken. The words came from a different typewriter, but they were charged with the authority of the master."[14]

During Cash's tenure as a student, Wake Forest became a crucible of the many religion and science educational controversies during the 1920s when its president William Louis Poteat endorsed the teaching of evolution, embroiling the college in an ideological war of words with Baptist fundamentalists. Poteat served as a hero for Cash by challenging the dominant religious views of fundamentalism that narrowed the minds of Southerners by prohibiting them from alternative sources of knowledge outside of Scripture. Cash was among the many students in the class of 1922 who formed an angry coterie that rallied in support of their president by attacking the fundamentalists who opposed him. Morrison illustrates the overarching and deeply personal significance for Cash in defending intellectual freedom against fundamentalism:

Evangelical Authoritarianism   *19*

There was no question that in reviling the fundamentalists, Wilbur was in part acting out his rebellion against John Cash and his puritanical code. The same was true of his independence in the matters of smoking cigarettes [. . .] of drinking [. . .] He held in deepest contempt the orthodox among the students at Wake Forest, which then was pushing toward an enrollment of about a hundred older men who had come to the campus as Baptist preachers and were dubbed "skies" in consequence. Cash would hang out the dormitory window and regale passers-by, especially the "skies," with—delicious scandal of a Baptist campus—marathon quotations from the arch agnostic Colonel Robert G. Ingersoll.[15]

The culture war that ensued between Wake Forest and its fundamentalist critics proved an opportunistic time for Cash to write many combative, Menckenian editorials as co-editor of the *Old Gold and Black* student newspaper. His 13 February 1922 editorial echoed Mencken's South-baiting against his home state of North Carolina: "It is a desert—a barren waste, so far as the development of culture and the nature of the beaux arts are concerned, and North Carolina comes near being the dreariest spot in the whole blank stretch. In all the long years of its history the State hasn't produced a half dozen writers who might, by any sort of standard, be called worthwhile. Worse—it hasn't even raised up readers for books that others have written."[16]

Responding to the fundamentalist opposition to Poteat's support of evolutionary biology, Cash wrote a scathing 21 April 1922 editorial appropriately titled "Intolerance," mocking Baptists as anti-intellectual. "The forces of intolerance are never asleep," he proclaimed, employing clever metaphors derivative of evolutionary teaching to describe his fundamentalist opposition: "Conceived in the primitive slime of ignorance, it seeks to thwart and retard the march of truth and knowledge by playing upon fears of the credulous and the willful blindness of the prejudiced." A follow-up piece on 5 May 1922 titled "Possibilities," satirically suggested that the college replace Poteat with William Jennings Bryan (the famous populist politician who would in just a few short years become the object of derision in Dayton, Tennessee, as the chief prosecutor in the Scopes Monkey Trial) or Wilbur Glenn Voliva (who believed the earth was flat) as a fundamentalist successor. Cash's editorials in defense of Poteat were celebrated and publicized by regional newspapers such as the *Morning Herald* (Durham) and the *Times* (Raleigh), providing the young writer his first taste of what would be a mercurial career challenging the authoritarian ideology of evangelicalism in the South.[17]

Cash would continue to associate evangelical religion with anti-intellectualism as the chief culprit for the South's entrenched ideology; his views were certainly borne out through his own experience in Southern education beyond Wake Forest. In a letter to Mencken, Cash noted how working as an English teacher at Georgetown College (his first post after graduation), a Baptist institution in Kentucky during the 1923–24 academic year, revealed the necessity for him to separate from religious institutions: "There I lost such illusion as had survived college, suffered an incipient nervous breakdown, and discovered that I had no business in sectarian institutions." It seems Cash found little intellectual stimulation at what he deemed a "jerkwater" college. In the 1924–25 academic year, Cash tried his hand at secondary education, teaching at the Hendersonville School for Boys, a high school closer to home in North Carolina. These two years teaching secondary and postsecondary English only confirmed his views that the entire system of Southern education was anti-intellectual as he confided in a letter to the sociologist Howard Odum that very few students held "any genuine interest in the ideas that begin to circulate in them, and that the great mass is satisfied with football, rah-rah, and Commerce A."[18]

With his frustrations mounting about the South and its culture, Cash moved to Chicago to work for the *Post* as a reporter. The newspaper's downward spiral was immediately evident by its paltry circulation of 48,000. Cash returned to North Carolina in 1926 to work as a reporter for the *Charlotte News*. Returning home to the South, according to Clayton, "brought [Cash] daily reminders that religion permeated his world." Clayton's historical presentation of this pivotal juncture of Cash's life reveals the North Carolina Piedmont as an authoritarian South of evangelical conformity. Cash was expected to attend services at the Boiling Springs Baptist Church, and even the news media, by Clayton's account, betrayed evangelical expectations: "Articles on religion regularly dotted the pages of local newspapers, reminding folks that church membership or attendance was up or down (it was usually up) or that the Sunday school classes conducted by the town's leading citizens were always packed." To assert his independence, Cash would have to resist the assumptions of the culture that surrounded him on all sides.[19]

Before he would make his mark as a journalist, Cash had to reckon with a hyperthyroid condition that induced bouts of irritability and near nervous collapses. Seeking relief for these symptoms, Cash followed the advice of his physician to seek solace abroad in Europe in the summer and fall of 1927. As he bicycled and walked throughout the continent, Cash had two similar experiences when he beheld the beauty of French cathedrals. Chartres Cathedral in northern France invoked a profound emotional response, which he recalled to a friend: "As I stood looking at the magnificent blue lancets, and then at the rose window, I found myself crying. I didn't believe a word of the notions that inspired such a masterpiece, but I kept on weeping and damn-near dropped to my knees. At last I blew my nose hard and went out and walked around that massive structure and I started crying again." Strasbourg Cathedral in eastern France induced the same emotional response, leaving him perplexed "as to why, stepping out into the little square beneath the soaring tower of the great cathedral at Strasbourg, I should suddenly (and though some finer cathedrals had left me cold) have been stricken with a nearly irresistible impulse to burst out bawling—I can't tell you, for all my diligent searching of Freud." Cash's biographers offer little commentary on the religious significance of young Cash's confessed experiences. Morrison calls them a redress for the "overexposure to the Baptist fundamentalism of his youth."[20]

It is crucial to note how Cash, at the age of twenty-seven, who was raised by evangelical Baptists and well versed in the Bible, did not seek (by his own account) to understand in any theological sense these emotional encounters with religious monuments. While the sheer beauty of these cathedrals might be reason enough to induce such intense feeling, perhaps Cash was lamenting his inability to mentally assent to the religious beliefs in which he was indoctrinated as a child. Such beliefs would have provided Cash a tidy, interpretive framework for understanding his emotional response as he encountered these shrines for religious worship. One could also speculate that the sadness comes from the recognition that these houses of worship no longer bear any relevance to their original design; rather, they are merely tourist sites to see the ruins of history. Yet Cash eschews spiritual explanations in his recollection of the events in favor of modern psychological explanations, signaling an important shift in the young intellectual's perspective; his account evinces the deconversion he underwent at Wake Forest, where he unlearned and discarded the evangelical worldview of his Baptist childhood. As Clayton observes, the young man's "emancipation from religious orthodoxy had begun at least as early as his college days, and it may have begun much earlier." Morrison perhaps best captures how Cash's own "self-education, in college and after, was devoted to unlearning virtually every tenet of 'Southern patriotism' that had been taught him in those early days of the century."[21]

After his extended trip abroad, Cash returned to the *Charlotte News* to write book reviews and weekly editorials titled "The Moving Row." The journalist's column afforded him the opportunity to write critically about the "mint julep school of southern historians" that romanticized the Old South and to take swipes at conservatives whenever he saw examples of political autocracy and cultural intolerance. One example is a 25 March 1928 editorial ("What Constitutes Decency?") in which Cash lampoons a controversy generated by local fundamentalists in Greenville, South Carolina, who were protesting the public display of a plaster-cast replica of the Apollo Belvedere—an ancient depiction of the Greek god releasing a death-dealing arrow—whose genitalia were exposed. Cash relished the opportunity to exploit the protesters' evangelical obsession with sin, nakedness, and shame, as he hyperbolically summarizes their position: "The statue would corrupt youth, wreck homes, lure fair Greenville down the poppy path to the ignoble doom of Nineveh and Tyre. So forsooth, they demanded that Citizen Apollo either go in the ashcan or put on pants." Cash's commentary displays an amusing mixture of biblical and mythological symbols in mocking the philistine sensibilities of local fundamentalists: "The Citizen Apollo, you understand, is a most immodest gent. He's naked—and how! Fig leaves wouldn't grow on the barren summit of Olympus." Cash uses the debacle to expose the fundamentalists' misunderstanding of the relationship between art and morality. Cash distinguishes morality, which is "concerned with those things which inspire actions, toward themselves, which may either be harmful or beneficial to the social body," from decency, which is "concerned with taste, with offenses against senses." Claiming that art is "essentially outside of morality," Cash explains how such responses of repulsion to aesthetic displays often reveal more about the beholder than the object: "Morality lies in the mind, not in the exciting agent." Cash contends that the real problem resides in the minds of repressed fundamentalists, who "may so react to the sight of a shoe, an umbrella, a pail, a dagger." Repression of desires in the puritanical mind creates a perverted attitude that perceives indecency in nude art, according to Cash. Instead of seeing beauty and form in the Apollo, the repressed fundamentalist sees only a phallus. As Cash explains, the Lions Club was able to alleviate public concerns, thus allowing the statue to continue being displayed in its original, nude form. Cash turns the tables on the fundamentalists in his conclusion of the matter: "Whatever of itself fixes interest of those things which arouse disgust and shock in the normal mind, free of over-emphasis on sex or any other bogey of society, is, I should say, indecent. Whatever does not do that is decent. The Apollo stands absolved."[22]

Cash found that cultural intolerance among Southern evangelicals also pervaded the political sphere with profound consequences. As his neurasthenic symptoms reappeared, Cash was forced to resign from the *Charlotte News* and move back home to Boiling Springs where he continued "The Moving Row" columns for the *Cleveland Press,* a biweekly country newspaper in his home county. His most striking coverage included the 1928 presidential election between Republican Herbert Hoover and Democrat Al Smith. Smith's Catholicism incited a cultural backlash among Southerners in North Carolina, as politicians, evangelical clergy, and the Ku Klux Klan all coalesced in a vitriolic attack upon the candidate's suspect non-Protestant faith. While Prohibition and immigration seemed to be the primary issues of the election, Clayton observes how Cash perceived the conservative positions as manifestations of a religious authoritarianism: "But the Klan's scurrilous attacks on Smith and the outraged utterances of Baptist and Methodist clergymen convinced him that the real issue in Cleveland County and North Carolina was religious intolerance and bigotry and that Prohibition, in particular, was a smoke screen that allowed the 'best people' to mask a bigotry the Klan openly espoused." Cash realized that evangelical religion was magisterial in Southern politics.[23]

When North Carolina Methodist Bishop Edwin Mouzon published a manifesto detailing Catholic persecution of Protestants and called upon the entire Methodist church in his jurisdiction to preach against the "lawless elements in the great cities against American civilization" that embodied Smith's candidacy, Cash used his column to savage the bishop and other religious leaders who disregarded the separation of church and state, charging them as supporters of a theocracy. Cash became embroiled in a war of words with local religious leaders and political figures; he had positioned himself as a maverick, and the locals of Boiling Springs (including his family) were without a doubt suspicious of the young intellectual. When Cash looked back upon the fall of 1928, he acknowledged later to Knopf that his columns involved him in a bitter fight with local authorities that he was not able to handle emotionally. "In that climate of hostility," Clayton writes, "young Cash needed all the psychic strength and courage he could muster. And in that region for a young native son, living in a home where truth was lodged in the Baptist church, the mills, and the Democratic Party to smite bishops, the Klan, and the Senator, would require extraordinary courage and emotional strength."[24] Ironically, when responding to Morrison's speculation that Cash likely overdramatized his fearless independence, Clayton echoes the Freudian sentiments that Morrison's earlier biography posited by attaching significance to the young Cash's rebellion against his evangelical father: "Killing the father(s) may be a prerequisite to becoming a man, as Freud said, but it can exact a heavy emotional price. If the price Cash paid was sickness, can the charge be sustained that he overdramatized his fearlessness or independence?"

During the fall of 1928, Cash had experienced a profound alienation among his own people in the religious South. Clayton's deft analysis of this period must be quoted at length:

> Religion honeycombed life. Prominent men taught Sunday School. Hoey's and Gardner's Sunday School class frequently attracted more worshipers than the sermon and service that followed. Piedmont pastors, usually Baptists or Methodists, occasionally Presbyterian, prayed over new store openings, county fairs, and high school football games. Such was normal and good; such was assumed, unquestioned, and thus honored by being taken for granted. And all this Cash had rejected. He had, mainly by his intellectual quest and journey, emotionally distanced himself from that world of religion, the world of his father and mother. Was he aware? Did he know how great, how unbridgeable, the emotional gulf had become between his psyche and that of his people, the very people he was trying to lead? If he knew—and one suspects that his knowledge was nine-tenths intellectual and still beyond his psychic understanding—if he knew, then he also knew that anyone who attempts to speak a critical word of truth in a land where the mind is mired in myth, illusion, and racial prejudice—and enveloped in religious certainty—was fundamentally at odds with the very people he would lead. If that truth-teller happens to have, as Cash did, a passionate, one might even say religious, need to speak the truth, the way is made straight for sorrow, perhaps for tragedy.[25]

Shortly after the presidential election (an expected Hoover landslide), Cash's symptoms returned, once again forcing him to quit the newspaper. The patterns of Cash's poor health already seemed to suggest psychosomatic elements, but an even heavier (and lengthier) cost would be exacted when he set to writing *The Mind of the South*.

It would be more than a decade between the appearance of Cash's essay in the *American Mercury* and the full-length book by the same title. This germination period during the 1930s saw Cash publish six additional essays in the *American Mercury* while writing editorials again for the *Charlotte News* exclusively on international affairs; the publisher hired Cash with explicit instructions that he was "not to write about local matters or state politics" after his firestorm coverage of the 1928 election.[26] One particular essay written in 1933 for the *American Mercury,* "Close View of a Calvinist Lhasa," embodies Cash's most devastating religious critique during this period and signals his recognition of evangelicalism's connection to authoritarianism. The essay portrays Charlotte, North Carolina, as an authoritarian society where God and Babbitry coexist harmoniously without question. As Cash muses upon the self-assured evangelical Calvinism embodied in the Southern city's Presbyterian history, he equates the denomination's signature doctrine of predestination with white supremacy: "They were enormously strait-laced, they looked upon industry and the getting of goods of pious exercises peculiarly pleasing to Heaven, and they had all the smugness, all the complacency and self-righteousness, natural to the belief that they were handpicked for Grace. They exhibited all these qualities in the measure common to their race." The doctrine of predestination functions as a manifest destiny, and Cash playfully uses biblical metaphors by comparing the untamed forest of the frontier as "pagan—the obvious symbol of Satan" to the wilderness wanderings of the Israelites—God's chosen people. "To mow it, to burn it in great heaps, to bend the earth to their will—that was at once to slake their lust for acquisition and to acquire favor on high. And the proof of that favor was that they prospered." Indeed, Cash keenly notes the convenience of the Calvinist doctrine that likens acquisition of land and wealth as a divine endorsement—a perfect theology for an authoritarian New South economy of Rotary and the chamber of commerce. Cash ironically asserts that such theology must be considered divine and therefore never to be question: "Theology and the hog literally make one flesh, and that, so far as the natives go, without any alloy of dreadful hypocrisy to sully their innocent confidence. To question Babbittry is to question God, and to question God is to question Babbittry." By satirically elevating the stakes, Cash reveals the way evangelical theology marshals conformity by imbuing business and politics with eternal implications.[27]

Cash asserts that the culture of Charlotte was "one continuous blue-law" of evangelical uniformity in not only deed but also thought: "One takes what the pastor of the First Presbyterian Church is thinking, one takes what the Duke Power Company is thinking, and one arrives at the editorial page of the *Charlotte Observer*—the very living mirror of the Charlotte mind and a catechism for all true believers. 'The Bible,' it appears, 'is the best textbook of biology.'" Cash indeed draws a disturbing picture of evangelical authoritarianism in Charlotte where the general mass of citizens are "chronically and greatly frightened—of themselves," and many pleasures and liberties must take place "behind the privacy of their locked doors"; consequently, "life degenerates to a dreary ritual of the office, golf, and the church—becomes nearly unbearably dull even for Presbyterians not wholly pathological." In many ways, "Close View of a Calvinist Lhasa" served as a dress rehearsal for *The Mind of the South*, affording Cash the opportunity to run through his ideas about evangelical authoritarianism enslaving the Southern mind in one particular city, which he would extrapolate on a grander scale in the published masterpiece of 1941.[28]

Cash finally completed his 800-page manuscript of *The Mind of the South* on 27 July 1940, accompanied by a cover letter to his publisher, Alfred Knopf, which reflects candidly upon the painstaking twelve-year process. Cash said that the pages of the manuscript were "written in blood," and included the most revealing detail as to why it took him so long: "I have never been able to approach the task of continuing it without extreme depression and dislike." Clayton speculated that each word was wrung from the writer's imagination, straining the writer's psyche along the way. The process was a "herculean task" that required the author to "plunge deeply into his feelings for an understanding of his people," a process all the more excruciating, Clayton observed, "because he had undertaken a sweeping critique of his own people." Cash's plight as a Southern artist was akin to William Faulkner or Thomas Wolfe, yet the stakes were higher in the nonfiction genre, exposing him to even broader scrutiny. Cash constructed a narrative history bearing the conspicuous marks of memoir that depicts the writer's upbringing as a Southern white in the Carolina Piedmont—experiences that he would often project onto the entire Southern region, much to the dislike of later historians who followed the lead of C. Vann Woodward's critique that Cash's thesis of singularity and continuity ignores the particularities and complexities of other souths. While he thoroughly researched everything he set down, Cash unabashedly acknowledged to Knopf "that ultimately the book is one man's view—a sort of personal report—which must rest in large part on the authority of my imagination and understanding at play on a pattern into which I was born and which I have lived most of my life." In a fifty-year retrospective, Clayton wrote that Cash was "thumbing his nose at professional assumptions, audaciously [seeking] to get at the very essence of the collective mind." Clayton asserts that by presenting the Southern psyche as "the prisoner of religiosity," Cash enacted a rude but artistic rejection of "the world of his mother and father and those who were bone of his bone and flesh of his flesh. No wonder he had trouble making himself sit down and write that book."[29]

By taking aim at the forces most complicit in fostering a closed society of white supremacy, Cash's narrative resistance presents a compelling framework for understanding the South's dominant evangelical culture. Throughout his uncompromising analysis, Cash traces the role of evangelical authoritarianism through issues ranging from slavery to race relations to cotton mills with the intent to subvert an established order. Using his own evangelical upbringing, Cash proffers a template for the South's religious pattern: Celtic by nature ("the chief blood strain"), susceptible to suggestions of the supernatural, and drawn to the anthropomorphic God of the Old Testament (*MS* 56).[30] Cash presents the Southerner as both romantic and hedonistic, his idle nature given to imaginings, flights from reality, and an overall self-absorption inducing him to inflate everything with a higher sense of purpose (*MS* 57). Cash contends that as the South evolved, the Southerner was repelled by intellectualism, refinement, understatement, and Stoic characteristics, resulting in a decline of Anglicanism; conversely, the religious Southerner was attracted to emotional, anti-intellectual, extravagant, gasconade, and individualistic characteristics, resulting in a rise of Baptists, Methodists, and Charismatics. The evangelical emphasis on a "personal God of personal salvation for the personal self" triumphantly emerged as the Southern religious orientation, set aflame by the great revivals and camp meetings of the nineteenth and early twentieth centuries (*MS* 58–59). Such a personal emphasis on religion would have significant ramifications in both the political and social realms.

As Cash notes, the South's religion and politics can both be understood as manifestations that grew out of the region's revivalism in the nineteenth century. With the coaxing of evangelists, revivalism stressed the importance of the individual in making life-altering decisions; as evangelical historian Mark Noll asserts, "great men and women of American evangelicalism have been those who knew best how to persuade." The same strategy was employed by demagogues who mastered the art of rhetoric and emotional manipulation to elicit political assent in democratic societies. Noll describes evangelical engagement in politics by using William Jennings Bryan as a prototype embodying populist ("spoken argument over published treatises"), activistic ("sought to protect community values through the exertion of individuals"), and mythmaking ("preferred ideals from the primitive past instead of patient examination of history in general") characteristics that prove immensely consequential in securing conformity among large groups of self-identifying conservatives.[31]

In a 29 April 1936 letter to Knopf, Cash made insightful observations concerning the primary role evangelical clergy play in assuring this type of mass conformity among white Southerners: "Since childhood I have had an unconquerable aversion to parsons because of their cocksure certainty in a world in which nothing is certain but that nothing is certain; because their professions have always seemed mawkish; and because their inquiries have always struck me as indecent: a man's soul, if he has one, ought obviously to be his own private concern." Clayton noted how such episodes as the clergy-led anti-Smith campaign in the 1920s demonstrated a conspicuous self-assurance as "confident parsons were even more intent on telling others how to live and think. When Cash wrote *The Mind of the South,* he maintained a consistently critical attitude towards preachers and religion, particularly their role in fostering a spirit of fanatical intolerance during the 1920s."[32]

Cash argues that evangelical religion also shaped Southern thinking about industry, capital, labor, and other economic considerations. Cash contends that evangelical doctrine enabled the god of "industry and capitalism" to reign supreme despite the adverse impact of disease, sickness, death, and retardation from the cotton mill. Local ministers chalked up these empirical evils as the byproduct of original sin; therefore, the lower- and middle-class workers never questioned the leaders of industry, for their businesses were "direct visitations from the hand of God" (*MS* 214). Illustrating the crucial role that evangelical religion played in preserving the South's traditional economic policies that were harmful to the very people who were members of the congregations, historian Charles Reagan Wilson explains:

> While southern religious leaders and their institutions had a sense of social responsibility, they believed in the preservation of the status quo. Social concern, in short, meant a conservative interest in the preservation of religious, political, societal, and economic orthodoxy. Thus the churches organized and agitated for moral reforms enforced by the power of the state, and they avoided any involvement in such social issues as the rights of labor, the poor, and Blacks. Ironically, the two dominant southern denominations, which had begun as dissenting, non-established sects, emerged as virtually the recognized religion of the South. They learned to use the state to gain their goals.[33]

Cash goes on to note how even pastors emerged as business owners in the New South with the "stamp of Babbitt upon them" (*MS* 228).

Cash's discussion echoes a contemporary Southern liberal journalist, Clarence Cason, who skewered Southern ministers that forged bonds with secular businessmen to strengthen their authority. In 1934, Cason satirically described scenarios of ministers dancing at country clubs and marking the turfs of golf courses with business tycoons to ensure his prominent position of influence: "Any slackening of the churchward procession in recent years has been compensated by a concourse of ministers around the festive noontide board of Kiwanis."[34] Using a business model, churches in the New South economic climate committed to the "bigger is better" mentality, competing with other churches in growth, size, organization, and revenue. The rich who tithed most were made deacons, according to Cash, despite being a "pirate in commerce" and displaying "unholy" character in public; as long as they gave public declarations of doctrinal adherence on essentials, they remained in good stead (*MS* 228).

Consequently, the Southern churches provided fertile ground for business by encouraging conservative policies and static social ranks. Leaders of business became more evangelical because the conditions "presented a nearly perfect stage for the working out of their personal ambitions—precisely because of the gathering perception that the southern mind was a bulwark for its preservation" (*MS* 229).

Cash observes how most evangelical leaders condemned those who pursued social justice. Alexander McKelway, a champion of child-labor laws in the South (and Presbyterian clergyman), was labeled an "un-Christian" class agitator who set brother against brother, violated parental prerogative mandated in Scripture, and usurped God's sovereignty to work things out in his own "due time" (*MS* 230). Cash highlights the materialistic self-interests of ministers who opposed labor unions, siding with captains of industry because they tithed the most money and therefore paid much of the ministers' salaries (*MS* 360–361). It is during this high time, according to Cash, that Southern evangelicalism equated the South, as both a region and an idea, with orthodoxy, thereby sanctioning laissez-faire capitalism, exploiting cheap labor, and becoming a sworn enemy of socialism (in both Europe and America). When it came to economic considerations, evangelicals championed the privatization of religious life away from any sense of social justice. Yet such privatization of religion would be conveniently ignored when it came to legislating their own brand of morality.

As the quid pro quo between ministers and businessmen continued, church and industry, eager to please one another, harmonized to form a Southern hegemony—a "decisive element" in evangelicals legislating their particular morality across the region of the South (*MS* 231–233). Evangelical morality was legislated to the entire Southern populace regardless of religious beliefs as evidenced in Prohibition and blue laws. Southerners would publicly support Prohibition, while privately consuming alcohol. The "clandestine" quality of a duplicitous life, according to Cash, became the "necessary ingredient of the highest enjoyment" (*MS* 233). Channeling the Apostle Paul (Romans 7:8), Cash suggests that the law of Prohibition deeply aroused the sensations of these secret sins of imbibing, creating an "exciting drama" (*MS* 233). Continuing in the Pauline vein, Cash argues that the drama unfolds as the guilty pleasures of the Southerner's private life likewise serve to bring about an even greater sense of sin, further heightening the emotional experience in "orgiastic" churches that dominated the South (*MS* 233).

The combination of a privatized religious faith and the authoritarian nature of evangelicalism fostered a split that subsequently emerged in the Southern religious psyche. According to Cash, the Southern psyche comprised two personas: the public puritan and private hedonist—a necessary compartmentalization of identity when confronted with palpable social pressures and expectations that come with being a Southerner in a religious community. Cash's analysis of the split-psyche is strikingly similar to Robert Louis Stevenson's celebrated allegory of *Jekyll and Hyde*. The Jekyll-Hyde motif of public moralist and secret sensualist—a necessary split of identity—served as a condemnation of the stifling authoritarian Calvinist culture of Stevenson's native Scotland. In Stevensonian fashion, Cash labels the "puritan" as the public moralist during the day and the "hedonist" as the private sinner lurking in the shadows of the night. Cash seems amazed at the parallel streams of contradiction present in the Southern psyche, a consequent tension resulting from evangelical hegemony. Cash states the duality of tensions—"streams" as he put it—ironically "could and would flow forward side by side, and with a minimum of conflict" (*MS* 59). Cash's analysis of the conflicting streams illustrates an unlikely coexistence in the face of stark contradictions; moreover, Cash contends the Southerner "succeeded in uniting the two incompatible tendencies in his single person, without ever allowing them to come into open and decisive contention" (*MS* 60).

Cash provides a profound psychological diagnosis of the Southern mind that would lay some important groundwork for Lillian Smith (who is examined in the next chapter) to further explore: "One might say with much truth that [conflicting streams] proceeded from a fundamental split in his psyche, from a sort of social schizophrenia" (*MS* 60). Theology served as the handmaiden of politics, as the South's duplicity fleshed out an "ostentatiously religious" diagnoses of class, whereby the Calvinistic doctrine of God's sovereignty (to encourage stasis) was combined with an Arminian doctrine of man's free agency and responsibility (to encourage hard work and economic upward mobility) that permeated the New South creed (*MS* 236). This theological duplicity is wrought with contradictions since no Arminian would affirm the former, nor would Calvinists affirm the latter. This absurd syncretism is just another manifestation of the split Southern psyche, an alloy justifying the Southern way of life. Oppressed individuals and groups among Southern society might have questioned the authoritarian status quo when faced with contradictory empirical realities; yet, as Cash continually demonstrates, poor Southern white people remained facile. Dualities of tension went unquestioned because of the power wielded over the Southern mind by evangelical culture. The exploitation continued by way of church and industry, splitting the Southern psyche in ways that could not be fully comprehended.

To better understand Cash's work in context, I find it appropriate to return to Clarence Cason to examine a contemporary who was also plagued by the authoritarianism of Southern society. Cason's *Ninety Degrees in the Shade,* a 1934 exposé of Southern culture, served as a forerunner to *The Mind of the South.* Like Cash, Cason was deeply troubled by the cultural conformity of the South that arrested any attempts at social justice. In his treatment of Southern religion and its role in sacralizing an authoritarian society, Cason argued that churches are "indeed so well integrated with the southern culture that they have become, in too many instances, powerful factors in support of southern complacency and resistance to social improvement when foreign influences are concerned." Cason observed how Southern ministers strengthened their authority by forging bonds with secular businessmen. Cason was troubled by the symbiotic relationship between religion and politics, observing how religious-political rhetoric constructs a form of psychosis where Southerners remain "under the delusion that their champions are fighting the battles of the common people." Musing on this "tragedy," Cason delivers a memorable close to his discussion of politics by looking to European Fascism and seeing the parallels in the American South.[35]

The troubling comparisons were drawn not only from the South's race relations, but also from its propensity to be controlled by persuasive rhetoricians who demagogue constituents by demonizing opponents as evil outsiders. Highlighting Southern political history, Cason writes, "One is almost forced to believe that a peculiar type of Fascism has been at work below the Potomac, although the southern states have not yet produced a Mussolini or a Hitler."[36] One fateful day in May 1935, inside his campus office at the University of Alabama, where he served as professor and chair of the Journalism department, Clarence Cason committed suicide with an automatic pistol—just days before *Ninety Degrees in the Shade* was to be published. Cash himself commented on Cason's suicide as a signifier of the anxieties one feels living in an authoritarian society: "Poor Clarence Cason, who taught journalism at Alabama, felt compelled to commit suicide, in part at least because of his fear of the fiercely hostile attitude which he knew that both the school authorities and his fellow faculty members would take toward his criticisms of the South in his [*Ninety Degrees*] *in the Shade,* published by the University of North Carolina Press a few days after his death" (*MS* 334). These words proved hauntingly resonant for Cash. On 30 June 1941, only a few months after *The Mind of the South* was published, Cash complained to his wife while in Mexico that Nazi spies were following him. After disappearing, Cash was found dead the next day, hanging by his necktie on a bathroom hook in the Reforma Hotel.

Some scholars believe that the proximity of Cash's suicide to the publication of *The Mind of the South* is no coincidence, despite the contrary claims of Cash's biographers. V. O. Key had Cash in mind when he famously remarked in his 1947 study, *Southern Politics in State and Nation*, that "a depressingly high rate of self-destruction prevails among those who ponder about the South and put down their reflections in books. A fatal frustration seems to come from the struggle to find a way through the unfathomable maze formed by tradition, caste, race, and poverty."[37] While Morrison and Clayton both dismiss Key's thesis, other notable scholars found something plausible in his estimation. Acknowledging the isolation of intellectuals in the Southern agrarian region, historian Bertram Wyatt-Brown argues that Cash seemed acutely aware of his own alienation from society and the consequences of his social criticism, resigning himself to gloomy conclusions. Wyatt-Brown argues persuasively that Cash's twelve-year process of writing *The Mind of the South* was an agonizing affair characterized by nervousness, depression, anxiety, and paralysis—all induced by the fear of rejection he anticipated from his regional homeland and in particular, his religious father:

> Having rejected the faith of his parents, the author, a stern moralist for himself and his region, no doubt found it hard to proceed in the vein of the biblical jeremiad. Perhaps it even further inhibited his progress in writing—his awareness of how disapproving the old man would be of his apparent perversity, by southern standards. For Cash was ridiculing "sin" in the manner of the old prophetic tradition upon which he was raised. The transgressions to which Cash referred were not the ones his father and other white men of the South would recognize. Rather, in Cash's anti-Baptist theology, they were racial bias, blind materialism, violence, and paganlike conventions—all offenses of a Bible-thumping culture, Christian only in the narrowest sense.[38]

Wyatt-Brown keenly notes the identification of Cash with the South he was criticizing—his inability to employ the air of scholarly separation and objectivity from his subject matter—was precisely what led to the mental anguish he internalized throughout the writing process. Hobson agrees with Key's observation, noting the connection between Southern criticism and self-destruction. In writing his seminal study, *Tell About the South: The Southern Rage to Explain* (1983), Hobson was struck by the fact that four of the subjects in his book (Edmund Ruffin, Hinton Rowan Helper, Cason, and Cash) committed suicide. Contending that these critics of the South appeared to self-destruct at their "most heightened moment of Southern self-awareness," Hobson observes that "three of the four suicides came at that moment—or just after it—when the writer had most deeply pondered the meaning of the South and his own identity as Southerner, and had gone on record with his feelings and conclusions."[39] Even though Cash's book initially received unanimous praise and minimal criticism, Rubin speculates that Cash must have felt some sense of postpartum depression that led the writer to reenact an internal struggle he anticipated would happen—yet never did—with the authoritarian Southern culture over which he obsessed. In the absence of an external struggle, Rubin continues, Cash may have decreed "his own persecution, convincing himself that Nazi spies were stalking him and about to close in on him."[40]

The suicides of Cason and Cash in such close proximity to publishing courageous critiques of Southern culture reveal the immense pressure of resistance in authoritarian societies; one can easily imagine the compartmentalization and anxieties with which each man lived, out of sheer necessity, in a region enforcing conformity in life and thought. Even if such oppression is imagined, catastrophized by depression, or enacted on a subconscious level, these desperate actions reinforce the profound conservative conformity that exists in Southern culture. Cash was not the only writer to publish nonfiction that resisted the authoritarian culture of the evangelical South. Lillian Smith would publish her provocative 1949 memoir that explored the oppressive culture of Southern evangelical churches by foregrounding its damaging impact upon childhood training and development. Like Cash, Smith would write from the authority of her own imagination and experience to further resist an evangelical pattern of thinking in the South.

Chapter 2

Deconversion and Redemption in Lillian Smith's *Killers of the Dream*

Over the course of three decades spanning the mid-1930s to the mid-1960s, Lillian Smith proved to be one of the most pivotal figures in Southern intellectual life. Her work, as Charles K. Piehl notes, is now regarded by historians to be a crucial bridge "from the [Southern] renaissance years into the turmoil of the civil rights revolution."[1] Smith's "mediating functions" were encompassed in her dual work as civil rights leader and writer, which she often described as the two parts of her nature by invoking a biblical story.[2] The tenth chapter of Luke's Gospel tells the story of Jesus and his disciples visiting the home of Martha (the sister of Lazarus, whom Jesus raises from the dead):

> She had a sister called Mary, who sat at the Lord's feet listening to what he said. But Martha was distracted by all the preparations that had to be made. She came to him and asked, "Lord, don't you care that my sister has left me to do the work by myself? Tell her to help me!"
> "Martha, Martha," the Lord answered, "you are worried and upset about many things, but few things are needed—or indeed only one. Mary has chosen what is better, and it will not be taken away from her." (Luke 10:39–42)

Smith was certainly not the first to appropriate the story as metaphor: The contrast of Martha and Mary has been discussed and recycled for centuries. Martha embodies the worker who tirelessly and practically tends to the business at hand, while Mary represents the artist-thinker type inclined to creativity. The story embodied the fragmentation of Smith's own personhood, the split-psyche that defined not only her work as a social reformer, but also her life. While Smith considered both of her roles critical, she valued her Mary side more; nevertheless, the Martha side kept her grounded and focused on the duties and obligations to her family. Smith's breakthrough—what she characterized as that human striving for wholeness—would come once she learned how to harness her creativity as a writer to engage in a lifelong struggle to reform the South and put an end to segregation. These two natures within Smith highlight her strategies to approaching the major issues facing Southerners, segregation, and herself; moreover, the concept of splitting and estrangement became a central motif throughout her writings—the origins of which were inspired by her Southern evangelical upbringing.

The previous chapter examined W. J. Cash's narrative depiction of Southern evangelical authoritarianism and its role in shaping the mind of white Southerners. *The Mind of the South* comprises a foundational understanding of the evangelical underpinnings of authoritarian ideology and its political impact. This chapter looks more thoroughly at the psycho-social consequences of an evangelical region by studying Cash's friend and advocate Lillian Smith, whose 1949 memoir, *Killers of the Dream,* undertakes a devastating social critique through the use of psychoanalysis and personal confession. In doing so, Smith expands upon Cash's resistance by portraying the evangelical South as an ominously constrictive environment, one posing a threat to her own sense of selfhood—and every other Southerner by proxy.[3]

Southern memoirs comprise a genre well suited for understanding narrative resistance; by exploring subjective identity in relation to an established cultural matrix, Southern memoirs offer the direct approach of an author inscribing personal agency to engage in social criticism while preserving the narrative qualities of fiction. As we saw in the first chapter, history itself is a narrative that often functions through oppressive uses of the past. The genre of Southern memoir comprises many examples of discursive interventions into history with the aim of either continuing or altering that narrative. The white Southern autobiographical tradition can be classified under Fred Hobson's "rage to explain" thesis, which illuminates why so many Southern writers were preoccupied with locating themselves both narratively and ideologically in relation to Southern culture. In *Tell About the South,* Hobson categorizes the Southern autobiographical tradition as divided largely into two groups and defined largely over the issue of race: the Southern party of remembrance found in the nostalgic conservatism of William Alexander Percy and Ben Robertson, and the party of guilt and shame exemplified by the outspoken liberalism of Katharine Du Pre Lumpkin and Lillian Smith.[4]

The textual exploration of "writing the self" functions as a resolution for each autobiographer's Southern identity within the region. John Hussey claims the genre of nonfiction primarily focuses on the metamorphosis of the author as protagonist, providing a prescriptive lens for the reader's interpretation of the

Deconversion and Redemption   37

surrounding culture. Most works of autobiography and memoir, Hussey argues, portray a normative pattern involving a "hero-narrator engaged in a solitary quest for spiritual and/or psychological renewal." In this sense, memoir should be regarded as rhetorically fictive; conversely, Hussey contends that its nonfiction designation preserves the chief aim: "They wish to preach."[5]

The overriding theme of Smith's literary work was the struggle against fragmentation in a quest to achieve wholeness. The title of her unpublished novel based on her experience living in China was "Walls"—one that would have been appropriate for *Killers of the Dream*. Echoing the nonfiction of Cash's *The Mind of the South*, Smith's *Killers* depicts the confrontational interplay between author and culture by exploring the religious expectations that come with life in the South; such expectations exert tremendous pressure on the individual, often necessitating a compartmentalization of public and private identities. Smith problematizes white Southern identity by positing a split-psyche, which emerges necessarily from the subjective interplay and tension between the author-protagonist and the evangelical culture of the South. By deploying the fictive qualities of memoir, Smith's narrative resistance casts evangelical culture as an oppressive and stifling antagonist, a roadblock to the protagonist's authentic self. As a result, Smith as the author-protagonist must achieve a sense of authentic identity, or wholeness, in spite of Southern evangelicalism.

Smith claimed that her intent in writing *Killers of the Dream* was "not to give answers but to find the big question that I could and must live with in freedom"—a sentiment even she noted was comparable to St. Augustine's *Confessions* since hers is also a narrative of confession and conversion. Smith referred to her memoir as "an act of penance [. . .] a step toward redemption."[6] With this sentiment in mind, Hobson examines Southern memoirs as secular conversion narratives by treating a number of white Southern writers (Smith chief among them) who wrote confessional autobiographies, in which they come to terms with racial guilt of both the writer and the region. Hobson labels this form of Southern self-expression as the white racial conversion narrative, a phenomenon Charles Lloyd Cohen referred to as "psycho cultural," which began appearing in the 1940s and continued through the end of the century.[7]

Conversion narratives have held a prominent place in American letters, dating back to seventeenth century New England, and reaching its zenith in Cotton Mather's *Paterna* (ca. 1727) and Jonathan Edward's "Personal Narrative" (1765). The origins of the conversion narrative itself date as far back as *The Confessions of Saint Augustine* (ca. 397–400 CE).[8] Conversion narratives depict a personal journey from darkness to light, from sin to salvation. The journey commences with the recognition of sinfulness, accompanied by feelings of guilt, misery, despair, and unworthiness, followed by taking responsibility for sin and asking forgiveness. The conviction of sin prepares one for the light of grace by which God forgives, thus converting the sinner into a saint. This conversion (literally "turning") sets the individual on a new path of righteousness, resulting in daily renunciation and reconstruction, as one gradually actualizes the spiritual transformation through discipleship, worship, prayer, Bible reading, and church membership (accompanied by tithing). The conversion narrative then becomes one's own personal testimony, bearing witness to God's transforming grace and serving as proof of the conversion itself.

Hobson notes the similarities between the religious Puritan narratives and their secular Southern counterparts that likewise exhibit "a recognition and confession of the writer's own sins and the announced need for redemption as well as a description of the writer's radical transformation—a sort of secular salvation. But the guilt that motivates the confession—the 'conviction' of sin, as the Puritans termed it—is no less real, nor is the deep need to tell one's story, nor the changed lives that these narratives relate. The impulse is the same—to witness, to testify."[9] James Cox notes how even slave narratives that deal with the issue of race, such as Frederick Douglass's autobiography, have been categorized as conversion narratives.[10] Hobson takes a bold step in comparing the white racial conversion narratives he treats in his study by referring to them as "slave narratives," noting how they also depict escapes from bondage, flight from the slavery of an authoritarian society of prejudice and restriction, "into the liberty of free association, free expression, brotherhood, sisterhood—and freedom from racial guilt." However, Hobson does not acknowledge the active role evangelicalism—whose template of conversion narratives he borrows—enacted through its justification and sanctification of a "closed society of racial prejudice and restriction," which induced such "turnings" away from its Southern matrix.[11]

My argument inverts Hobson's by treating Smith's memoir as a deconversion narrative, which resists evangelical religion as an oppressive ideology that inflicts psychic damage on white children who grow up in the South; consequently, Smith's journey to wholeness, so to speak, results from her "turning away" from Southern evangelicalism toward independence of thought and life. Smith's deconversion narrative, as we shall see, was neither a simple nor definitive renunciation of her evangelical upbringing, but rather a lifelong process of negotiating faith and reason, community and independence, duty and desire, conscience and creativity.

Lillian Smith was born 12 December 1897 as the seventh of nine children

Deconversion and Redemption   39

in Jasper, Florida, a small Southern town between Tallahassee and Jackson-ville known for its swampy areas and referred to by the Indians as "trembling earth." The Smith house sat across the street from the Methodist church, where her deeply religious father, Calvin, served on the board of stewards, fulfill-ing the duties of a lay preacher and hosting evangelists who would come to preach revivals at the church. With a family library that contained an illus-trated Bible, Charles Monroe Sheldon's best-selling novel *In His Steps: What Would Jesus Do?* (1896), and sermon collections by Dwight L. Moody, DeWitt Talmadge, and the fire-and-brimstone preacher Sam Jones, Smith became well versed in reading what she recalled as "an odd assortment of truth and error" (Loveland 5–6).

Smith recounted her evangelical upbringing as one of intimacy with God, who seemed to exist as another person in the family: "We had family prayers once each day. All of us children read the Bible in its entirety each year. We memorized hundreds of Bible verses and repeated them at breakfast, and said 'sentence prayers' around the family table. God was not someone we met on Sunday but a permanent member of our household." Smith described her evan-gelical childhood as "the strain of living so intimately with God" (*KD* 32).[12] Such intimacy both reflected and induced an abiding sense of guilt and anxiety over whether she was truly saved. These feelings were likely exacerbated by the rejec-tion she felt as child from her mother, who turned Lillian over to a Black nurse, Aunt Chloe, after her younger sister, Esther, was born; desperately seeking the approval of both her mother and a heavenly Father, Smith found it impossible to feel assured of love and salvation.[13]

It should come as no surprise, then, that her father loomed large as a godlike figure during Lillian's childhood. Smith recalls her father as an entrepreneur in naval and lumber stores, who "owned large business interests, employed hun-dreds of colored and white laborers, paid them prevailing low wages, worked them the prevailing long hours, built for them mill towns (Negro and white), built for each group a church, saw to it that religion was supplied free, saw to it that a commissary supplied commodities at a high price, and in general man-aged his affairs much as ten thousand other southern businessmen managed theirs" (*KD* 33). In addition to providing bread and circus to his mill towns, Calvin employed his political machinations to see to it that Prohibition was en-acted; he once boasted to his family how he lined up his mill force on election afternoon, handed each man a silver dollar, and marched them to the ballot to vote liquor out of Hamilton County. Smith further describes her father as a champion of God and mammon, "with never a doubt that God was by his side whispering hunches as to how to pull off successful deals. When he lost, it was his own fault. When he won, God had helped him" (KD 34).

Perhaps the most troubling story of Calvin Smith during Lillian's childhood occurred when the mill was on fire; with the alarm sounding and panic ensuing, Calvin continued kneeling with his family for evening prayers, showing no interest in the devastation of the moment. When he received a telegram informing him that his favorite son was killed in the fire, he simply "gathered his children together, knelt down, and in a steady voice which contained no hint of his shattered heart, loyally repeated, 'God is our refuge and strength, a very present help in trouble. Therefore will we not fear, though the earth be removed, and though the mountains be carried into the midst of the sea.'" Even on his deathbed, Smith remarks that her father, when he was dying of cancer, "whispered to his old Business Partner in Heaven: 'I have fought a good fight . . . I have kept the faith'" (KD 34). Smith often spoke and wrote about the parable "Two Men and a Bargain," which she used to explain how poor white people remained facile in the face of poor economic conditions. Smith depicts a grand bargain that Mr. Rich White makes with Mr. Poor White to "Jim Crow everything"; by appealing to an ideological sentiment of white supremacy, Mr. Rich White distracted Mr. Poor White from agitating for better working conditions. One wonders to what extent Mr. Rich White might have been a projection of her godlike father.

As she grew older and more independent, Smith recalled an important teenage thought that would plant the seeds for her eventual deconversion: "It never occurred to me until I was fourteen or fifteen years old that [God] did not chalk up the daily score on eternity's tablets" (KD 32). After graduating high school in Jasper in 1915, Smith and her family moved to their summer home in Rabun County in the Blue Ridge Mountains of north Georgia to open a small inn, the Laurel Falls Hotel, on Old Screamer Mountain after Calvin's business failed. The nearby town of Clayton provided Lillian with firsthand exposure to the extreme poverty of rural white people. After spending a summer teaching in Dillard, Georgia, Smith enrolled at Piedmont College in Demorest, Georgia. The following year her family began operating a hotel in Daytona Beach, Florida, where Lillian played the piano with an orchestra—a talent she had been honing since the age of eleven. Met with unanimous praise for her musical ability, she began attending the Peabody Conservatory in Baltimore—an experience that exposed her to painting, sculpture, books, and music. In 1922, she accepted a position as head of the music department for the Virginia School for Girls in Huzhou, Zhejiang, China, a Christian missionary school where she taught wealthy Chinese

Deconversion and Redemption   *41*

girls for the next three years. According to Anne Loveland, by the age of fifteen or sixteen, Lillian "rebelled against her Methodist training; by the time she went to China she had become agnostic" (19).

Indeed, leaving the South at three crucial intervals provided Smith the necessary distance to undergo her deconversion: studying music at the Peabody Conservatory in Baltimore for four years (1917–1922); sailing for China where she taught music for three years (1922–1925); and visiting Columbia University where she studied psychology for two winter semesters (1927–1928). During her studies at Columbia, Smith received her first exposure to psychology and psychoanalysis. Over the ensuing decade, Smith read all of Freud, whose books, she explained later to Robert Coles, "were a raft that I hopped on and escaped from the whirlpools by clinging to." Freudianism enabled Smith to come to grips with the false feelings of self-imposed guilt that came with her evangelical upbringing, helping her to loosen the bond of obligation that she felt to her family, which Smith maintained, "made me feel I must always be the 'Martha' in every situation, although I longed to get away from family." As Loveland points out, Freudian psychology provided a means of liberation for Smith and many others in her generation from the fears and anxieties instilled during childhood. These eight total years removed from the South enabled Smith to see the region more objectively; her conscious detachment would be essential for her to return again to take measure of the evangelical South as cultural critic and reformer.[14]

Smith returned to Georgia in 1925 to help her parents who had fallen ill and poor, and she directed the Laurel Falls private summer camp for girls. After spending the last eight years nourishing her creative "Mary side" in Baltimore and China, Smith would revert to her conscience-stricken "Martha side" to assist her parents with the practical duties of running Laurel Falls Camp. Smith found herself unable to extricate from her family obligations, which increasingly filled her with resentment; in truth, she believed she was killing her own dreams as an artist and musician by returning to the South to help her family.[15] The catalogue of decisions Smith made to help her family and obey her Martha side included turning down a second-year scholarship at Piedmont College to stay close to home and help her parents; returning home to Clayton, Georgia, from China to help run Laurel Falls Camp; moving to Fort Pierce, Florida, for two winters to care for her older brother's two-and-a-half-year-old daughter after his wife died; giving up her winter residency in Macon, Georgia, where she lived and worked as a writer (which she began in 1930 after her father died) in 1935 to move back to Clayton permanently to care for her mother in the last three years of her life.

Smith became increasingly aware during this period of obligation and resentment of the deep split in her nature, which she continued to characterize as her Martha and Mary personas. Again, the Martha side embodied Smith's sensitivity to conscience and duty, demanding she relinquish her independence and freedom for the interest of family; her Mary side, on the other hand, pursued the pleasure and artistic principles that enabled her to discover her own voice as a writer and artist, while rebuking the overzealous conscience that haunted her until both her parents died. The push and pull of this split made Smith feel imprisoned and pressured, and it became nearly unbearable for her to manage in the 1920s and 1930s. As she herself claimed, writing helped her to "burst out" by expressing her fragmented life in "an effort to reconcile the two sides of her nature." Eventually, the more Smith embraced her writing as a vocation, the easier it would be to overcome the tension between conscience and creativity. Smith would come to appreciate the manifold uses of writing as a means to indulge her creative impulses, assert her independence, and satisfy the demands of her conscience.[16]

After purchasing Laurel Falls Camp from her family in 1928, Smith became more aware of her talents as a writer when she began a little newspaper for the camp called the *Laurel Leaf*. She also became good friends with one of the counselors, Paula Snelling, a high school math teacher from Macon, who shared an interest in literature and began encouraging Smith to write more. A pivotal moment occurred when Snelling had a near fatal accident riding a horse that required spending the winter of 1935 with Lillian and her mother at Old Screamer. In the spring of 1936, Lillian and Paula began a literary magazine, *Pseudopodia,* which the following year would be renamed *North Georgia Review* and, in 1942, would become *South Today*. The magazine's purpose was to advance the concerns of the literary South beyond the Old South polarizing fetishisms of either romanticizing or demonizing the region. Concerned "with whatever seems to us artistic, vital, significant, which is being done by writers who have their cultural roots here whatever their present locale and interest may be, and by those from no matter where who have been grafted to us and are now bearing fruit nourished by our soil," Smith and Snelling desired to provide a forum for such writers that were not published in larger circulations. Both women were frustrated with groups such as the United Writers of the Confederacy (UWC) and the Agrarians, dubbed "the Beauty Shop of Old Southern Culture" for their sterile escapism of the South's troubled history of white supremacy, ignorance, racism, and poverty. On the other hand, they seemed even more troubled by the "Dixie Dirt Dobbers," like Erskine Caldwell who fell into a rut of faultfinding that obsessed over one facet, the filth of Southern life, to the exclusion of others.[17]

In 1939–1940, Smith and Snelling received a fellowship from the Rosenwald Fund that enabled them to investigate "the Real South" about which Smith believed the Agrarians and the Southern Review knew nothing. Smith's travels across the region were a conscious attempt to broaden her exposure and experiences to minorities, impoverished sharecroppers, miners, orphanages, penitentiaries, universities, and colleges—two years that helped her to break down the walls (economic, social, and psychological) that separated her from the people of her region. As a culmination of their travels and investigation of the real South, Smith and Snelling published "Across the South Today" in the Winter 1941 issue of the North Georgia Review. Their report on Southern culture advocated for reform and criticized institutions that restricted the region's ability to progress.

Chief among these Southern institutions was evangelical religion. In "Do You Know Your South?" Smith characterized Southern evangelicalism as "at its worst a strong support of an exploitative status quo with no spiritual content; at its best a means of achieving various ameliorations of society's surface ills and of giving mystical comfort to those who can take it." Smith consistently pointed to the importance of childhood training among families, churches, and schools in propping up notions of white supremacy and Black segregation. In her writings in the 1940s, Smith formulated a psychocultural theory of segregation; she believed that white people overesteemed their skin color as a form of infantilism—a continuation of a child's self-centeredness that was fostered by family and church. Childhood training stressed the notion of superiority, which was supported by Calvinistic doctrine of election and the dominance of "the Protestant God-the-Father image." As Smith wrote in the *Saturday Review of Literature,* "Over-esteem of one's skin color, whether in individuals or in masses of men is a regressive narcism [*sic*], a symptom of psychosexual maladjustment that involves sex, religion, family life, and yes, money also."[18]

Smith stressed the notion of psychic damage that segregation inflicted on white people. Growing up and living under segregation stunted the emotional and psychological growth of white people who were incapable of becoming fully human, for such a doctrine of predestination denied the idea of human growth and development, thereby cutting off white people from organic, healthy relationships:

> In trying to shut the Negro race away from us, we have shut ourselves away from the good, the creative, the human in life. The warping distorted frame we have put around every Negro child from birth is around every white child from birth also. Each is on a different side of the frame, but each is there. As in its twisting distorted form it shapes and cripples the life and personality of one, it is shaping and crippling the life and personality of the other. It would be difficult to decide which character is maimed the more—the white or the Negro—after living a life in the southern framework of segregation.[19]

What set Smith apart from Southern liberals was her insistence that ideology, not economics or politics, was at the heart of the segregation problem; therefore, the notion of white supremacy, in Smith's view, needed to be fully acknowledged and confronted directly. As Loveland notes, Smith distinguished herself from other racial equality movements in the 1940s by emphasizing "the notion of white superiority as the root of discrimination and segregation, her stress on the damage segregation did to whites, and especially her conviction that a psychological approach was the best way to eliminate it by changing white attitudes and behavior."[20]

Smith would go on to illustrate the psychic damage that segregation enacts upon Southerners in her 1944 novel, *Strange Fruit*. Set in the fictional town of Maxwell, Georgia, *Strange Fruit* dramatizes the impact of racial segregation and white supremacy upon all its citizens. The white protagonist, Tracy Deen, falls in love with a Black woman, Nonnie Anderson, while stationed in Marseille during World War I. Upon returning home to the American South, however, Tracy proves incapable of interacting with Nonnie apart from the beliefs and customs of racial hierarchies learned as a child. Despite brief respites from a segregated world only through private sexual encounters with Nonnie in a deserted cabin, Tracy is haunted by his own psyche that recalls words and ideas that embody the prejudice of his upbringing.

After a pivotal meeting with a Black reverend upon his return to Maxwell, Tracy falls back upon his familiar, indoctrinated upbringing, as he realizes that his relationship with Nonnie can only be an illusion. Through the use of free indirect discourse, Smith underscores the power of ideology, as she takes us into the mind of Tracy who conceptualizes his relationship with Nonnie as somehow irrational despite the empirical evidence and attraction that he feels naturally; therefore, Tracy's return home to the South is a return to the conditioned racism and controlling ideologies, which Smith ironically frames as his return to "rationalism" and the familiar by using her signature imagery of enclosure, walls, and separation:

Why it was so, why the accidental meeting with the Reverend and Roseanna could have done this, he did not know. All he knew was, as he stood there looking at them, a door slammed in his mind, shutting out the new world, shutting out Nonnie with it. He was just there on the sidewalk, where he had always been, feeling the feelings he had always felt. He had been somewhere . . . in a dream maybe; maybe crazy. Maybe it had been shell-shock. He laughed. Or plain amnesia. That's better! Maybe he'd lost, not his memory, but his white feelings. Ought to be thankful he hadn't lost his memory too. Well, he was sane now—the dream was over. Whatever he had forgot how to feel, Roseanna had made him remember. He had come back to Maxwell. Yes, the Reverend had said it, he had come back home. (*SF* 51)[21]

The role of the religion looms large in Smith's novel, as Tracy acquiesces to both his mother and Brother Dunwoodie in their pressures for him to join the church, marry the girl next door, and live a conventional Southern life. Upon discovering that Nonnie is pregnant with his baby, Tracy solves this dilemma by paying Henry, a Black servant of the family, one hundred dollars to marry her. Nonnie herself is stunted by her Southern upbringing; despite being a college graduate, she works as a nursemaid and pretends that racial discrimination no longer exists but is rather something invented. Despite her own family reproving her for naïve denial of her own race, Nonnie proves to be the one who denies reality, thus inventing a dream world in which racism and segregation no longer exist.

Strange Fruit proposes no solutions to the damaging effect of segregation, for the characters in the novel prove incapable of overcoming the damaging consequences of racial ideology. By portraying characters as conditioned by a culture in which they have grown up and by emphasizing the role of the unconscious in determining human behavior, the novel precludes positive resolution. At the conclusion of the story, the lynching of Henry, wrongly charged with Tracy's murder, appears inevitable—the consequence and culmination of wrongs, misconceptions, and disasters borne out a culture of segregation. As Loveland keenly observes, "*Strange Fruit* illustrated one side of the argument Lillian had developed by the early 1940s, that racial segregation and the notion of white superiority were maintained by the training children received in the South—and the resultant fears and anxieties—as well as by the region's special brand of evangelical religion and Victorian morality, and that segregation did as much harm to whites as to Blacks" (66).[22]

Smith depicts both characters (white and Black) as psychologically crippled by the system of segregation. Denying that she wrote a "race book," Smith insisted that the story was "about human beings and their relationship with each other." Claiming that the characters could have lived anywhere segregation occurs, Smith positioned them in the South to explore how evangelical culture shapes the values and actions of humans. The impact of an authoritarian culture was one of shaping and twisting the development of people and their personalities in what Smith compared to a "steel frame within which they could grow, but only according to the limits defined by the rigid design of the frame." Of course, *Strange Fruit* was partially autobiographical, as Smith noted, "I was trying to put down the South as I had personally known it to be." The book reflects the splits and estrangements of her own life experiences, just as she described her characters as "torn and ambivalent," who were mirrors of herself; Smith recalled that "every tension was an echo of a tension in my own life."[23]

These tensions arise when individuals come to the realization that the walls of segregation in Southern culture separated humans from each other and other experiences that would enrich their development. Smith wrote about the pattern in which she knew, the Southern evangelical frame that bound its inhabitants in their feelings of love, fear, and hatred, to the extent in which even their dreams conformed.[24] Smith would turn to nonfiction to intervene by confronting these issues more boldly and directly; her 1949 memoir would shake the Southern evangelical establishment by portentously declaring in her first sentence: "Even its children knew that the South was in trouble" (*KD* 25).

Lillian Smith's *Killers of the Dream* (1949) comprises a critical tour de force examining the fractured Southern psyche. Taking up one of the many concerns from W. J. Cash's *The Mind of the South*, Smith advances his theory of the split-psyche in a much bolder fashion.[25] Smith incorporates Cash's approach of treating the "man in the center" as her subject by writing about those experiences she claims, "most white southerners born at the turn of the century share with each other" (*KD* 27). Smith described the process of writing *Killers of the Dream* as a deconversion—a shedding of old beliefs that proved transformational in both act and identity, which she detailed in her 1961 foreword twelve years after its initial publication:

> Coming back to the book after these years, I opened it wondering if what I was about to read would seem authentic to me. For I have changed since writing it. I am different. Because I wrote it. In the writing I explored the layers of my nature which I had never touched before; in reliving my distant small childhood my imagination stretched and enclosed my whole life; *my beliefs changed as I wrote them down.* As is true of any writing that comes out of one's own existence, the experiences themselves were transformed during the act of writing

by awareness of new meanings which settled down on them [. . .] But I see it, too, another way: the writer transcends her material in the act of looking at it, and since part of that material is herself, a metamorphosis takes place: *something happens within:* a new chaos, and then slowly, a new being. (*KD* 14)

The rhetorical strategies Smith details in the above passage, Scott Romine argues, embody a "dialogic tension" between Smith as interrogative narrator and the prevailing cultural mores of the South. As Romine argues, this tension seems present in Smith's "dual intention" of both Southerner within the culture and usurper of the culture, enacting a "de-centering of traditional Southern rhetorical tropes." Theoretically, the spatial distance between Smith as the narrating subject ("I") and Smith as the object of study should be large; however, Smith reduces this phenomenological split by proving her essential Southernness early on in the memoir, thus allowing herself to function as synecdoche for the entire South.[26]

The key rhetorical shift, according to Romine, arrives when Smith presents herself simultaneously as a Southern outsider, or at least one capable of transcending the cultural limitations to didactically take measure of the South. Romine claims that Smith—by isolating herself from Southern culture—proceeds "in dialogue with her former self, and by extension, the South," which frees her up to "deconstruct the rhetorical undergirding of southern oppression." This interplay often equates Smith's former self (as a child raised in the South) with the prevailing cultural sentiment, only to interrogate those values with the newer, more critical self. This strategy of resistance succeeds in disarming her readers by inscribing herself as the subject, or human receptacle containing learned ideologies, which she can, in turn, interrogate as an adult in her path to liberation. Romine rightly identifies Smith's narrative persona in *Killers of the Dream* as "evangelical in a cultural sense, attempting to invoke the culturally conditioned concept of religious sin within in a social context. In constructing a narrative persona with such evangelical overtones, Smith assumes the voice of one who can tell the white South what it cannot tell itself as a means of effecting a cultural rebirth and salvation."[27]

In the first chapter, "When I Was a Child," Smith carefully lays out the centrality of ideology packaged in the form of childhood training; here again, like Cash, she places an emphasis on the Southern mind and its resistance to criticism by using the metaphor of walls that simultaneously enclose and protect. Ideology is instilled through what Smith repeatedly refers to as "lessons," which every Southern child learns through family, school, and church, "who so gravely taught me to split my body from my mind and both from my 'soul,' taught me to split my conscience from my acts and Christianity from southern tradition" (*KD* 27). Smith cleverly uses the language of Darwinian evolution to describe herself as haunted by the memories of an evangelical childhood, in which "forces press[ed] [her] into conformity with primordial patterns"; such language makes sense when she confesses her faith crisis in isolation as representative of Southern children who, like herself, ventured privately, "up the stairs to the library where you cloistered yourself from questions you could not help asking but found no answers to: Who is God? what is eternity? why is death? where are heaven and hell? where did I come from? and where am I going? when is the end of time? and where is the end of space? and who am I? beside a name, what else? And who is this other Self that watches me? Does it go to sleep when I do?" (*KD* 12). Indeed, the most important lessons in a Southern childhood are "driven by an invisible Authority," by centering upon evangelical religion. Smith details with irony the centrality of a Southern evangelical worldview that managed to hold contrasting elements of love, hate, segregation, sin, sex, damnation, and redemption together:

> I do not remember how or when, but by the time I learned that God is love, that Jesus is His Son and came to give us more abundant life, that all men are brothers with a common Father, I also knew that I was better than a Negro, that all Black folks have their place and must be kept in it, that sex has its place and must be kept in it, that a terrifying disaster would befall the South if ever I treated a Negro as my social equal and as terrifying a disaster would befall my family if ever I were to have a baby outside of marriage. I had learned that God so loved the world that He gave His only begotten Son so that we might have segregated churches in which it was my duty to worship each Sunday and on Wednesday at evening prayers. (*KD* 27–28)

As these lessons prove contradictory to children in their development, they become what Smith calls "a rigid frame too intricate, too twisting to describe here so briefly, but I learned to conform to its slide-rule measurements. I learned it is possible to be a Christian and a white Southerner simultaneously; to be a gentlewoman and an arrogant callous creature in the same moment; to pray at night and ride a Jim Crow car the next morning and to feel comfortable in doing both" (*KD* 29). Such contradictions persist, according to Smith, "by closing door after door until one's mind and heart and conscience are blocked from each other and from reality" (*KD* 29). Compartmentalizing the self proves necessary; as Smith explains, either she had to close those doors, or they would be closed for her (*KD* 29). In the face of contradictory and segregated living, Smith's parents palliated her rhetorically by speaking in "excessively Christian and democratic terms" (*KD* 32).

Smith's examines these splits more in depth when she discusses the "first lessons" of sex and race taught to white girls in the South, revealing a duality of tensions that she appropriates throughout her discussion. The lessons she learned—that masturbation was wrong, and segregation was right—combine two seemingly incongruous ideas, wrapping sexuality and race together to expose the untenable taboos kept sacred in word, but violated in deed. By secretly breaking these rules, Southern girls told themselves they had not done so; this rationalization sundered their sense of selfhood: "Our minds had split: hardly more than a crack at first, but we began in those early years a two-leveled existence which we have since managed quite smoothly" (*KD* 84).

Smith explores the rhetoric that reinforced the internal splitting of the Southern psyche. Mystery and terror functioned as tools by which evangelicals maintained order. For example, Smith mentions how ministers were fond of mentioning the one unpardonable sin in the Bible: blasphemy against the Holy Spirit. Of course, no one knew what this meant exactly: That was the genius of it, for this "sin," Smith maintains, invoked both mystery and terror, ensuring that one tread lightly lest it be committed (*KD* 86). Evangelicalism preached a "terrible poetry" of contradictions: of love and punishment; of redemption and the unpardonable sin; of the body as the temple of the Holy Spirit and sinful as a tomb of death; of pain permitted and pleasure forbidden; of alcohol as evil and food as good; of drunkenness as evil and gluttony as permissible (*KD* 86–88). Returning to the body, Smith recalls the mixed message of her white skin being a symbol of purity, a miracle of sorts, yet she remembered the flesh being called sinful (*KD* 89). After evangelical Christianity devalued the human body, the one thing left to affirm was white skin color, thus racial binaries of Black and white became theological categories: sin and purity; evil and righteousness; darkness and light (*KD* 90).

Smith's most germane criticisms of evangelicalism reside in the chapter "Trembling Earth," an extended meditation on revival culture and itinerate evangelists. She opens the chapter with a pertinent statement regarding the strength of Southern religion: "We cannot understand the church's role as a teacher of southern children without realizing the strength of religion in the lives of everybody, rich and poor" (*KD* 99). In writing about the circuit-riding evangelists, Smith wants to make sure that her reader understands their centrality in shaping white Southern identity: "Such men there were in both Methodist and Baptist churches (whose combined membership is about eighty per cent of the South's churchgoing people)—eloquent, fiery, compelling—and for more than a century they shaped and gave content to the conscience of southerners, rich and poor" (*KD* 103). While there were certainly Southerners who went to church for the social aspect, Smith assures that they got more than they bargained for, particularly during revival meetings in August: "Guilt was then and is today the biggest crop raised in Dixie, harvested each summer just before cotton is picked" (*KD* 103). Smith colorfully characterizes Southern culture during a hot summer as a "combination of a warm moist evangelism and racial segregation" (*KD* 101).

Itinerant evangelists, wielding profound manipulative power in the culture of the South, reaped these harvests of religious guilt. Smith reflects on the legacies of the Wesley brothers and George Whitfield who blazed a trail for the most powerful figure in Southern culture, the evangelist:

> We can hardly overestimate the influence of these three preachers of God on the mind of the South, for they were men of powerful personality, burning with a powerful belief in the importance of the common man's uncommon soul, and a powerful talent for making men believe in their soul's sacredness by giving size to their sins. It was a curious inversion, this proving a man's stature by the great black shadow he cast, but it worked. Men believed in their importance by believing in the importance of their sins and grew a pride in possessing a conscience that persecuted them. (*KD* 101)

It is striking to note how Smith echoes Cash here by highlighting the narcissistic aspects of personal salvation, which ironically swell the conscience with pride. Both Cash and Smith suggest that a man is made to feel great by the size of his sins, yet Smith identifies the evangelist as the culprit who cultivates this religion of narcissism. The Southern evangelist preached asceticism but with the words of a libertine, according to Smith, glorifying the sin while simultaneously condemning it (*KD* 104). Smith seems to suggest that this awkward binary of lust and hate for sin casts the evangelist as a rhetorical pornographer, one who accentuates sin by making it more sensual and enticing: "*Whore, harlot, unnatural sins, self-abuse*—words we had never heard in our homes and would not have dared repeat outside the church, became an August vocabulary that was pressed deep in our memory. Adolescents, whose parents could not bring themselves to tell them where babies came from, sat on the edge of benches, wet-lipped and tense, learning rococo lessons in Sin from the revivalist who seemed magnificently experienced in such matters. The sermon titled *For Men Only* lifted the lid from the flaming pit of things one should not know" (*KD* 108). Smith portrays the evangelist as sadistic in his powerful instinct for sex and hate, claiming that he is in love with sin and admires it as his own creation (*KD* 105). Smith elaborates on evangelicalism as a narcissistic faith, concerned only with the solipsistic themes of body and soul. For most Southern evangelicals, sin was located solely in the human heart rather than institutions; therefore, the South was devoid of concern about social issues. "The spirituality of the church" was a convenient doctrine that maintains the status quo of racial, gender, and economic inequality (*KD* 105). Like Cash, Smith argued that Southern religion constructed an environment of stasis that trapped many Southerners, forcing them to split their psyche through public (outer) and private (inner) identities. After inducing this split-psyche, evangelical preachers exploited the sundered identity of Southerners. The exploitative power of the evangelist, according to Smith, resided in a projected faith of having conquered the inner struggle of the average layman—a faith that "released an enormous energy which in most of us is locked tight in a struggle between the two halves of our nature" (*KD* 103).

Smith expresses cautious admiration for these itinerant evangelists who proved to be talented entertainers, channeling a rhetorical energy that exaggerated stories of great sins and even greater salvations. Endowed with sheer magnetism, evangelists manipulated crowds to foster a cult of personality. Smith admires the godlike persona projected by the evangelist, one "free of personal anxieties," harnessing the power to "whistle back at will" the "ghosts" everyone else feared within (*KD* 106). Again, employing the twisted psychical language, Smith perceives that the evangelists "were curiously indifferent to cultural patterns or else in violent loyalty defended the barbed wires crisscrossing our age on which their own lives had been wounded" (*KD* 105). Even their physical attributes made them appear imposing: "They were fine looking men, strong, bold, with bodies of athletes" (*KD* 106). Smith also casts the evangelist as a psychologist, palpating the source of anxieties within the subconscious and drawing out buried sins and memories from a captivated audience (*KD* 106–107). The evangelist also incorporates the language of sales culture in his repertoire, offering "propositions" through invitations to the Gospel, holding out "compensations" of salvation. These bait and switch tactics worked, for these subjects felt the euphoria of being "saved," as if an epiphany or revelation was at hand (*KD* 107). Smith equates Southern revivalism with the theater or circus, full of concert-like performances and entertaining side shows of sensationalism and extravagance (*KD* 108–109).

To complicate matters, Smith illustrates how the dialectical culture of the

South mirrored the split-psyche of the Southerner in its mixed signals and contradictions. The palliative consolations of family and warm hospitality set off feelings of immense confusion in the Southern child, according to Smith, as racist taboos "padded" in good will were nearly suffocating in a conflicting system of values. These mixed messages of friendly hospitality and harsh segregation served to shunt the psyches of children like Smith: "But once under it, these children too were squeezed by its weight, shaped by it as were all until they, like the rest, became little crooked wedges that fit into the intricately twisting serrated design of life which THEY WHO MAKE THE RULES had prepared for us in Dixie" (*KD* 92). In a memoir largely centered on childhood, Smith seems conflicted when she proclaims, "We were petted children, not puritans" (*KD* 93). The easy manners, liberal love, and harsh discipline all served to reinforce the splintered psyche: "Sugar-tit words and sugar-tit experiences too often made of our minds and manners a fatty tissue that hid the sharp rickety bones of our souls" (*KD* 93). Smith ends this dialectical confusion with a rhetorical question in exclamatory fashion: "How can one dig down deep enough into such a childhood to find the sharp needling lessons that sometimes gave a death-prick to our souls!" (*KD* 93). Smith illuminates the Southern home as a duality of warm kindness and rigid values, an environment preventing the Southerner from recognizing and treating her split-psyche.

Smith presses her dialectics of Southern language and culture further in her famous chapter, "Three Ghost Stories." In this section, Smith explores the contradictions between Christianity and the Southern life, and how, echoing Cash, Southerners adjusted themselves in a world of contradictions through slippery rhetoric and willful ignorance. According to Smith, "people said what they did not mean, and meant what they dared not say" (*KD* 114). The cultural contradictions and the crushing weight upon one's psyche were resolved through "intellectual deafness," impeding one from hearing the dissonant, "antiphonal choruses of white supremacy and democracy, brotherhood and segregation, love and lynching, and so on" (*KD* 115). The dialectical language also mirrored the psyche, and thus, as Smith contends, the Southern mind split itself into "logic-tight compartments," separating belief from action, or better, faith from works (*KD* 115).

Smith employs other dialectics in the chapter, such as the back-yard/front-yard duality that haunted the Southern white man. In yet another split of body and spirit, Smith presents the front yard as the province of puritanism and the back yard as the sphere of sensuality. According to Smith, the front yard idealized whiteness as abstract perfection, leading to a cult of Southern womanhood—an apotheosis of white women as a goddess and beacon of morality. The more angelic she became, the more disconnected the white man felt somatically; therefore, he turned to the back yard to fulfill his private lusts. The back yard, according to Smith, embodied temptation, sensuality, pleasure, liveliness, play, sex, laughter, and unashamed nakedness; the exotic province of Black enslaved families provided an outlet for the white man's hedonistic pleasures that were suppressed in the Southern cult of white womanhood. By dehumanizing Black women as sexual objects, white men indulged their private pleasures and momentarily unfettered their split consciences. Smith considers the psychic impact of this duality: "The white man's roles as slaveholder and Christian and puritan were exacting far more than the strength of his mind could sustain. Each time he found the back-yard temptation irresistible, his conscience split more deeply from his acts and his mind from things as they are" (*KD* 120–121).

Another ghost she advances is the specter of mixed children. To the extent that a white man rejected his mixed child, he rejected one part of his own psychic life, performing violence to it as though it did not exist (*KD* 125). To deny the existence of a soul in a mixed child, a white man essentially denied some aspect of his own soul, if not all of it, thus further splitting his troubled Southern psyche. The implications of mixed children posed an existential dilemma by either affirming the value of both races or denying both outright. Such a duality proved too disturbing for the white Southern mind to sustain (*KD* 120–121).

Another ghost splitting the Southern psyche was the dialectic of white mother and Black mammy. Being nursed and physically cared for in the most crucial stages of childhood by a Black mammy, the white Southerner developed a powerful bond that, at some stage, must be broken in adulthood by cultural necessity. This movement from innocence to racial awareness required white people to make a conscious decision to break with their Black mammies and label them as other and inferior. These pivotal moments had profoundly damaging consequences, according to Smith. Engaging in piercing Freudian analysis, Smith claims that this compartmentalizing of Southern identity provides "a source of profound anxiety," plunging into a more clandestine state in the pursuit of pleasure (*KD* 128).

Smith's insights concerning the oppressive nature of evangelical religion and the subsequent psychic damage can be appreciated better by understanding the ways in which evangelicalism has historically thrived on cultural modernity and adaptability. At its core, evangelicalism can be conceived as a religious byproduct of modernity, splitting itself from many of the traditions of Christendom. Martin Marty's essay, "The Revival of Evangelicalism and Southern Religion," contends that evangelicalism exemplifies modernity in its "chopping up of life." While premodern Christianity emphasized a holistic approach to religion, evangelicalism from its origins has embraced modernity in what John Murray Cuddihy terms a "differentiation model." Borrowing from Cuddihy's *The Ordeal of Civility,* Marty appraises the cultural impact of modernity in its "differentiation of home from job . . . of fact from value, of theory from praxis . . . of art from belief . . . sundering cruelly what tradition had joined."[28]

This sundering has become an essential characteristic of evangelical identity, not just its ideological consequences, as Smith maintains. While evangelicalism may minister to the "hunger for wholeness" in its congregations, according to Marty, it relishes separations and concentrates on the private dimensions of life: "With genius it chose to specialize by differentiating portions of life. Evangelicalism concentrated in private vices and virtues, saving souls even at the expense of care for the whole life of humans, seeing the ecclesiastical sphere as one of special concentration on private, leisured, familial, and personal life no matter what happened to political, social, or cultural meanings." Marty warns us not to be fooled, however: Behind the separationist facade, evangelical leaders smuggle legislation and coercion through the back door of community-majority rule on issues such as prayer in public schools, appealing with nostalgia to the "better" times when Christianity dominated.

Evangelicalism further exemplifies modernity in its emphasis on choice and decision. Contrasted with premodern Christendom of progeny and tradition, evangelicalism champions the decision of voluntary agents in not only choosing faith, but also their own suitable church. In a capitalistic American society that stresses allocation and commodities, Marty claims that evangelicalism fits eloquently into such a culture: "The Evangelicals are the pioneer religious moderns, with their pietist ecclesiola in ecclesia—the chosen little church inside the given great big surrounding one—as a model. They still remain in the avant-garde in the electronic age as they adopt the most rigorous secular advertising and entertainment styles for the gathering of television clienteles, the final development of 'chosen' religion." In addition to its emphasis on voluntarism, commodification, and choice, evangelicalism exemplifies modernity by stressing intensity. To attract converts in a modern society, evangelicalism radiates with impassioned pleas for authentic spiritual experience, striving to be "accessible and instantly open to experience and interpretation by common people in the industrial city, on the frontier, or in the suburb." Insisting on the experiential and emotional side of religion, evangelicalism advances sensational rhetoric contrived by its evangelists to create a powerful, watershed moment for the impressionable. With an emphasis on "hot understandings" and an infallible Bible, evangelicalism commands clearly defined boundaries for the psyche with an emphasis on conversion and biblical authority, thus providing an ordered existence "in times of identity diffusion." By embracing and maintaining separatism, evangelicalism's marketplace mentality induced more "chopping" when it comes to choosing a church. Though one might expect a weakening effect of this fragmentation, sectarianism has actually served to strengthen a movement that thrives on novelty and choice, thus making evangelical faith the most suitable religion for modern Americans.[29]

Daniel Singal considers Smith's *Killers of the Dream* the clearest articulation of an anti-Victorian ethos prevalent in the 1940s, noting specifically how Smith treats psychic forces as sustaining segregation by pinpointing "the Victorian dichotomy, with its separation of mind and body, as the chief culprit."[30] Contemporary reviews of *Killers of the Dream* in the late 1940s were mixed. While some wisely praised its bluntness in confronting segregation, others took issue with what they regarded as repetition and oversimplification of Freudian psychoanalysis. Nina Ridenour's review for the National Committee for Mental Hygiene complained that Smith seemed "to have taken her psychiatry in great raw hunks which have remained as yet undigested." Ellsworth Faris naively wrote how Smith was obsessed with sex in a review for the *Christian Century,* arguing that Smith's distorted view of the South was based upon the author's own Freudian projections and childhood trauma. Like Faris, Ralph McGill claimed that *Killers* revealed Smith's own personal psychological agony and warped interpretation of the South. Such critical resistance to Smith's psychoanalytical and strident criticisms of the segregated South also reflected a late 1940s scholarly preference for more "scientific objectivity," rather than Smith's passionate plea for social correction. Taking a more subjective approach to cultural analysis put Smith out of step even with other liberal social critics and certainly set her apart from the mainstream.[31]

Smith suspected that the critical reception of her work betrayed other underlying forces at work. Despite also achieving popular and financial success as a writer for her best-selling novel of interracial romance and violence, *Strange Fruit* (1944), Smith believed she was being "curiously smothered," not because of her gender—since contemporaries Caroline Gordon, Katharine Porter, Eudora Welty, and Flannery O'Connor had no such problems—but her outspoken and uncompromising activism, which made both the conservative and moderate establishments recoil: "When Southern writers are discussed, I am never mentioned; when women writers are mentioned, I am not among them."[32]

Margaret Rose Gladney identifies Smith's lesbianism as another explanation for her alienation from the literary establishment. Gladney argues that lesbianism in the evangelical South was even more taboo than the miscegenation Smith imagined in her fiction, for it subverted the sacred, biblically prescribed roles of gender and sexuality. And while Smith confronted such taboos as miscegenation and the Southern cult of womanhood, her silence about her own sexuality underscores the profundity of her evangelical upbringing and context. Hobson speculates that Smith's lesbianism circumscribed a social alienation that allowed her to identify even more with Black Southerners since she, too, experienced a form of destructive invisibility.[33]

Of course, Smith did not possess the wider perspective of how her legacy as woman who, despite the political, literary, and cultural walls that separated her, would endure as one of the most important voices of Southern liberalism in the twentieth century. Throughout American history, women activists have often shrewdly used their enforced detachment from the centers of political, economic, and editorial power to their advantage; the absence of public roles also meant that institutional ties did not bind them. Coming out of what had been a largely religious tradition of Southern feminine activism, Smith exploited this to her advantage as an uncompromising liberal prophet and crusader to end segregation by contrasting herself against the likes of McGill and Hodding Carter. Journalist Harry Ashmore rightly referred to Smith as "an outright evangelist" for the cause of desegregation, traveling the Southern circuit to preach the cause of civil rights, while McGill and Carter tread cautiously as Southern moderates (a political calculation they believed would prevent agitation among their constituents and thus preserve their cultural relevance as authorities on the race issue). Smith herself even remarked how she and Paula Snelling behaved "like missionaries with a solemn purpose."[34]

In 1954, Lillian Smith felt compelled to write another work of nonfiction at the age of fifty-five that would detail her search for meaning and purpose in the latter years of her life. *The Journey* comprises Smith's quest to find an image of the human being that she could feel proud of, "something to believe in; something that intelligence and heart can accept" (*J* 6–7).[35] The work reveals Smith's belief in the dignity and worth of humankind, whose integrity lies in an attempt to overcome brokenness by reaching for wholeness. Such efforts to achieve wholeness, according to Smith, embody what makes us fully human (*J* 8).

The book's significance lies in Smith's discovery and descriptions of her newfound basis for religious faith. Smith recalls how as a young woman she rejected the Southern evangelical Christianity of her upbringing and became an agnostic by exchanging old-time religion for the scientific positivism as an alternative worldview. Smith employs Darwinian metaphors to reflect back on her deconversion experience: "I felt, as did so many of my generation, that we were at last stepping out of a dark tangled swamp of medieval superstitions and beliefs where mankind had been lost so long, where many were still lost, into a sunny open plain where facts could be clearly seen" (J 50–51). Smith came to believe that science offered proof and facts, as opposed to religion, which thrives upon mystery and the unknown; for Smith, science provided practical solutions to real-world problems in the here and now, while evangelical religion concerned itself with personal, spiritual salvation and the life to come.

Smith's deconversion initially led her to a positivism that overvalued science to the exclusion of religious faith. By the time Smith had written *The Journey,* she arrived at some middle ground between the two. Smith explains this spiritual return as a "flight from the unknown." In a 1959 letter to her friend and attorney Donald Seawell, Smith described her return journey to religious faith in greater detail: "We begin to understand that we can never have absolute knowledge of God and yet He is not 'relative.' It is simply that our knowledge is incomplete and while it will increase as we grow, always there will be the impenetrable between man and God."[36] In his review of *The Journey* for the *New Yorker,* Anthony West was correct in his assessment of Smith's statements concerning religious faith: They echoed the same "irritating fuzziness" present in the postwar boom of inspirational books that espoused a superficial, civil religion.[37]

Writing for the *New Leader* in 1951, Smith insisted that Southern white people remained "profoundly troubled by the split between their ideals and acts, burdened by the authoritarian pressures of white supremacy, fearful of what the practice of segregation is doing to their own children's growth as human beings."[38] While rural white people were more prone to demagoguery due to poverty, guilt, and frustration, according to Smith, their evangelical orientation offered some hope for change: "The rural southerner cherishes some pretty evil beliefs, but he holds stubbornly to some fine ones." Alongside white supremacy, the rural Southerner cherished the Sermon on the Mount, an inconsistency, Smith maintains, that displayed white evangelicals' desire and potential to be morally upright: "However vague [that] concept of goodness, however narcissistic, its over-concern with body mortality, the *desire to be good* exists, and plays a dynamic role in Southern psychology" (J 4–5).

Smith eventually came to regard evangelical belief in Christian brotherhood and charity as common ground upon which she could make appeals for equality; the real obstacles preventing social change among rural Southern white people, Smith argued, were political leaders, both conservative and moderate, who grossly underestimated their own constituents with derogatory and inaccurate judgments about the region's "readiness" to accept racial equality. Smith believed that segregation was a psychological mechanism—ideological walls used by men to shut out alien people and ideas. Just as ideology was learned, it could be unlearned and overcome by an act of the will; therefore, Smith maintained that social change in the South required the active participation of individuals to change their own thought patterns. With the view that these ideological walls could be deconstructed, Smith continued her tireless work bridging and preparing future citizens of the South for better days ahead until her death from breast cancer in 1966; in her view, teachers, preachers, politicians, artists, and writers were essential in the pursuit of creative and constructive solutions to social equality. Even the evangelical religion that informed Smith's conscience as a child could be reconfigured and redeemed in her personal quest to achieve wholeness for herself and the South.

Part Two

Narrative Satire

Chapter 3

Evangelical Sales Culture
in Flannery O'Connor's *Wise Blood*

In part one, we studied the narrative strategy of resistance found among Southern memoirs in the 1940s; the nonfiction of W. J. Cash and Lillian Smith directly confronts an evangelical worldview that enabled an authoritarian culture of white supremacy to flourish in the American South. Their strategies typify a path of transcendence and subsequent judgment concerning the intellectual and moral shortcomings of Southern evangelicalism. Both writers' Southern evangelical upbringings authorize their critiques by dramatizing the psychological consequences of ideology, the means of liberation, and hope for reform. As cultural insiders, their resistance bears greater weight and consequence.

In this section, we examine the strategy of narrative satire by looking at two famous Catholic writers in the evangelical South. Flannery O'Connor and Walker Percy shared a unique insider-outsider status that afforded both proximity (Southern) and distance (Catholic) from the region and culture in which they lived and wrote. As Southerners, they were intimately familiar with the language, rhythms, and customs of the region. Despite sharing many essential doctrines, both writers' Catholic faith isolated them from the cultural hegemony that evangelicalism exerted over the region. Yet for all their similarities, O'Connor and Percy employed different approaches in their fictional works to satirize the same compromises and shortcomings of evangelicalism in the region. As we shall see, their satiric renderings illuminate the repercussions of evangelical ascendancy in Southern culture.

Critics understand satire as a rhetorical device to critique contemporary culture. For this reason, some conceive of satire as a conservative inclination to parody social norms that deviate from a romanticized past. While often true of poetic satire, narrative satire parodies not only prevailing social norms, but also opposition to such norms. In his essay, "Discourse in the Novel," Mikhail Bakhtin coined the term heteroglossia (multivoiced) when discussing the novel as an exploration of the relationship between language and ideology; examining Dostoevsky's characters as bearers of ideology, Bakhtin revealed how the linguistic dynamics of heteroglossia constitute dialogical parody. Bakhtin celebrated folklore and carnival as parodic forms that mock rigid social norms. Such carnivalesque antithesis disrupts by opposing and unmasking the status quo, leaving the audience with unresolved juxtapositions of conflicting frameworks.[1] As Frank Palmeri asserts, dialogical parody cuts both ways by asserting an "antithesis to orthodoxy and then the negative of that antithesis; it describes a dialectic without synthesis."[2]

Narrative satire's open-endedness excludes compromise and middle ground in its depictions of both status quo and opposition, making it different from the genre of comedy with which it's often conflated; consequently, narrative satire forecloses resolution. This framework informs my analysis of satirical novels that resist resolution by depicting the adaptability of Southern evangelical culture awash in postwar American consumer capitalism. In her essay, "The Fiction Writer and His Country," Flannery O'Connor contends that the duty of a fiction writer is to make her vision apparent by exaggerating societal distortions that a reading audience has come to regard as natural. O'Connor believed that Christian novelists like herself wrote in territory consisting largely of unbelieving audiences who were hostile to religious faith; consequently, distortions should be employed to startle spiritually complacent readers. In what might be her most cited prose, O'Connor argues that when a Christian writer determines that her audience does not share the same beliefs, she must make her "vision apparent by shock—to the hard of hearing you shout, and for the almost blind you draw large and startling figures."[3]

The territory shifted after O'Connor wrote her essay, which has led me to wonder how her fiction might speak to an evangelical reading audience that resides in the mainstream of American culture. As another Catholic who shared many of O'Connor's religious concerns as a writer, Percy lived long enough to witness the emergence of evangelical Christianity into the mainstream of American culture. Percy's novel *The Second Coming,* arrived seasonably in 1980 with the rise of the Christian right in Reagan's new presidency; signaling this emergence, the protagonist Will Barrett returns home to the North Carolina of Billy Graham "where everybody was a Christian and found unbelief unbelievable." In a novel chiefly concerned with religious inquiry, *The Second Coming* presents a Southern culture of evangelical hegemony. Will states that he might find Christianity more compelling if only there were fewer Christians around; illustrating

Evangelical Sales Culture   63

his point, Will writes to a friend: "Have you ever lived in the midst of fifteen million Southern Baptists?"[4]

With the belief that O'Connor's fiction still has something to say in a territory that is quite at home with Christian faith, this chapter shows how her first novel, *Wise Blood* (1952), provides satirical distortions that startle an evangelical audience whose vision has been dulled in its engagement with American sales culture. To achieve this startling effect, O'Connor created a minor character to satirize the salesman-evangelist persona commonly manifested in evangelical culture. The key to understanding O'Connor's malgré lui protagonist, Hazel Motes, lies in seeing him as reactionary to the religious indifference he sees around him. Asa Hawks, the speciously blind preacher, functions as a crucial foil to ignite Haze's backward journey of fulfilling his inherited destiny as a preacher. Haze's initial obsession with Hawks is due to Asa's striking contrast with the religiously complacent culture of Taulkinham. Hawks's seemingly anomalous devotion—crystallized by an alleged act of self-blinding—provides a stumbling block to Haze's own determination to dismiss the Christian faith. Ironically, when Haze discovers that Hawks is a fraud, he plunges recklessly toward his own conversion while evangelizing about a new "Church Without Christ" in his attempts to shock not only the complacent onlookers in Taulkinham but also the blind street preacher and his assistant, Sabbath, who hand out tracts and beg the public to give money for Jesus with such ease. Yet Haze's provocative preaching to shock the religious sensibilities of his listeners proves to be an utter failure and much to his consternation, continually meets with the public's indifference. Other indicators are employed—such as blasphemous exclamations by multiple characters—in more subtle fashion to further illustrate a self-satisfied culture that nettles Haze's Christ-haunted psyche.

One of these more subtle indicators arrives with the introduction of yet another foiling preacher, Onnie Jay Holy (a.k.a., Hoover Shoats).[5] In a chapter 9 episode outside a picture show, there are only three people listening as Haze is preaching atop his Essex. Haze's badgering is quite appropriate, revealing much of his disgust with what he perceives as an insipid faith among the people of Taulkinham: "[Do] you care? Are you going to pay any attention to what I've been saying or are you just going to walk off like everybody else" (*WB* 84)?[6] Most audiences dismiss confrontational evangelists loitering on street corners, but many will stop and listen to an easy, appealing message of reassurance. Enter Holy, who interjects to fill the sentimental void by framing his rhetoric in familiar American sales-speak. Holy serves as a critical contrast by embodying the facile Christian culture that Haze so strongly despises. This essay traces the evolution of Holy's character through the early unpublished manuscripts[7] of *Wise Blood*, providing readers of O'Connor's first novel an important glimpse into her process of creating such a memorable minor character to engage the cultural and religious themes that evolved over subsequent drafts. By examining the drafts of *Wise Blood* manuscripts, the evolution of O'Connor's novel reveals itself to be a work that not only explores but satirizes an evangelical culture saturated with marketing and consumerism. An examination of this colorful character provides incisive critiques of an American evangelicalism subsumed by sales culture and demonstrates that while O'Connor might have been sympathetic to evangelicals, readers would be mistaken to perceive her as uncritical of them.

John Turner's study, *Bill Bright & Campus Crusade for Christ: The Renewal of Evangelicalism in Postwar America,* provides an eye-opening assessment of the indelible mark that evangelicalism has made upon mainstream American culture. Turner specifically examines this engagement through parachurch organizations that exist alongside institutional congregations. Examples of parachurch organizations include Bill Bright's Campus Crusade for Christ, James Dobson's Focus on the Family, Pat Robertson's 700 Club, and the Billy Graham Evangelistic Association—all of which generated hundreds of millions annually in revenue by appropriating marketplace strategies and creative technological usage. I note the significance of parachurch organizations for two reasons. First, parachurch ministries have functioned to make the most significant evangelical impact in the twentieth and twenty-first centuries. As Turner argues, it is difficult to overstate the significance, influence, and power of evangelicalism in light of its parachurch organizations. By possessing a cultural adaptability unfettered by denominational boundaries and bureaucracy, evangelical parachurches alter their strategies of cultural engagement to shape not only the character of religion but also political policies in many regions in the United States.[8] Second, it is important to note that all religious activity that occurs in O'Connor's *Wise Blood* takes place outside of and beyond the church; in fact, despite all the talk of religion—Christianity, Jesus, souls, conversion—there are no actual churches in the entire novel, only references to them.

Evangelicalism's impact upon American culture arose from a conscious commitment to mainstream its methods and identity. The evangelical talent for promoting the faith in familiar yet fresh language can be traced back to the Great Awakening, when George Whitfield advanced pamphlets, sensational press, and advertisements prior to his arrival in towns to preach. This appropriation of technology and media hype rose to new heights in the Billy Graham Crusades, with its innovative preaching techniques, "barrages of publicity, and the use of emerging media." Today, evangelical art forms amass huge revenue in a country starving for spirituality, which has moved evangelicalism toward the center of American society in a virtual "baptism of American culture." Martin Marty notes that while contemporary evangelicalism may still employ the rhetoric of converting the world and taking the country back for Christ, in reality, it actually "now serves as a means of providing ritual process for applicants to the approved world, in a day when the President of the United States, business leaders, celebrities, athletes, beauty queens, and civic figures attribute their worldly success to the fruits of conversion."[9]

Such mainstream cultural engagement opened evangelicalism up to scrutiny. R. Laurence Moore contends that a marketplace methodology has sapped evangelicalism's "transformative power." While Turner contests Moore on this point, he agrees that compromises have been made by many evangelicals to achieve cultural gains and create a friendly environment for the movement to continue to flourish. D. G. Hart argues that this mainstream success has actually proven to be the movement's demise. In *Deconstructing Evangelicalism,* he contends that the very ease with which the movement has mimicked mainstream consumer culture renders its impact shallow and inconsequential because such assimilation fails to solidify into a generative tradition. An excerpt from Hart's polarizing conclusion is worth quoting at length:

> The "ministries" to which born-again Protestants have such easy access on the radio or Internet are brilliant examples of entrepreneurial and organizational genius, but they are also arenas in which celebrities thrive, thus creating genuine obstacles to the formation of a tradition. How does one hand down the celebrity of Billy Graham or a James Dobson, for example? At the same time, the music that born-again Protestants enjoy in the privacy of their cars and homes and to which they sway on Sunday mornings is as dependent on the structures of celebrity as the parachurch. Even Contemporary Christian Music has little to commend itself as a form of tradition.

While Hart's critique appears sound, he proves a bit overeager in declaring the demise of American evangelicalism. If we agree that evangelicalism—through mass media and parachurch ministries—transformed American culture (and it clearly has), we should also consider how American culture has transformed evangelicalism.[10]

Before engaging in a reading of *Wise Blood* as a satirical critique of evangelicalism, I want to acknowledge the dangers of this approach. O'Connor's preface to the second edition of *Wise Blood* and her many letters and essays make her authorial and thematic intent all too clear.[11] O'Connor's startling figures drawn for a perceived audience of unbelievers demonstrate that she, a Catholic, was sympathetic to the evangelical faith she observed in the Protestant South: "When you write about backwoods prophets, it is very difficult to get across to the modern reader that you take these people seriously, that you are not making fun of them, but that their concerns are your own and, in your judgment, central to human life." Furthermore, O'Connor felt a sense of kinship with Southern evangelicals and appreciated their fervor and sincere religious feeling. On the other hand, O'Connor recognized that the individualistic tendencies of Protestant evangelicalism often produce "distorted images of Christ" that take a believer to "strange places" far away from ancient Christian orthodoxy. While O'Connor was sympathetic to her fictional evangelical characters, it would be a mistake for readers to minimize or entirely miss the satirical distortions of them.[12]

This is precisely why Michael Kreyling's introduction to *New Essays on Wise Blood* remains crucial, as he asserts that O'Connor's fiction has been canonized by Christian critics due to her oft-discussed Catholic faith in her prose and letters, her untimely death from lupus analogous to martyrdom, and her obvious scorn for those who misread her fiction in a way that was not aligned with her own religious views. All these factors have ensured a dominant segment of O'Connor criticism to be religious, often narrowing O'Connor criticism to Christian apologetics and leaving little to no room at the table for secular readings of her fiction. To characterize O'Connor's fiction as subversive to evangelical Christianity would certainly be a misreading; however, it would also be shortsighted to perceive O'Connor's vision as wholly uncritical of evangelicals.[13]

O'Connor was troubled by the ease with which the lines between American religion and sales culture were blurred. In addition to her writing regiment in the morning, lunching at the Sanford House, and receiving guests in the afternoon, O'Connor read the local newspaper and watched television on a daily basis. Such regular exposure to popular culture and media provided humorous conversation with friends and fertile material to satirize in her fiction. In the postwar years of commercial and consumer excess, celebrity ministers flooded the channels of media. In *Selling Catholicism: Bishop Sheen and the Power of Television*, Christopher Owen Lynch examines the emergence of celebrity clergy within the context of America's postwar success, using Bishop Fulton Sheen's television ministry as a conduit for his study. Sheen's television program, *Life is Worth Living,* enjoyed a wildly successful run from 1952–1957 by combining "an evangelical message of turning to Jesus for salvation with American patriotism and anti-communism"; consequently, it became the only religious program ever to be commercially sponsored and compete for ratings. Sheen would open his program addressing his listeners as "Friends," and begin with "some icebreakers—usually anecdotes about young children—and then speaks extemporaneously for a half hour on a topic such as the dangers of communism, the values of family love, the duties of patriotism, or the need to examine one's conscience," only to conclude with "Bye now, and God love you!" Lynch contends that Sheen succeeded by taking the same approach as Billy Graham ("the prophet of America's ideology"): stressing the importance of religiosity while minimizing church affiliation and doctrinal specifics.[14]

In a 6 September 1955 letter to Betty Hester ("A"), O'Connor referred to Sheen's dumbed-down approach as supreme "vulgarity," and sarcastically remarked "that the vulgar must be saved and that generally this is to be accomplished by the vulgar, or the vulgarer than they." O'Connor also joked to Robie Macauley that her television interviews supporting the made-for-TV movie version of "The Life You Save May Be Your Own," would corrupt her into a combination of Gorgeous George Wagner (celebrity professional wrestler) and Fulton Sheen; it was clear that O'Connor was skeptical of the sheen that celebrity ministers and televangelists contrived to manipulate their respective audiences.[15]

In printed media, O'Connor was an avid reader of pop psychologist George W. Crane's "The Worry Clinic," a daily column that ran in the *Atlanta Constitution* from 1954 to 1957. Writing to Hester again on 30 September 1955, O'Connor shared a story she recently read about a child who questioned his mother about why he should consider Jesus's words authoritative; the mother replied, "Because He was a gentleman." O'Connor's elaboration proves illuminating: "It might have been Billy Graham or Dr. Crane but I wouldn't accuse them as I'm not sure. Do you read Dr. Crane? I never miss him. He is an odd mixture of fundamentalism (against the grape), psychology, business administration and Dale Carnegie. The originator of The Compliment Club. He appears in the Atlanta Constitution on the same page as the comic strips. He is always telling Alma A. how to keep her husband by losing 75 pounds."[16] In a separate letter to Macauley, O'Connor mentioned their shared disdain "of Dr. [George] Crane, my favorite Protestant theologian (salvation by the compliment club). I was glad to hear this because I think the doctor ought to be more widely appreciated. He is really a combination minister and masseur, don't you think?" Loxley Nichols argues that Crane's "The Worry Clinic" provided O'Connor not only amusing fodder for her repeated satire of American consumerism, but also a "literary antithesis and the background against which she wrote." "Anti-intellectual, xenophobic, smug, provincial, capitalistic, sentimental, mechanistic, reductive, commercial, and ludicrously Protestant," George Crane, Nichols contends, "provides a composite portrait of what O'Connor satirizes in her fiction."[17]

Nichols unearths an impressive catalogue of Crane's columns and analyzes how O'Connor satirizes his American pop psychology in a minor character written in her 1960 novel, *The Violent Bear It Away*. Meeks, a copper flue salesman, embodies the Crane philosophy that preaching is selling. Meeks, or "the salesman," offers his best advice for success to young Tarwater as he sets out into the world: Feign interest in people (i.e., customer or convert) from whom you want to get (i.e., sell or preach) something. "He said love was the only policy that worked 95% of the time. He said when he went to sell a man a flue, he asked first about that man's wife's health and how his children were." Nichols's reading is complimented with a quote from The Worry Clinic on 23 April 1954 that could just as easily come from Meeks. According to Dr. Crane, "Preaching, as well as school teaching is really salesmanship of ideas, instead of merchandise. And the first law of salesmanship is to win friends, for you can't sell solid 24-carat gold bricks to enemies, even at bargain prices." To win friends, one must pay compliments—a central concept for Dr. Crane, who challenged his Chicago Temple Bible class (the "compliment club") to pay three daily compliments for a month to achieve success and happiness in life. By embodying the Crane sales philosophy, Meeks becomes the object of satire in O'Connor's fiction.[18]

The centrality of paying compliments and winning friends, however, is not a concept that originated with Dr. Crane. Dale Carnegie's best-selling classic, *How to Win Friends and Influence People,* provided a blueprint for the sales tactics of flattery and manipulation even before its publication in 1936. Self-help seminars in hotel conference rooms all started when Carnegie delivered success talks, from which he later organized into one of the most influential books of the twentieth century. Carnegie's book reads like an evangelical Sunday school or sermon series, where a few points are made among a seemingly endless supply of feel-good anecdotes. Each chapter contains principles in "handling" people and endearing yourself to them. In "Part One: Fundamental Techniques in Handling People," Carnegie provides a fundamental principle applied in the vocation of sales: Arouse in the other person an eager want; he shrewdly claims that "the only way on earth to influence other people is to talk about what they want and show them how to get it." The outcome of focusing on others' desires

Evangelical Sales Culture   69

proves immense for the salesman to endear himself, as Carnegie concludes: "He who can do this has the whole world with him." As an aforementioned letter to Hester in September of 1955 made explicit, O'Connor lumped Dale Carnegie, Fulton Sheen, Billy Graham, and George Crane into the same unflattering heap of evangelical-business hybrids who inflate egos and in turn increase their influence and celebrity. Such pretense both humored and haunted O'Connor, and it is apparent in the writing of her first novel that the assimilation of such tactics in evangelical religion remained an abiding concern in her art.[19]

The manuscripts of *Wise Blood,* housed in the Ina Dillard Russell Library's Special Collections at Georgia College and State University, reveal an early novel that is strikingly different than the published version. The manuscripts are divided into folders, referred to as entries containing O'Connor's typed work and handwritten notes. *Wise Blood* encompasses entries 22–151, half of the entire manuscript collection.[20] In the first entry (22a), O'Connor provides a synopsis of the first four chapters that she frames as a struggle between religious contemplation and a conquest of the city, which is reminiscent of Augustine's binary between the city of God and the city of man. O'Connor's binary is negotiated by the protagonist, Hazel Motes, as he joins an evangelical group called David's Aspirants who are led by the missionary Asa Hawks. David's Aspirants provides a clever allusion to King David. At first glance, an aspiration to be like David implies being a person after God's heart, yet the actions of this group reveal their true aspirations to secure the wealth of a king. Growing uneasy with a spiritual compromise that fuses the city of God with the city of man, Haze's sense of guilt increases, leading him to flee from worldliness to find something resembling Eastrod, the idealized hometown of his childhood. Haze seeks to situate himself safely from the encroaching world of modernity. In this sense, the setting of Taulkinham functions as a city of vapid relativism where life is reduced to a world of consumption—a metaphor for modern American culture. O'Connor's satirical depictions appear absent in this early draft; moreover, Haze comes across as a more straightforward religious seeker rather than the man who wants to escape the ragged figure who beckons him to a life of faith.

In the early versions of chapter 8, O'Connor had a working draft of a character named Mercy Weaver (108 c–f). The earliest drafts depict this character as a fat, fleshy white man, who regularly examines his hands on both sides, while delicately prodding his pocket containing a pale gold watch. In one draft, he is all flesh and no bones, as though he were a swelling growth. After Haze leaves a diner where he did not eat his breakfast, Mercy imposes upon him in an aggressive manner, leaping into the Essex uninvited for a ride home. What is fascinating about this episode is the description of Mercy's body language: laying his arm over the seat of Haze and later putting his hand on Haze's shoulder. Mercy possesses a creepy smile and claims that he and Haze can understand each other. In another draft (108e), Mercy asks what Haze's name is; Haze lies, telling him it is Henry. Mercy responds in a suggestive manner, exclaiming that he loves the name Henry, and he once knew a man by that name.

Another draft (108c) depicts Mercy Weaver as a homosexual who aggressively attempts to lure Haze back to his apartment. This entry incorporates many of the parts found in the other three involving this character (108 d–f), including the last entry that casts him as an insurance salesman. O'Connor employs sexual imagery to describe an adjacent street car as a zipper closing behind them to illuminate Mercy's intentions with Haze. Mercy again invites Haze up to his apartment, noting that he can serve him breakfast since Haze did not finish his own at the diner. Upon the sudden realization of Mercy's sexual intentions, Haze tells him to get out before he kills him. A different entry (108e) of this dramatic episode contains only a half-page excerpt of Mercy's advances toward Haze; most interesting about this fragment are the handwritten notes by O'Connor in ink and all caps that allude to Haze being a traveler who is wounded—perhaps in a more spiritual or emotional sense.

The most provocative of the early drafts depicts Mercy Weaver as an outright sexual predator who touches Haze in the car and propositions him sexually. O'Connor uses this episode as an epiphany for Haze's understanding of himself (108f). In this entry, the sexual contact and innuendo that reveal Mercy's sexuality are no longer foregrounded; rather, the awkward moment, combined with nature and his surroundings, serves as a self-realization for Haze: He is isolated, lonely, vulnerable, and emotionally wounded. This wound is evident to people like Mercy who prey upon the vulnerable. Mercy's misinterpretation of Haze's condition functions as a projection of his own sexual orientation that makes him feel alienated from the community. Mercy reaches out to Haze for a connection, a means of intimacy and understanding. Haze realizes his own vulnerability as an exposed loner and outsider. Haze's condition is exacerbated by his life as a traveler who attempts to escape internal conflicts through external flight. It is important to note the difference in which Haze dismisses Mercy from the car in the more-developed entry of the working drafts: He simply pulls the car over, reaches across and opens the door for Mercy to get out. With an unspoken, peaceful understanding, Mercy gets out of the car without Haze's exhibition of violent threats and disgust. In this entry, O'Connor casts a more complex and sympathetic Haze, one who does not cast blame upon

Mercy for misinterpreting his own loneliness. Haze's isolation is existential, not sexual.

Another working draft (108a) alters the episode entirely. The fat man is now named Macy Weaver—a probable allusion to the American department store that marketed itself to be the largest in the world during the 1950s. A different proposition is aggressively advanced to Haze, one motivated more by business than sex. Macy Weaver sells insurance. This depiction of Weaver's character, while less provocative, seems more consistent with the published novel's overall themes. The conversation in Haze's car is steered by Macy to discuss two abstract and pliable concepts: happiness and security. When Haze mentions his discontent with Taulkinham, Macy tells him—with the same suggestive language as Mercy while implying something material rather than sexual in this context—that many people are happy here and eventually find what they are looking for. Meanwhile, Haze is driving recklessly through the busy traffic, no doubt nervous by Macy's overbearing presence in the car. Macy uses this opportunity to pitch him accidental insurance. Macy does not tell him to drive more safely or slowly; no, Haze just needs to pay a little more money to insure his preferred way of life. For only a few cents a month, the people we harm or injure with our lifestyles will not cost us a cent when the time comes to repair damages, according to Macy. When this pitch does not work on Haze, Macy ratchets up the rhetoric by injecting fear and sensationalism—an often effective sales ploy—to suggest that Haze might kill someone with his driving. When the appeals for happiness no longer work, the salesman resorts to fear as an incentive to purchase the product immediately.

O'Connor's choice of insurance salesman is fascinating: Macy is trying to sell a policy needed only in the case of a disaster; meanwhile, the customer continually dumps money into the policy in the event something bad might occur. For most who never have that accident, it is paying for an illusion of security, the sort of happiness that provides enough incentive to purchase. The development of Weaver from sexual predator to overbearing insurance salesman demonstrates an interesting connection. This chubby, charming, and preening character embodies sinister qualities that threaten to deceive and manipulate the vulnerable of society. O'Connor sensed a connection of sorts between sexual and sales propositions—both scenarios highlight crafty predators attempting to lure their prey through charm, flattery, and persuasive rhetoric.

While Weaver's character, in name, was ultimately scrapped, further examination shows that he evolved into yet another character found in the published version of *Wise Blood*. In chapter 9, Haze first notices Onnie Jay Holy winking at him every time he looks his way (*WB* 83). Other details of Holy include pulling at Haze's pants leg (*WB* 84), brandishing a lavender handkerchief (*WB* 88), and speaking to Haze in a "soft voice" when they are alone together in the car (*WB* 88). Holy is described as "plumpish," having "curly blond hair that was cut with showy sideburns" (*WB* 83). Throughout the episode, Holy communicates feelings of inadequacy and alienation from his family and community, similar to Mercy Weaver's attempts of solidarity with Haze's outsider persona. The chapter 8 Essex episodes from the early, unpublished drafts begin with Mercy (or Macy) Weaver's self-invitation to ride with Haze and engage him in a conversation. In the same manner, Onnie Jay Holy, realizing that Haze is getting away, "ran off just as the Essex began to slide again. He jumped on the running board and got the door open and plumped in, panting, beside Haze" (*WB* 88). Identical to the early manuscripts with Weaver, Haze reacts with disgust, ordering Holy to "get out," while "reaching across and opening the door for him" (*WB* 89).

In both the early drafts and the published version of *Wise Blood*, we see Haze as a loner isolated from his surrounding culture. Haze's isolation serves to attract the sexual and sales predators found in the characters of Mercy Weaver, Macy Weaver, and Onnie Jay Holy, who all seek to exploit his loneliness for their own gains. The early drafts reveal O'Connor's deliberate process in writing a minor character that evolves from sexual predator to insurance salesman to fraudulent, sentimental street preacher. O'Connor's creative process reveals fascinating correlations she perceived between sexuality and salesmanship, a connection readily visible in American marketing and sales culture today.

Jon Lance Bacon has examined the permeation of sales culture in America depicted in *Wise Blood*, arguing that O'Connor was deeply troubled by the expansion and power of corporations. O'Connor's satirical critique of consumer culture is found in her depictions of Taulkinham, an urban city too busy shopping to notice the majesty of creation. Illustrated in both the signs around town and the language of business, happiness is defined by advertising with salesmanship as the deferment of true selfhood. Bacon contends that O'Connor's criticism of American consumerism extended to the mainstream religious culture: "To affirm the possibility of dissent, however, O'Connor had to distinguish her form of religion from the ones that dominated American culture during the 1950s. *Wise Blood* attacks the dominant forms, suggesting that American religion had been appropriated by the "salesman's world." In the world of the novel, faith itself becomes a commodity."[21] O'Connor hones her satiric aim upon marketplace religion by exemplifying its ethos in the celebrity minister-salesman, Onnie Jay Holy.

Evangelical Sales Culture   73

The descriptions of Holy serve as a burlesque of many celebrity evangelists who exude cloying self-awareness. The narrator employs verbal irony with the use of a simile: "He was not handsome but under his smile, there was an honest look that fitted into his face like a set of false teeth" (*WB* 83). This initial description encompasses a characterization of Holy as one wielding the guise of friendliness and honesty as a means of manipulation. Even when sharing a weakness or a traumatic story, Holy still maintains his winning persona. The narrator satirically suggests that Holy's outward show of humility signifies an inner arrogance: "He had a winning smile and it was evident that he didn't think he was any better than anybody else even though he was" (*WB* 86). Holy's first words divulge an interesting emphasis: "Come on back heah, you folks," he said. "I want to tell you all about *me*" (*WB* 84). In the early drafts, O'Connor underlined the final first-person pronoun with a pencil for special emphasis, which shows in italics in the published version. This emphasis subtly reveals how the success of many evangelists often hinges upon a charming and engaging personality. Holy's manner is alluring, and despite his empty, falsely humble pleadings to the contrary, *he* is the message and the product being sold to the crowds.

Holy proves commercially savvy, as his advertising language equates material consumption with a real sense of importance. Holy's marketing approach to evangelism serves as a form of reassurance, affirming the audience's essential goodness and limitless potential.[22] The narrator states that Holy looks at his audience as "if he were appealing to the good judgment that was impressed on their faces" (*WB* 84). Holy enacts a key move from the salesman's playbook: Appeal to the superior judgment of the customer. This logic of sales flattery is ironic, for if a customer's judgment is, in fact, so superior, then why is it necessary to be persuaded by salesmen? The sales vocation implies just the opposite—namely, that left to oneself, the customer will make the wrong decision, thus requiring the prodding and better judgment of salesmen. By appealing to his audience's superior judgment, Holy deceives them into thinking they are making their own informed decision about what they want: a sense of identity achieved through consumption.

Holy summons novelty as a sign of relevance and authenticity, selling his church as if it is the latest piece of technology: "This church is up-to-date! When you're in this church you can know that there's nothing or nobody ahead of you, nobody knows nothing you don't know, all the cards are on the table, friends, and that's a fack" (*WB* 87). Holy agrees with Haze that a new Jesus is needed, one that is up-to-date (*WB* 90). This falls in line with Holy's fascination with pop music, as he proclaims that he can say things much sweeter with his guitar

(*WB* 84). Music possesses mainstream appeal, providing Holy with a conduit to move his audience with an easy spirituality that O'Connor witheringly characterized as "one big electric blanket" of sentimentality.[23] Indeed, contemporary music and worship emerged to the forefront as effective evangelical tools. This utilization so prevalent in evangelicalism reveals the alluring qualities of pop culture; apart from the some of the words of the songs, it might be difficult to distinguish between some contemporary evangelical worship services (clapping, dancing, lifted hands) and typical secular music concerts. Responding to Haze's accusation that he "ain't true," Holy commends his radio program called "Soulsease" that provides "real religious experiences" (*WB* 88).

Holy's theology asserts that humans are innately good, endowed with a "natural sweetness": "Every person that comes onto this earth is born sweet and full of love" (*WB* 85). The trials of life caused by experiences and people, particularly our families, drive that sweetness inside us to where it cannot be seen anymore. All we need is someone to help us "bring it out" (*WB* 86). Holy's message of self-help and self-love was quite popular in the 1950s when Norman Vincent Peale's *The Power of Positive Thinking* (1952) promised happiness and fulfillment by urging people to harness their inner powers by thinking positively rather than getting bogged down in the difficulties of life. Holy's preaching emphasizes passive surrender and abandonment of effort, giving the true "self" a rest. This pep talk, what William James often characterized as "mental hygiene," is a much easier pill to swallow because it appeals to human vanity and an eagerness to defer personal responsibility.[24]

Stirring his audience to make a commitment, Holy fabricates a sensational testimony of life before he met the prophet: "I was ready to hang myself or to despair completely. Not even my own dear old mother loved me" (*WB* 85). Robert Brinkmeyer analyzes the use of evangelical sermons in O'Connor's fiction to highlight the preacher's use of a "highly rhetorical style punctuated by illustrative stories and anecdotes to electrify his listeners' sensibilities and ensure his success." Sensationalism manipulates listeners to make an impulsive commitment, an effective move in closing the sale. In his most defining passage, Holy explains to Haze that moving an audience to make a commitment is a work of art: "You ought to listen to me because I'm not just an amateur. I'm an artist-type. If you want to get anywheres in religion, you got to keep it sweet. You got good idears but what you need is an artist-type to work with you" (*WB* 89). It is astonishing how such "artists" can permanently alter the lives of so many impressionable people in such a brief encounter. Holy exemplifies the manipulation of evangelists who use their magnetic personalities to prey upon unsuspecting listeners, his awkward pseudonym implying the deception of his message and approach. Even though he turns out to be an opportunistic fraud, Holy's image, actions, and rhetoric embody a saccharine evangelicalism in which charming personalities prey upon the impressionable in a skillful simulation of sales tactics: Endear yourself, create a want, and close the sale.[25]

Joel Osteen, also known as the smiling preacher, embodies the continued success of contemporary televangelists and self-help gurus; he serves as the pastor of Lakewood Church, easily the largest evangelical church in the America with a congregation of more than 45,000 attending weekly in Houston, Texas. The sanctuary of Lakewood Church is located in the Compac Center—the former arena of a professional basketball team, the Houston Rockets. Every Sunday service kicks off with concert hymns and multimedia presentations on jumbo, hi-definition screens, followed by Osteen's reassuring sermons whereby he smilingly addresses his audience as "friends." These pep talks are eventually bundled together and published in a book, selling millions of copies with Osteen collecting a hefty advance before it releases. His 2004 bestseller, *Your Best Life Now: 7 Steps to Living at Your Full Potential,* contains the core of the health and wealth gospel found in his sermons: that anyone can achieve prosperity and happiness by imitating Osteen's own positive outlook. In the book, Osteen urges his readers to implement the following seven steps for their own success: Enlarge your vision, develop a healthy self-image, discover the power of your thoughts and words, let go of the past, find strength through adversity, live to give, and choose to be happy. It is interesting to note that none of these seven steps contains anything exclusively or explicitly Christian in their aims to achieve abundant life. Osteen serves as an abiding reification of O'Connor's "combination minister and masseur" by reinforcing an American culture of self-regard, rendering God to be a genie who grants wishes to his happy followers.[26]

As a fiction writer, O'Connor pursued an artistic commitment to depict the world in which she lived, even if that vision were unflattering to Christians and ran the risk of being read as subversive. If this meant unattractive, comical portrayals of evangelicals, so be it. In a 1963 letter to Sister Mariella Gable, O'Connor responded to complaints that her fiction did not "make Christianity look desirable." O'Connor responded that her duty as a writer was not to romanticize faith, for "ideal Christianity doesn't exist, because anything the human being touches, even Christian truth, he deforms slightly in his own image always toward the abstract and therefore toward allegory, thinness, and ultimately what they are looking for is apologetic fiction." Because O'Connor's figures are, in her own words, so largely and clearly drawn, readers familiar with evangelical culture will recognize her prophets and preachers are as much realistic as exaggerated. And while Hazel Motes was certainly created to startle an unbelieving audience, Onnie Jay Holy ought, in a different manner, to startle an evangelical audience.[27]

It is not the duty of the Christian artist to provide assurance to an evangelical audience that resembles American sales culture. If the Christian artist does not perform the duty of startling the complacent audience, then she might as well give them over to the "advertising agencies," for as O'Connor declared, "[t]hey are entirely capable of showing us our unparalleled prosperity and our almost classless society, and no one has ever accused them of not being affirmative." In conclusion, O'Connor's satirical fiction startles an evangelical audience who are largely at home in American culture. Returning to where we started this chapter, Walker Percy was also concerned about the deformities and compromises he observed in evangelical Christianity. Percy commended the virtues of satire for the Catholic writer to ridicule "the inhuman in order to affirm the human." Percy would continue O'Connor's legacy for the next three decades in a more calculated manner. We now turn to the writer who took aim at an evangelical culture he felt was all too at home in the Southern region.[28]

Chapter 4

Diagnostic Satire
in Walker Percy's Fiction

Once described as "the chief diagnostician of our American anomie," Walker Percy devoted his fiction to examining the loss of individual and cultural identity. Drawing from an initial medical career as a pathologist, Percy would use his writing to diagnose the ills of society. Echoing Thomas Aquinas, Percy defined art as a "virtue of the practical intellect, which is to say making something." When a novel aims to make somebody behave morally, it functions as a tract, not literature, according to Percy: "The South is by and large in no mood for messages from Walker Percy, being, for one thing, too busy watching *Dallas*, *Love Boat* and the NFL on the tube. Or Jimmy Swaggart." Percy often avoided prescribing solutions to his readers; however, he believed that Americans suffered from a spiritual anomie and suggested that religious faith was the panacea.[1] Most consequential to Percy's development was his adult conversion to Catholicism after being diagnosed with tuberculosis and prematurely retiring from the medical profession. Percy's Catholicism augmented his diagnostic outlook in such a way that his fictional concerns can be regarded as chiefly religious.[2] With the prominence of religious issues that permeate six novels, three anthologies of essays, and two collections of interviews—all reinforcing Percy's Christian commitments—one would assume that an author so outspoken about his faith would have his fiction exhausted with religious readings. Yet compared to his contemporary, Flannery O'Connor, it is striking to see the minimal amount of religious criticism of Percy's fiction.[3]

Like O'Connor, Percy's Catholic faith positioned him to write critical and imaginative fiction about the South. While the author shared many of the essential doctrines of Christianity with Protestant believers in the region, his Catholicism secured his outsider perspective in a region dominated by evangelical religion. Though Percy can be considered both Southern and Christian, he harbored concerns about the evangelical hegemony dominating the region.

In his 1982 Flora Levy Lecture, "How to Be an American Novelist in Spite of Being Southern and Catholic," Percy confessed to being a Southern writer in the Christian tradition, and that such a position afforded him an advantage of seeing the region from within, as well as the larger nation from an outsider perspective. Being a Catholic writer in an evangelical region also provided Percy with a more objective vantage point to cast his critical gaze upon the region's dominant religious strain. This critical distance can be understood not just by his position outside the evangelical community, but also the ancient Catholic tradition that predates the more culturally tractable evangelicalism that flourishes in the South. It was precisely the cultural ease with which evangelical religion flowed alongside the social mores of consumerism, racism, complacency, and self-absorbed individualism in the American South that deeply disturbed Percy.

Percy devoted his career to finding narrative strategies that drew his audience's attention to philosophical and theological concerns. In "Percy's Bludgeon," Robert Brinkmeyer identifies two strategies the writer used in his fiction to reach his audience, both of which can be found in the author's 1975 essay collection, *The Message in the Bottle*. Percy's approaches are informed by the premise that his audience exists in a state of alienation caused by modernity's failure to live up to its promises of human progress and happiness. According to Brinkmeyer, Percy's audience can be divided into two parts, requiring a strategy for each: "an alienated reader who knows he is alienated and an alienated reader who imagines he is not." Percy's narrative strategy for the self-conscious, alienated reader is embodied in the first two novels, *The Moviegoer* (1961) and *The Last Gentleman* (1966). This strategy is illustrated in Percy's "The Man on the Train," which prescribes the subtle approach of connecting with the reader who is already in touch with his alienation, forming what Brinkmeyer calls an "alliance with the character and author." Percy proffers a narrative strategy as an aesthetic reversal of alienation whereby an alienated commuter reads a book about another alienated commuter. The experience is affirmative by giving voice to the alienated person's experience. This reversal through re-presentation alleviates the alienation and suggests that religious faith might be the answer.[4]

While this first narrative strategy might establish a profound connection with the sentient reader, the effects upon those more assured in their religious convictions might prove superficial. Consequently, the second strategy, found in his last four novels (*Love in the Ruins, Lancelot, The Second Coming,* and *The Thanatos Syndrome*), comprises a conscious narrative attempt to shock the self-assured sensibilities of the modern reader. This latter approach, which is outlined in Percy's "Notes for a Novel about the End of the World," places a premium on conjuring up catastrophe to awaken the reader out of slumber:

> A serious novel about the destruction of the United States and the end of the world should perform the function of prophecy in reverse. The novelist writes about the coming end in order to warn about present ills and so avert the end. Not being called by God to be a prophet, he nevertheless pretends to a certain prescience. If he did not think he saw something other people didn't see or at least didn't pay much attention to, he wouldn't be wasting his time writing and they reading.[5]

While the first strategy of subtlety can be classified as diagnostic, this latter strategy of shock can be considered prophetic in its attempts to startle complacent readers. In this sense, Percy's fiction after *The Moviegoer* and *The Last Gentleman* began to emulate the prophetic mode of O'Connor, whose stories drew large and startling figures to force her readers to see the religious dimensions in her fiction.[6]

Yet, it is important to distinguish how each Catholic writer startled readers into considering the religious sphere. Percy's fiction tenders compelling conflicts between religious and secular ideologies, often with more complexity and sympathy than O'Connor, whose fiction consistently casts academic, intellectual, and secular characters as pretentious and stubborn. Secular humanists in O'Connor stories characteristically have some type of violent or embarrassing outcome that humbles and prepares them to perceive religious truth. O'Connor's narratives rarely, if ever, accept secular ideas as legitimate alternatives to her Christian worldview. O'Connor unsettled her readers by writing grotesque characters who often undergo violent ordeals; Percy, on the other hand, relied more upon the harm that ideas enact upon the human psyche. While there are certainly violent ordeals in Percy's narratives, he was far more interested in depicting the spiritual condition of alienated modern man. Using his protagonists to both internalize and dramatize philosophical dilemmas, Percy aimed to write prophetic literature that bore witness to Western society's rejection of ontological realism rooted in the Incarnation—the divine Logos revealed in human history. Percy wrote about spiritual and psychic confusion, fragmented and polarized communities, and the subsequent devaluation of language as consequences of this rejection throughout his fiction. Percy's willingness to explore scientific empiricism, philosophical skepticism, and nihilism on their own terms through sympathetic and sophisticated characters often ran the risk of being misinterpreted as deconstructing the faith he ultimately hoped to advance.

Percy believed the nature of Southern fiction was to "probe, challenge, attack, and satirize" the cultural norms of the region. Because evangelical Christianity was the established cultural norm of the South, Percy's satire was unsparing to his own religious worldview. "Satire," according to Percy, "attacks one thing in order to affirm another. It assaults the fake and the phony in the name of truth. It ridicules the inhuman in order to affirm the human. Satire is always launched in the mode of hope." By ridiculing widely cherished ideas and institutions, satirical literature's aims are therapeutic: to reprove and reform. At times both critical and humorous, Percy's fiction achieves effective satire by situating independent-minded protagonists to engage in a struggle with the complaisant evangelical culture of the South. As Linda Whitney Hobson notes, the Percy protagonist always seems to be "rendered something of an invalid by the power of his radar; by his despair at conventional wisdom, behavior, and religion." This radar, according to Hobson, allows each protagonist to see connections that the uncritical or contented would never see. Doreen Fowler presses the alienation of each protagonist as being crucial in their ability to appraise their culture objectively: "Percy's characters seem whole and healthy exactly in proportion to their estrangement from society." Diagnosing the pathologies of religious compromise, Percy's satire treats the anomie present in Southern evangelical religion.[7]

This chapter explores how Percy's fiction satirizes Southern evangelicalism, exposing cultural compromises that are subtle yet visible underneath the smiling surface of a religious institution whose divine vocation is to be in the world but not of the world. The compromises that Percy ridicules stem from the cultural hegemony white evangelicals have enjoyed in the South. The subsequent sense of entitlement contributes to the spiritual anomie of which Percy's protagonists seem wary. This chapter begins with a discussion of a posthumously published essay of Percy's that directly outlines the writer's reflections upon the cultural conformity of the American church. I then examine the writer's life growing up in an evangelical South that proved insufficient to the writer's intellectual or spiritual development. In fact, Percy's education, health, and personal search led him to convert to Catholicism, which provided an alternative to the dominant evangelical orientation of the region. While Percy never embraced evangelicalism, he was ever aware of its profound cultural impact across the Southern region. The chapter examines the satirical depictions of Southern religion in Percy's first two novels, *The Moviegoer* and *The Last Gentleman*. By using alienated and critically minded protagonists as his narrative personae, Percy hoped that his readers would imitate their self-awareness of the modern malaise of cultural conformity. Percy's satire was launched in a mode of hope that Christians would embrace their mission to transform the surrounding culture by reviving a language that had become derivative, irrelevant, and stale.

Much of Percy's fiction, interviews, and essays indicate pressing concerns about evangelical hegemony in Southern culture. Percy's direct commentary on the impact of religion in contemporary culture illuminates the constructive aim of his satire. In "A 'Cranky Novelist' Reflects on the Church," Percy laments the present religious "devaluation of language, a cheapening of the very vocabulary of salvation," which serves to dumb down the faith among American, and more pointedly, Southern evangelicals. Percy argues that there are "three enemies of the Good News in American society, wolves in sheep's clothing" who subvert the message of the church and render society indifferent. According to Percy, these three enemies constitute idolatry in their subversive impact. The first idol of society is the "consumership mentality" that is fostered through the American addiction to technology and media. Noting how most Americans watch several hours of TV each day, Percy claims that these seemingly innocuous diversions influence human behavior in ways that we have yet to understand. Percy argues that we should not expect these people to be receptive to the Christian gospel when their short attention spans are satiated with conflict resolution in thirty-minute sitcoms. The second idol is the occult, a pseudoscience that Percy argues has taken the mantle of subverting Christianity from real science. Christianity used to contend with actual science on the battlefield of metaphysics; now, the occult fuses pseudoscience with spiritual mysticism in fields such as astrology. Percy could only hope such trends might result in a premodern return of harmonizing science and religion to resist this new Gnosticism.[8]

The third idol of American society is Percy's most compelling: fundamentalism. Percy claims that fundamentalists in the South "utter the name of the Lord loudest and most often are the most evident in both in media and in marketplace, whose schools are proliferating at a rate exceeding both private and parochial schools." Percy levels a devastating critique at evangelicals, arguing "they do a disservice by cheapening the vocabulary of Christianity and pandering to a crude emotionalism divorced from reason."[9] The anti-intellectualism and emotionalism of Southern evangelicalism precipitated a "crisis" of young people abandoning the apostolic faith for novelty, according to Percy, who injects his "cranky" commentary: "[T]he young person who turns his back on the apostolic Catholic faith with its two-thousand-year-old synthesis of faith and knowledge, art and science, with the sacramental presence of God Himself on the altar, to take up with some guru or Bible thumper who has no use for sacrament or reason, this young person has in fact sold his birthright for a mess of pottage—or, as some wag put it, a pot of message."[10]

Percy echoes the sentiments of other theologians who argue that popular evangelists and writers are dumbing down the message of the Gospel to a "lowest common denominator theology" in order to garner mass appeal and conversions. Evidence of this dumbing down, according to Percy, is found in the absurd yet successful crusade by evangelicals to cast doubt upon sound evolutionary science in the belief that they are preserving creationism and the soul of mankind. These cultural wars waged by the religious right only serve as an embarrassment to the church, similar to its opposition to Copernicus' heliocentric theory as another unbiblical heresy. In a 1986 interview with Charlotte Hays, Percy lamented that evangelicals often constitute the dominant voice of Christian policies in public discourse. While Percy was an ardent pro-life supporter, he expressed misgivings about evangelicals representing Christianity: "I have reservations, though, when people make that a litmus test but have absolutely no interest in preserving the sanctity of life in such areas as the prevention of war, capital punishment and helping women—the young, poor women—who get pregnant. I notice that a lot of people who are extremely opposed to abortion don't want to do anything to preserve life in other areas. I'm proud that the Catholic Church is on the side of life and not death—in all areas." The criticism seems appropriate with the current political culture comprised of evangelicals and Republicans in unison on issues such as preemptive war, cutting welfare, and supporting the death penalty. Percy asserts the theological and political consistency of Catholicism ensures that Christian policies are informed by orthodox doctrine. One of loudest voices of the Republican social platform to emerge in Percy's career was the religious right, an evangelical coalition of biblical literalists who pushed for a stronger Christian presence in the legislative, judicial, and governing processes. Evangelical leaders such as Pat Robertson, Jerry Falwell, and James Dobson galvanized Christians by pressing hot-button issues such as abortion, homosexuality, prayer in schools, and even textbooks in public schools. Such galvanizing has been far more acute in the South. As Percy argues, many of the problems with Southern evangelicalism occur when a "cultural manifestation of the Church often gets confused with its historical and apostolic mission," reflecting far too often a product of a culture that is more Southern than Christian.[11]

Walker Percy was born on 28 May 1916 in Birmingham, Alabama, where he spent the first thirteen years of his life. His father, LeRoy, grew up Episcopalian while his mother, Mattie Sue, was Presbyterian. The Percy family held membership in the Independent Presbyterian Church in Birmingham where LeRoy taught Sunday school, served on the deacon board, and helped lead the church in building a new sanctuary. The Independent Presbyterian Church in Birmingham began when pastor Henry M. Edmonds was censured by the North Alabama Presbytery for theological liberalism (e.g., he was skeptical of supernatural events in Scripture and generally emphasized the ethical teachings instead) at the South Highlands Presbyterian Church; the Percys were among the core members who followed Edmonds to his new church. Pastor Edmonds's liberal theology provided Percy's introduction to the Christian faith, and despite the family's heavy involvement, he would be at loss to say whether this formative exposure had any real impact on his life.[12]

Percy's experience in Birmingham represents, among other things, a charged symbolic encounter between an archetypal Old South family and a prototypical New South city, and this encounter played a crucial role in shaping the author's character and imagination. Despite professional success, a burgeoning family, and a house on a golf course to provide leisurely distractions, all was not well with his father, LeRoy Percy. Living in the shadow of his own father's suicide and struggling with the same clinical depression, LeRoy killed himself in the attic of the Percy home with a shotgun on the morning of 9 July 1929. After LeRoy's suicide, Mattie Sue moved the family to Athens, Georgia, briefly, then eventually moved in with LeRoy's cousin, William Alexander Percy ("Uncle Will"), the poet, lawyer, planter, and war hero in Greenville, Mississippi, during the summer of 1930. While Mattie Sue encouraged her children to attend Presbyterian Sunday school, Walker eventually stopped going when he sensed that evangelical faith did not provide the answers for his life.[13]

Tragedy again struck the Percy family on 2 April 1932, when Mattie Sue mysteriously drove over the side of a bridge with her youngest son, Phin, in the car, plummeting twenty feet into the water of the bayou. While Phin was able to escape the submerged car, he was not successful in pulling his mother out. Uncle Will adopted the three Percy boys, and he tried to instill a proud sense of education, high culture, and social responsibility. While Uncle Will was nominally a Catholic, his worldview, in reality, was more informed by an ancient Stoicism that stressed heroic virtues of grace and honor that stood firm in the face of a tragic and crumbling civilization. For the development of a Southern intellectual and writer to be, Walker found sanctuary in the household of Uncle Will that shielded him from the dominant evangelical culture of Greenville, of which he would later deride as a culture of "genteel repressed Southern Presbyterian sexuality." Percy's formative teenage years were described by Tolson as "looking for certainties, and though he attended Greenville's Presbyterian church along with his brothers, he did not find them in religion or even in the Stoicism of Uncle Will. He found his answers, increasingly, in science—or, more accurately, in that exaggerated faith in science that is called scientism."[14]

Upon entering the University of North Carolina at Chapel Hill, Percy wrote that he was Presbyterian on one of his entrance forms, indicating he still viewed himself as a Protestant before his collegiate studies began. Though he never went to church in college, he was inspired by the devotion of his roommate, Harry Stovall, a Catholic who faithfully attended Mass early every Sunday. Percy considered Stovall's behavior countercultural, a key witness planting seeds for his eventual conversion to Catholicism. During his sophomore year at Chapel Hill, Percy wrote four articles with *The Carolina Magazine* on literature and contemporary culture that displayed early on his penchant for satire. Commenting upon a January 1935 essay Percy wrote about Willard Wright, a once-esteemed cultural critic who later wrote popular detective fiction, Tolson observes an emerging skill in the younger Percy that would mark the keen satirical orientation of his eventual novels. Tolson notes how the essay, "reveals Percy's fascination with the "decadent artist" as the man who engages thoughtfully, even daringly, with popular culture. There is more than ambiguity in Percy's attitude toward this engagement. There is sympathy. The idea of the intellectual who masters a popular form in order to beguile a wide readership clearly fascinated the precocious sophomore. How could it fail to? This, after all, was a person who, between Schiller and Shakespeare, eagerly submerged himself in Hollywood's latest fare." Percy recognized how popular culture possesses a powerful sway over Americans in certifying their lives and experiences; regardless of how crude the artifice, entertainment and the lives of celebrities vicariously provide an excitement to the ordinary malaise of human existence.[15]

Once he graduated from Chapel Hill, Percy attended medical school at Columbia University. Percy continued to be attracted to Catholics for what he perceived to be an air of certainty and solidarity with American culture. Finding himself drawn to another Catholic friend and classmate at Columbia University's medical school, Frank Hardart, Percy was fascinated by his quiet confidence and spirituality. After finishing his coursework, Percy began an internship in pathology at the Bellevue Clinic in New York. The young physician contracted tuberculosis, which forced him to enter various sanatoriums in New York. Undergoing a rest cure at Trudeau Sanatorium on Saranac Lake, Percy endured a long period of isolation where he immersed himself in books. Having no other options as a patient but to lie or sit, Percy read obsessively and contemplated deeply about his life. Acknowledging that his scientific education taught him much about humanity, he felt that many answers about human existence were not sufficiently answered. Tolson notes that it was during this isolated and depressing period that he discovered the kind of literature that suited him best:

> Rather than novels brimming with society, Percy found consolation in fiction that featured lonely, cut-off, even somewhat aberrant types. He would later give precise formulation to the paradoxically cheering effect of gloomy literature, but at Saranac Lake all he knew was that he found himself reading Kafka's bleak parables and Dostoyevsky's novels of tormented spiritual seekers with something close to joy—as well as kindred sympathy. There was also a teasing simultaneity about reading these books at this time, a time when confidence in Western culture and civilization was being most darkly challenged.[16]

Percy's philosophical quandary led him to gravitate to many European existentialist writers. One writer in particular resonated with Percy during this time of reflecting upon his own mortality: "After twelve years of scientific education, I felt somewhat like the Danish philosopher Soren Kierkegaard when finished reading Hegel. Hegel, said Kierkegaard, explained everything under the sun, except one small detail: what it means to be a man living in the world who must die." Percy first encountered Kierkegaard when he read "The Difference between a Genius and an Apostle." Here, Kierkegaard asserts that difference between revelation and intellectual discovery; while both truths are important, the former is distinguished not as a genius who speaks with brilliance but as an apostle who has been authorized to speak ultimate truth through divine revelation. Both Kierkegaard and Gabriel Marcel attended to themes that concerned modern man's sense of sickness and homelessness—a loss of self that social science proved ill-equipped at diagnosing, much less treating.[17]

Bedridden, left only to himself and his books, Percy commenced to reconfigure his philosophical outlook, as he gradually made his way to Catholicism in search for an ultimate answer. During his stay at Saranac, Percy befriended another Catholic from New Jersey, Arthur Fortugno, who would spar with Percy in debates concerning religion. The debates with Fortugno led Percy to read Thomas Aquinas, whose systematic logic proved appealing. While Percy had yet to convert, he increasingly found Catholicism compelling, and he began attending services at St. Bernard's, a local Catholic church. Tolson states that Percy began to realize at Saranac that his vocation would not be research, but rather "the search" to discover the mystery that surrounds human life.[18]

During his rest cure in the Adirondacks of New York, Percy wrote regularly to Mary Bernice Townsend, whom he called "Bunt," and it was clear that the relationship was emerging into an abiding one. The relationship proved strongest at a time when Percy was reconstructing a completely new outlook that considered writing a potential vocation and Catholicism an attractive worldview. Catholicism, Percy believed, best answered the questions that nagged at him. Once his tuberculosis became dormant, Percy took a pilgrimage to Sante Fe where he traveled, explored, and pondered, while residing for several months on a dude ranch. Santa Fe embodied the pure possibility of the West—a place, according to Percy, where "what a man can be the next minute bears no relation to what he is or what he was the minute before" laid his existence bare. In such a place, Percy came to a decision as to what man he would be: "It was more a matter of coming to the end of a long line of thinking, and of waking up one morning in the early autumn on a ranch near Santa Fe and deciding [. . .] I've got to have a life. I'm going to be a writer. I am going to live in New Orleans. And I am going to marry Bunt."[19]

Percy, for the first time since boyhood in the Presbyterian church, began to read his Bible at the family's Brinkwood home in Sewanee, Tennessee, shortly after marrying Bunt in late 1946. He affirmed Kierkegaard's view about the writers of Scripture: Such people derived authority to speak the divine in human language. It must be noted, however, that Percy did not agree with Kierkegaard's "leap of faith" proposition when it came to conversion. As Tolson notes, Percy did not regard religious belief as absurd, but rather concurred with Aquinas that faith was "compatible with reason" and therefore a "form of knowledge." He would move to New Orleans as his community of choice in September 1947. New Orleans embodied the perfect place for starting his new life because of its sense of being queer and adrift from the normal cultural trappings of the conservative evangelical South.[20]

After moving to New Orleans, Percy began taking instruction with his wife at Holy Name Church. He converted and was baptized on 13 December 1947. The Catholic Church provided a rich intellectual faith for Percy during a time when he needed strength and stability. He believed that the modern age had come to a crashing halt, and that the ancient faith in God's incarnational entrance into history through Jesus Christ was the only source of salvation. Despite the disapprobation from his lifelong friend Shelby Foote that he was in "full intellectual retreat," Percy did not feel compelled to justify his newfound religious belief; as Samway discusses, "Walker preferred not to talk publicly about why he became a Catholic. He knew that his spiritual life was private and that discussion of religion, friendly or polemical, often ended up in confusion [...] And rather than wasting anyone's time, Walker preferred to retreat into silence by noting finally that he didn't have the authority to bear or proclaim the Good News."[21]

Percy's conversion to Catholicism was not unique, but part of a movement of many other literary figures who converted after World War II. Ann Waldron discusses the postwar boom of literary figures converting to the Catholic Church:

> The climate was favorable for conversion just then; there was a boom in Catholicism after World War II. Francis Sheed, an Australian convert, and his wife, Maisie Ward, a British cradle Catholic, were writing furiously, publishing Catholic writers at Shee & Ward, and even preaching on street corners. Bishop Fulton J. Sheen had become a television personality and had personally instructed converts like Heywood Broun, Fritz Kreisler, Grace Moore, Henry Ford II, the glamorous Claire Boothe Luce, and even reconverted Louis Budenz, managing editor of *The Daily Worker*. The Catholic Worker movement and French worker priests made the news magazines. It seemed easy, almost chic, to be a Catholic.[22]

Tolson notes that many of these writers, like Percy, shared a "dissatisfaction with the doctrinal fuzziness of Protestant creeds and with Protestantism's suppression of the ritual and even supernatural dimensions of faith. They admired the scholastic rigor of Catholic theology, and they respected the church's insistence upon obedience. Celebrating the lost unity of the medieval world, they also saw Catholicism as the best hope for restoring an organically connected society." Percy's conversion was a similar intellectual process, as Tolson elaborates: "He shared with the literary converts a certain disdain for the wishy-washiness of Protestantism. And he might even have been attracted to the idea of Catholicism as the foundation for a renewed human community, though Percy's concern for the social dimensions of his faith seems to have come somewhat later." Brinkmeyer also notes that Allen Tate, Caroline Gordon, and Percy converted to Catholicism as adults after their prolonged struggles with the positivism of modern thought that had stripped away traditional frameworks of meaning and morality. These writers saw their Southern heritage as another identity to define themselves in resistance to the modern world; the Catholic Church provided transcendence of modernity, restoring "myth, meaning, and mystery to what they saw as a morally irresponsible modern world." Tolson differentiates Percy from other literary counterparts who converted to Catholicism by illuminating the unique path the writer took "by way of science and scientism and involved a dialectical movement away from everything he once believed toward its apparent antithesis." As Tolson observes, Percy "never turned a hostile eye toward science and technology, as most of the literary converts did." Percy concluded that science—while valuable—could not fully account for the uniqueness of the human being and his individual existence.[23]

Living in New Orleans and then eventually settling into his lifelong residence in Covington, Louisiana, Percy commenced a second apprenticeship (the first being a medical student) as a writer. While *The Moviegoer* may have burst onto the scene by winning the National Book Award for Fiction in 1962, it took many years developing his craft solitarily (though with the remote assistance and feedback of Caroline Gordon and Shelby Foote) on two separate novels—*The Charterhouse* and *The Gramercy Winner*—that never were published. Percy had more success publishing articles extensively as early as 1954 on semiotics and the nature of language. Percy was not your typical Southern writer who was comfortable telling a story; his discourse consisted more in the realms of dialectic and argument—elements he would eventually incorporate into his own novels that wrestled with philosophical themes. Percy's spiritual and vocational conversions were now complete: His new life commenced as a Catholic writer. Like his contemporary, Flannery O'Connor, Percy possessed a Catholic faith that provided some critical distance to the evangelicalism that dominated his home region; he exploited this vantage point to his artistic advantage by writing effective religious satire that would diagnose the ills of a cultural Christendom that lulled Southern evangelicals into a complacency unworthy of Christ's institution.

THE MOVIEGOER

Percy's debut novel, *The Moviegoer*,[24] follows Binx Bolling, the protagonist and narrator, during the week leading up to his thirtieth birthday, as he embarks on a search for meaning to overcome the despair of everydayness that settles over his life like a malaise. As a stockbroker living and working in a suburb outside of New Orleans, Binx has settled into a comfortable life of consumerism and casual sex with his secretaries. Moviegoing provides Binx with an aesthetic escape from the alienating sentence of human existence. It is through films that Binx interprets the world and lives vicariously through the Hollywood-scripted triumphs. Binx becomes unsettled with his life at the outset of the novel, as he recalls a near-death experience as a soldier during the Korean War. As death seemed inevitable, he resolved to search for a meaningful life when he returned

Diagnostic Satire 89

home; however, like many postwar Americans, Binx settled down comfortably in the late 1950s making lots of money and devoting his life to consumption. Growing increasingly uneasy with this everydayness, Binx embarks upon his search—a central theme that Percy would explore in all of his fiction.

Winning the 1962 National Book Award, *The Moviegoer* was praised by the judges who voted for it unanimously, citing Percy's examination of "the delusions and hallucinations and the daydreams and the dreads that afflict those who abstain from the customary ways of making do," as the prime achievement. In a 1961 interview with Judith Serebnick, Percy further revealed his antecedents in European existentialism, which are embodied in the rebellion and alienation of his two main characters:

> My novel is an attempt to portray the rebellion of two young people against the shallowness and tastelessness of modern life. The rebellion takes different forms. In Kate, it manifests itself through psychiatric symptoms: anxiety, suicidal tendencies and the like. In Binx, it is a 'metaphysical' rebellion—a search for meaning which is the occasion of a rather antic life in a suburb of New Orleans (the action spans one week, Mardi Gras week, in New Orleans). The antecedents of this book are European rather than American: Dostoevsky, Rilke, and especially Albert Camus.[25]

Percy uses an epigraph from one such European existentialist, Kierkegaard, to suggest his own narrative strategy—made even more explicit in the epilogue—as a way of understanding how he engages in an indirect method of critiquing prevailing cultural practices (religion being chief among them). The quote from Kierkegaard speaks to the complacency and lack of self-awareness that Percy explores throughout the narrative: "The specific character of despair is precisely this: it is unaware of being despair." In his posthumous publication, *The Point of View*, Kierkegaard details his unique approach as a Christian author writing to critique a religiously complacent readership. Kierkegaard engaged this cultural Christianity by writing in two modes: religious works published under his real name and philosophical works published under pseudonyms. Kierkegaard considered his religious works a direct mode of authorship that functioned to edify Christian readers. The pseudonymous philosophical works—what he called "esthetic" writing—were considered an indirect mode that functioned more subversively to engage his audience through "godly" irony and deception. Between the years 1843–1848, Kierkegaard released both types of works concurrently within days of one another, whereby the esthetic writings would serve to prepare his readers often days in advance for the message of his religiously edifying works. I would suggest that both of Kierkegaard's modes are at work in *The Moviegoer* as narrator, Binx engages in the indirect, esthetic mode of reflection for the majority of the novel, only to become more direct and edifying in the epilogue. In fact, Binx refers to Kierkegaard specifically to suggest that he can no longer engage in the esthetic mode of "searching," and that he can only speak on such matters in a way that is "edifying" (*MG* 237). This passage provides one of many indications that Binx has embraced the Catholic faith of his mother's family by the novel's end.[26]

Kierkegaard considered the esthetic mode a necessary strategy based upon his belief that the masses of Denmark were under an illusion that they were Christians by virtue of living in a Lutheran country. Kierkegaard poses a rhetorical question to illustrate this illusion: "What does it mean, after all, that all these thousands as a matter of course call themselves Christians?" In view of their complacency, Kierkegaard understood he could not directly confront his readers with the accusation that they were deluded, for this would result in being labeled a fanatic and would only serve to reassure an already self-satisfied culture. The esthetic writings engaged in a Socratic method that "approached from behind" to deceive his readers into the truth. To clarify, Kierkegaard's godly deception entails an act of solidarity by which the Christian author poses as an outsider, a non-Christian who takes his audience's delusions at face value to engage in a search for understanding. This approach, again following Socrates, places everything in reflection to model for his reader the path to becoming a Christian. For Kierkegaard, "total thought is the task of becoming a Christian," a proposition that posits reflection at the heart of his esthetic writing; therefore, "everything is cast into reflection" and the author resides "in the background helping negatively" through indirect communication. Kierkegaard's esthetic method appears to be appropriated in all of Percy's novels: The reflective protagonists function indirectly by inducing readers to imitate their epistemological quest for ultimate meaning.[27]

Of all Percy's novels, *The Moviegoer* embodies the Kierkegaardian esthetic most fully. Binx's reflections, in many ways, can be considered the novel's ultimate concern. In describing the nature of his search, Binx alludes to the same Kierkegaardian quote found in the epigraph: "To become aware of the possibility of the search is to be onto something. Not to be onto something is to be in despair" (*MG* 13). Binx associates the despair with the everydayness in which most people are sunk, a condition whereby humans surrender any sense of reflection about the meaning or significance of their lives. Binx specifically highlights religious complacency in a poll that shows 98% of Americans believe in God and the remaining 2% as agnostics or atheists, leaving "not a single percentage point for a seeker" (*MG* 14). In Kierkegaardian fashion, Binx indulges the dominant culture's assertions at face value to consider that he is still searching for what everyone else has apparently found. Yet the satirical intention is suggested when Binx teases out the more likely explanation: Most people have abandoned any sense of reflection, opting instead to "settle down with a vengeance" (*MG* 14).

Binx's satirical perception reveals how many people thrive in the South by projecting moral superiority and self-assurance. While Binx caricatures these qualities directly in characters like the Lovells who, according to Nell, have examined their own values only to find them impregnable (Binx tries his best not to fart while listening), he uses a more subtle satire in his descriptions of Uncle Jules, the wealthy and bullish patriarch of the Cutrer family. Binx catalogues a checklist of Uncle Jules's credentials to certify his "total and unqualified" victory in the world (*MG* 31). Such a victorious lifestyle moves Binx to playfully admire the patriarch's sartorial qualities, remarking how he longs to nuzzle his nose in the soft-spun cotton of Jules's perfectly tailored shirts (*MG* 30–31). Such comedic observations provide Binx an opening to consider the spiritual ramifications of his uncle's worldly success: "He is an exemplary Catholic, but it is hard to know why he takes the trouble. For the world he lives in, the City of Man, is so pleasant that the City of God must hold little in store for him. I see his world plainly through his eyes and I see why he loves it and would keep it as it is: a friendly easy-going place of old-world charm and new-world business methods where kind white folks and carefree darkies have the good sense to behave pleasantly toward each other" (*MG* 31). Binx invokes the Augustinian binary of cities to typify "two distinct commitments of will—or two loves." Vernon Burke argues that *The City of God* provided Augustine with a theological template whereby all "human history and culture may be viewed as an interplay of the competing values of these two loves and of these two cities." For Augustine, the Christian life is defined by a tension between these loves, as one seeks to be in the world but not of it. As far as Binx discerns, no such tension exists in Uncle Jules.[28]

The implicit critique of Uncle Jules' religious commitments are voiced more explicitly by Binx's manic cousin, Kate. In detailing Kate's dialectical scrutiny of her parents as she grew up, Binx reveals that Kate was a daddy's girl early on in her childhood, but through the adolescent years of asserting her independence and rebellion, she gravitated to her mother, Emily, who embodied a sense of critical and free thought. Kate perceives Jules quite differently during this period of her life: "If she hadn't much use for her father's ways, his dogged good nature, his Catholic unseriousness, his little water closet jokes, his dumbness about his God, the good Lord; the everlasting dumb importuning of her just to be good, to mind the sisters, and to go his way, his dumb way of inner faith and outer good spirits" (*MG* 45). Binx's repetition of "dumb" expresses the facile faith that embodies Jules' unexamined religious life. Contented to shift the burden of Kate's dangerous mental issues onto Emily, Jules exhibits a hollow faith of platitudes and sterility.

Percy's satire aims to not only critique but also correct religious compromise by introducing key minor characters that provide viable alternatives—a strategy that he uses in all of his novels. Binx's half brother, Lonnie, only fourteen and stricken with a fatal illness that keeps him bound to a wheelchair, represents the sincerest character of religious faith in the novel. Binx's early description foreshadows the sacramental impact Lonnie will have upon the protagonist by the novel's end: "For one thing, he has the gift of believing that he can offer his sufferings in reparation for men's indifference to the pierced heart of Jesus Christ" (*MG* 137). Despite weighing only eighty pounds, Lonnie wants to fast and abstain during Lent. Lonnie's fasts are to "conquer an habitual disposition" of envying his older brother, Duval, who tragically died from drowning; Lonnie confesses that he feels joy at this misfortune and that he also hoped his talented and favored brother to lose in his sporting events (*MG* 163). After Binx convinces him to focus instead on the Eucharist, Lonnie informs Binx that he is still offering his communion for him (*MG* 165).

In the epilogue, Binx informs the reader that Lonnie died a few days after his fifteenth birthday from a massive viral infection. The day before he died, Lonnie whispered to Binx that he conquered his habitual disposition, a signal that the boy is prepared for death and eternity. Lonnie's death presents many clues of Binx's religious conversion, as the adversity provides an opportunity to bear the fruits of his religious faith at the end of the novel. Rather than sit by paralyzed with grief, Binx instead goes to check on the younger siblings (Jean-Paul, Mathilde, and the twins, Clare and Donice) who have been waiting in the car all morning. He tells the kids that Lonnie has been anointed and that he will no longer be in a wheelchair when the Lord raises him up on the last day (*MG* 240). Binx's affirmation of the resurrection and his service to the children provides a crucial allusion to Fyodor Dostoevsky's *The Brothers Karamazov,* in which the novel's Christian hero, Alyosha, also ministers to the schoolboys after the untimely death of their friend, Ilyusha, which also occurs in the epilogue. Christian ministry to children in both instances provides hopeful conclusions and bears the fruit of Christian spirituality. While Binx, like Percy himself, may not have "the inclination to say much on the subject" of his search or religious faith to his reader in the epilogue, he cleverly alludes to Kierkegaard again by stating that he can only hope to "edify" his readers—another subtle signal by Percy that though he may not possess the apostolic authority to preach, he can encourage or suggest to his readers a path to religious faith through concrete narratives (*MG* 237). Binx embraces Catholicism as he concludes his search at the end of his "thirtieth year to heaven" (*MG* 236).

THE LAST GENTLEMAN

In his second novel, *The Last Gentleman*,[29] Percy hones his satirical mode to extrapolate religious compromise onto the entire South. The most autobiographical of Percy's novels, *The Last Gentleman* traces the protagonist's travels from New York to Birmingham to Ithaca (fictional representation of Greenville, Mississippi), and concluding in Santa Fe—four cities that figured prominently in Percy's life. The protagonist is Will Barrett, a twenty-five-year-old from Ithaca, Mississippi. Will dropped out of college at Princeton and came home to Ithaca to read law one summer, but stopped when his father, Ed Barrett, a progressive leader in the small town, committed suicide in the attic of their home. After fits of melancholy and amnesia, Barrett serves two years in the army before moving to New York where he lives in the YMCA in Manhattan and works at Macy's as a humidification engineer over a console three floors underground. When he is not working, Will enjoys people watching in Central Park (the "Ground Zero" of humanist culture) with his Tetzlar telescope. This safe, scientific distance from humanity enables Will to transcend the world of human activity and observe, as the narrator often refers to him as the "engineer." While in New York, he meets the Vaughts who have brought their sixteen-year-old son, Jamie, from Alabama to treat his leukemia. The family finds Will so endearing that they invite him back with them to Birmingham to serve as a companion to Jamie—a request he gladly fulfills after falling in love with the daughter, Kitty. This arrangement provides several dramatic crises that cast Will back into the subjective world of human relations and force him to deal with his troubled past in the South.

When Will returns home to the South, he discovers many unexpected qualities: "The South he came home to was different from the South he had left. It was happy, victorious, Christian, rich, patriotic and Republican" (*LG* 185). The "formidable" and "almost invincible" happiness of the New South belies an unexamined alliance of God and mammon. Martin Luschei notes how the descriptions of the South in *The Last Gentleman* imply a facade to mask the region's religious compromise. The novel's treatment of religion after the New South campaign of economic prosperity reveals what John Desmond calls a "sharpening of [Percy's] critical analysis of the deep spiritual disorder" accentuated by contradictions. Percy, like his protagonist, believed that the Old South was informed by Stoicism and nominal Christianity, marking it with a poetic pessimism that took a strange satisfaction in the dissolution of its values. In a 1956 essay for *Commonweal*, Percy contends that the Old South's worldview was shaped more by Greek influences and the virtues of the "old Stoa" than Christianity. Percy asserts that the Decalogue, the Beatitudes, and the Incarnation were foreign doctrines to the Old South, which Percy claimed was comprised of a cultural Christendom (borrowing from Kierkegaard): "The Southern gentleman did live in a Christian edifice, but he lived there in the strange fashion Chesterton spoke of, that of a man who will neither go inside nor put it entirely behind him but stands forever grumbling on the porch." This cultural Christendom was not necessarily a bad thing, for noble virtues of grace and manners were upheld. In a 1968 essay, "The Failure and the Hope," Percy claims that the Stoic tradition came to an end around the turn toward the twentieth century; the subsequent vacuum was filled by a white-hot evangelical faith that would mark the South as the Bible Belt of America, fervently advancing a more fundamentalist orientation that shielded its eyes from the advances of science and modernity.[30]

The coherence of Stoic values found in the former South of Will's father has been exchanged for the New South of thriving businesses and churches, as Desmond observes how "Will's return to the 'New South' in search of the Vaughts—the happy, prosperous, hypocritically 'Christian' South—enables Percy to map with deadly satire the broader landscape of fractured community in America and its metaphysical incoherence." The new industrial order alluded to in the passage undermines the "network or relations which made possible the appearance of those values in the first place." As the South pursued material prosperity through northern industrial means, the region began to compromise its distinctiveness, becoming what Fred Hobson describes as the "successful, optimistic, prosperous, and bland" Southern region that characterizes the settings in Percy's fiction.[31]

The "newly exuberant, self-congratulatory South" was not celebrated by Percy, for the Southern region had become infected with the American problems of "alienation and disaffection" that result from the "shallowness and impersonality of modern life." In a 1985 interview with John Kemp, Percy discussed the ambiguity of the South's recent economic leadership—the fruits of the New South agenda—and how it has affected the Southern writer: "The so-called Southern novel also became victim of its own success. Southern writers are in a quandary about what to do now that the old defeated and exotic South has become a victorious and prosperous sunbelt." Observing all the Sunbelt progress, Percy grew increasingly uneasy at what he called the "Losangelization" of the South. Percy characterized the contemporary South as a region of the "LA-Dallas-Atlanta axis . . . an agribusiness-sports-vacation-retirement-show-biz culture with its spiritual center perhaps at Oral Roberts University." Malcolm Jones, after an interview with Percy, perhaps put it best: "In Percy's South, historical monuments and Hollywood fakery coexist cheerfully: Sunbelt newcomers pull on riding boots and take to drawling; the descendants of Civil War generals move to the suburbs and make fortunes converting slave quarters to $400,000 condos."[32]

The Last Gentleman provides Percy's best satire of an awkward economic and religious alliance: a South flaunting its prosperity and evangelical fervor. One might assume that evangelical religion would problematize the ethics of the New South economic agenda, yet proponents of economic supremacy tapped into the same religious fervor as the Confederate cause in harnessing a divine justification for the South's moral and religious exceptionalism. The narrator provides further description of a perplexing mixture that combines regionalism with a very un-Southern sense of national patriotism: "They had a history, they had a place redolent with memories, they had good conversation, they believed in God and defended the Constitution, and they were getting rich in the bargain" (*LG* 186). As Will travels deeper into the South, "he passed more and more cars which had Confederate plates on the front bumper and plastic Christs on the dashboard. Radio programs became more patriotic and religious" (*LG* 186). The fusion of Confederate sympathy, national patriotism, and rampant consumerism highlights the power of religious sentiment to induce cultural conformity. James C. Cobb highlights this awkward embrace typified in the Southern Methodist Publishing House's release of "*The Law of Success* which suggested that good Christians made good capitalists and vice versa by drawing on the experiences of a number of 'self made' southerners to emphasize 'the commercial value of the Ten Commandments and a righteous life.'" Appropriating spiritual things for material ends, the New South proponents argued for the inverted result: By establishing "material prosperity," Cobb observes, "religious and moral supremacy would result among southern churches."[33]

Percy's satire of Southern religion proves to be richer and more complex in *The Last Gentleman* than his first novel. The writer's strategy of using a third-person narrator to stand apart from the protagonist, along with the addition of more characters and settings, provides the reader an abundance of complications in which to navigate. Sutter Vaught embodies a compelling character for Will to contend with, as the protagonist is drawn to the neurotic and suicidal physician who gives language to the ontological problems that plague him. Will correctly senses that Sutter is onto the cultural malaise, as he reads the physician's casebooks, which function as confessional, philosophical journal entries that voice the competing ideologies that Percy wished to dramatize in the novel. Sutter has embraced the metaphysics of scientism, a reductive ideology that displaces the real of "things, persons, relations" by emptying them out through theory. Sexual contact becomes sacramental in such an abstract predicament, as Sutter asserts, "There remains only relation of skin to skin and hand under dress" (*LG* 279–80). Sutter's lewdness is foiled by his sister, Val, an earnest Catholic nun who has settled into an obscure and impoverished ministry to Black children in Southern Alabama (a sure sign of religious authenticity in Percy's fiction). Many of Sutter's notebook entries are addressed to Val, as Percy uses the two characters to dramatize the opposing viewpoints with which he wants his readers to struggle: "The only difference between me and you is that you think that purity and life can only come from eating the body and drinking the blood of Christ. I don't know where it comes from" (*LG* 282). John Desmond keenly observes that both Sutter and Val perceive and welcome "the demise of hypocritical Christendom." While Sutter refuses to believe God is present now in the flawed church of human community, Val embraces a life of faith and works to transform it.[34]

The young leukemia-stricken Jamie—eerily similar to Lonnie in *The Moviegoer*—is on a similar intellectual quest with Will Barrett, as they share an interest in science, enjoy traveling, and seem unconvinced by the religiosity surrounding them throughout the novel. Jamie's confrontation with death, however, forces him to reckon with the claims of Christianity. It is his reckoning during the last chapters in Santa Fe that Will (and the reader) witnesses a powerful deathbed conversion in the hospital. When Will realizes that Jamie is only moments away from dying, he calls Val, who charges Will with the duty to administer Jamie's baptism since she knows she will not make it to Santa Fe in time. Instead, Will finds a hospital chaplain, an older and reluctant priest to perform the duty. It is here that Percy writes one of his most moving scenes by depicting a baptism with cloudy tap water from a hospital bathroom administered to the dying and defecating Jamie; while Will fetches the water, Sutter assists the priest by bracing Jamie and giving his full name for baptismal pronouncement. This grotesque and undignified moment ushers in a shocking, sacramental act of grace breaking into a moment of natural decay. It is apparent that the scene has a profound impact upon both Sutter and Will, as both (along with the reader) are left to reckon with this mysterious and dramatic religious conversion. It is through characters of religious authenticity, such as Val, Lonnie, and Jamie, that we find Percy's "mode of hope" to which he alludes, as if they were written to dramatize a life of faith as a viable approach to a life of despair. Such characters reinforce Percy's belief that the Catholic Church provided a religious alternative to an evangelical Southern culture that devalued language and was hostile to intellectual and scientific inquiry.

In both *The Moviegoer* and *The Last Gentleman*, Percy satirizes the materialism and evangelical Christianity that flow alongside one another, compromising the South's religious authenticity. The Christendom that Percy satirizes is not the ecclesia of the New Testament serving poor people and widows, nor is it the religion of Jesus who proclaims, "it is easier for a camel to go through the eye of a needle than for a rich man to enter the kingdom of God" (Matthew 19:24). On the contrary, this is an evangelical South truly at home in the world. Most troubling to Percy and his reflective protagonists is the unfounded sense of religious assurance, as financial success and evangelical hegemony coexist harmoniously to create an odd mixture of Jesus, prosperity, and nationalism. Percy's satire illustrates how people are quite content to live their lives as consumers in today's society. The irony of many evangelical Southerners is that despite self-assured claims to having been redeemed from a fallen world, they embrace the same consumer lifestyle with little reflection as to how compromised they might be. While Percy certainly viewed Christian faith as providing a way out of the despair, he understood the cultural ease of Christendom embodied in Southern religion.

Part Three

Narrative Negotiation

Chapter 5

Descent and Vision in Dennis Covington's
Salvation on Sand Mountain

The first two sections of this study focus on Southern writers who depict evangelicalism as authoritarian (Cash), oppressive (Smith), manipulative (O'Connor), and compromised (Percy). Narrative resistance is a dualistic and oppositional strategy characterized by reaction and defined by negation. Narrative satire comprises a dialogic parody of conflicting ideologies, which forecloses resolution. Both strategies invoke ideological binaries that separate individuals and communities. While these sections may seem to construct a hero (Southern writers) versus villain (evangelical religion) motif, the final section of late twentieth century Southern writers—both nonfiction and fiction—will serve to complicate matters through sympathetic renderings and active participation in evangelical faith.

Narrative negotiation is characterized by hybridity and subjectivity. Negotiation cultivates complex and nuanced understandings of human subjectivity by elevating social engagement and emotion. Consistent with its Latin root, negotiation connotes a sense of unease by complicating existing categories, which become re-envisioned and repurposed toward different ends. Stephen Greenblatt describes negotiation as "complex, ceaseless borrowings and lendings" that move materials, including "well-worn stories," "from one culturally demarcated zone to another." In similar fashion, Thomas West and Gary Olson define negotiation as a "borderland" narrative strategy "connected to the ambivalent state of hybridity wherein the co-constitutive dimensions of identity and meaning formation are recognized and exploited." In the context of teaching composition, Henry Giroux characterizes negotiation as a "border pedagogy" that transgresses existing boundaries forged in domination through redefinition, which enables a "fashioning of new identities within existing configurations of power."[1]

The term "negotiation" often carries a neutered connotation for ensuring civility in public discourse by devaluing emotional expression. As Homi Bhabha argues, "The structures of feelings and the structures of affect are radically devalued in the language of political effectivity, cultural identity, and so on." Negotiation has historically been used as a hegemonic strategy that masks as civil interaction. In this context, negotiation suppresses emotion, unsanctioned thinking, and action; therefore, negotiation becomes synonymous with conflict aversion and compromise that reinforce the status quo. Making discourse polite discourages marginalized communities from passionately presenting their interests. According to this perspective, negotiation de-politicizes discourse by removing antagonistic passions. West and Olson characterize this notion as a "limp liberal conception" of compromise that smooths over tensions. Used in this way, negotiation becomes a floating signifier, devoid of descriptive power and open to subjective interpretation and appropriation. Liberal conceptions of tolerance and community can also hide inequitable power relations; these abstract notions inevitably manifest as a particular version or interpretation couched in demotic discourse.[2] Tolerance and community function rhetorically as virtue terms: imbued with positive connotations and deployed with minimal reflection.[3]

Because reality is rarely ordered or logical, narrative negotiation elevates the importance of subjective experience and emotion in creating a sense of meaning and identity; therefore, negotiation need not be associated with compromise, but rather the "process of translation and rearticulation, a rewriting or reinscribing." The hybrid quality of negotiation evokes ambivalence by trespassing established borders and transforming cultural codes into something new and different. Crossing boundaries entails some form of exchange, as writers borrow cultural materials to appropriate for their own purposes. Narrative negotiation entails more than merely trading and sharing cultural materials; negotiation involves translation, which West and Olson define as the "rearticulation of social and cultural codes" that requires "intense reflection on the affective relations and politics of difference" in order to modify how we feel about one another.[4]

The materials of evangelical religion are translated by the writers in this final section to negotiate themes of place and space, past and present, freedom and security. Their narrative strategies depict evangelicalism as a culture capable of providing nourishing communities as well as a strong sense of individual purpose and selfhood. Instead of dismissing evangelical faith for its transgressions, these writers see a wider spectrum within the religious tradition, appraising its capacity to satisfy human desires for love, companionship, and affirmation. By elevating the roles of emotion and subjective participation, their narratives obscure the lines between individuality and community as well as body and spirit.

Descent and Vision   103

Rather than resist or satirize the old-time religion of the South, the strategies of negotiation in this final section appropriate and reconfigure evangelical faith through compelling narratives of conversion, self-discovery, and community.

Dennis Covington's *Salvation on Sand Mountain: Snake Handling and Redemption in Southern Appalachia* documents a spiritual journey into the heart of an evangelical subculture. From the opening pages of *Salvation on Sand Mountain,* Covington centers on religion as a key to understanding the South's identity, and he takes great pains to present a fair and sympathetic perspective of not only snake handlers, but also rural white people. Covington negotiates snake handling culture by casting it as a marginalized community. This translation, so to speak, problematizes our understanding of white evangelicals as a monolithic entity that holds political power and cultural influence. Covington enables readers to see the class differences within white evangelical subsets: how Pentecostals differ greatly from the Baptists and Methodists that comprise a powerful majority in the South. In doing so, Covington reveals how these disparaged and diminished communities prove worthy of the "difference" designation employed by progressive scholars.

Covington's initial interest in snake-handling culture begins as a journalist for *The New York Times* covering the Scottsboro, Alabama, trial of Reverend Glen Summerford, who is convicted to serve ninety-nine years in prison for attempting to murder his wife with the same rattlesnakes used in the services of his church. Rather than viewing the trial as an amusing spectacle of Southern freaks, Covington becomes fascinated with the earnest faith of the snake handlers. Covington's interest is not merely driven by curiosity; he becomes charmed with the snake handling culture in what amounts to gonzo journalism at its finest. Attracted to "the passion and abandon of their worship," Covington engages a sect that is often derided as grotesque by mainstream culture; through compassionate investigation and active participation, Covington travels, worships, speaks in tongues, and eventually handles serpents in his quest to understand both the region and his roots (*SSM* 67).[5]

In what follows, I reveal how Covington employs a rhetorical strategy of self-writing that typifies Southern identity memoirs while differing from their epistemology of cultural isolation. While many of these memoirs differ from *Salvation on Sand Mountain* in their writing about racial injustice and violence, I show how Covington's subjective experience with evangelical spirituality enables him to negotiate the same cumbersome history and social issues that have long plagued the South. Offering an inversion of the prototypical approach to Southern memoirs that transcends the region to achieve selfhood, Covington generates a vision of Southern identity in memoir that comes at a price: His descent into soul and South involves a decentering of self, a negotiation that arises from participating in a snake-handling culture that also holds the key to his identity.

As we saw in chapter 2, Southern memoirs often follow a conventional pattern: A writer grows up in the South, experiences a crisis of identity with the cultural values, and eventually overcomes this tension by migrating North, through education, or some combination of both. A pattern typified by Katherine Du Pre Lumpkin and Lillian Smith, Southern memoirs often depict a writer who flees to find herself, only later to emerge as a more objective critic of the South. Such memoirs by Southern white people often come to terms with a moment of crisis centered on race. While these moments of racial awareness may center on pivotal childhood experiences—Lumpkin witnessing her father abusing a Black servant and Smith being told that white and colored children cannot play together—they are recounted by an adult who fled the South and returned through the writing of the memoir. In the second paragraph of *Killers of the Dream,* Smith explains, "This haunted childhood belongs to every southerner of my age. We ran away from it but we came back like a hurt animal to its wound, or a murderer to the scene of his sin. The human heart dares not stay away too long from that which hurt it most. There is a return journey to anguish that few of us are released from making."[6] While these childhood moments set such writers on a path for understanding themselves and Southern culture, the literal and figurative separation from the South enables these writers to discuss race in such a forthright manner. Depicting the South as antagonistic to their development, these memoirs of resistance make it imperative to transcend cultural constraints in order to achieve a sense of vision.

The conventional Southern memoir's dual function of self-expression and social commentary is best exemplified in Lumpkin's *The Making of a Southerner* (1946) and Smith's *Killers of the Dream* (1949). Jacquelyn Dowd Hall contends that Lumpkin's "turn to home" after her northern education functions as a redemptive mission of reconfiguring the South as both critic and citizen of the region. Allying herself with the causes of racial and economic justice, Lumpkin later returned home to the South as sociologist, historian, and autobiographer. On this return she would confront the South through demystification. To illustrate Lumpkin's status as a courageous "return migrant," Hall quotes Carol Stack's *Call to Home:* "You definitely can go home again. You can go back. But you don't start from where you left. To fit in, you have to create another place in that place you left behind." Scott Romine suggests that Lillian Smith's *Killers of the Dream* performs the same dual function in a complex rhetorical strategy that situates Smith as a Southerner who simultaneously critiques the culture as an outsider. In this respect, Smith inscribes herself as both subject and object, affording her "impeccable credentials as a Southerner but [one] who has eluded Southern constraints on verbal expression." The textual explorations of "writing the self" serve as a resolution for both Lumpkin's and Smith's Southern identity within the region. Within both memoirs, the writer mitigates the tension she feels in relation to the dominant culture by presenting herself as an outsider capable of overcoming cultural limitations to "didactically take measure" of the South.[7] By isolating the self from culture, the writer engages in a rhetorical interplay that equates her former self—a child raised in the South—with the prevailing cultural sentiment, only to interrogate those values with the newer, more critical self. Transcending the burdensome culture of the South seems to be a necessary strategy for these representative memoirs to achieve a clear vision of both the South and the self.[8]

While Covington employs some of the same rhetorical strategies, his inverted approach envisions Southern culture differently: Rather than bringing the present self back to interrogate the South's influence, he returns to find value there. This inverted pattern was set by James Agee and Walker Evans in their masterpiece, *Let Us Now Praise Famous Men* (1941). Eschewing what W. E. B. Du Bois called the "car-window" sociological approach to documenting poverty, Agee submerges himself in Southern culture by living with and among poor sharecroppers in rural Alabama. *Let Us Now Praise Famous Men* functions as a memoir about Agee's own metamorphosis—what John Hussey refers to as a "solitary quest for spiritual renewal." Agee's personal quest centers upon finding a sense of home, "a hallowed ground which nourishes and heals his fractured spirit."[9] The author's regeneration functions prescriptively for the reader to also share in the transformative experience and see Southern culture with better vision.

Agee's unflinching exposure of rural poverty seeks to imbue the reader with a social conscience that feels the weight of responsibility for the neglected conditions of the sharecroppers. Through his documentary process, Agee dramatizes the conflicts of negotiating subjective experience with discursive reflection. After agonizing over his role as a "spy" to the impoverished people he documents, Agee finally arrives at an epiphany—what I would call a sense of vision—by immersing himself into the lives of the sharecroppers. Agee captures this knowledge of immanence deftly in the following passage:

[A]ll that surrounded me, that silently strove in through my senses and stretched me full, was familiar and dear to me as nothing else on earth, and as if well known in a deep past and long years lost; so that I could wish that all my chance life was in truth the betrayal, the curable delusion, that it seemed, and that this was my right home, right earth, right blood, to which I would never have true right. For half my blood is just this; and half my right of speech; and by bland chance alone is my life so softened and sophisticated in the years of my defenselessness, and I am robbed of a royalty I can not only never claim, but never properly much desire or regret.[10]

While remorseful in tone due to an acknowledgment that he can never be one of them, Agee expresses a profound understanding and solidarity with the people he documents, producing not only a more thoughtful knowledge of Southern culture, but of Agee himself. The personal cost of discomfort living among poor Southerners, in Agee's estimation, is a cheap price to pay for such precious knowledge about himself.

Similar to Agee, Covington perceives his present journalistic vocation as hindering his ability to fairly depict the snake handlers, and he comes to realize how much he can learn from them: "The handlers showed me something, and I was ready to be shown" (*SSM* 67). Just as Agee and Evans began their project as a journalistic article of sharecroppers only to abandon it for something far more comprehensive, Covington conceives of a larger work that will present the snake handlers more fairly and deeply. This realization occurs when he apologizes to Brother Carl Porter, interim pastor of The Church of Jesus with Signs Following, for taking notes during a service in which Brother Carl preaches a sermon and handles a copperhead. Brother Carl encourages him to write a book about snake handling because it will be tantamount to spreading the Gospel and edifying the body of Christ. Covington's internal reaction proves crucial, his language illustrating a verbal irony that belies his own naïve sense of journalistic objectivity: "I nodded. But I wonder if Brother Carl knew then about the inevitable treachery that stood between journalist and subject. I wonder if he was ready for the dance that would have to take place between him and me" (*SSM* 20). As we shall see, Covington's narrative negotiation blurs the lines between journalist and subject by becoming both in a sensational account that documents his personal journey of descent.

In the prologue, Covington even places himself as an outsider from Southern culture despite his upbringing in the industrial city of Birmingham, Alabama. Reading the great writers of Southern fiction revealed "how little [he] knew about real life" in the South (*SSM* xvi). Covington states that he grew up in a "quiet, sober neighborhood, where the families of grocers and plumbers and office workers tried to secure a hold on middle-class respectability" (*SSM* 8). Part of this class awareness can be found in the Methodist church that Covington attended as a boy. During annual revivals, Covington received his first taste of the more daring religious temperament of sweaty itinerate preachers from southern Appalachia. Those early days, he explains, "were filled with desperate innocence and with a spiritual light," providing the boy with a perception of danger and spirituality fused, and this during an impressionable time that he could not shake in his adult life. Covington continues, "And if my experience in that church did nothing else for me, it accustomed me to strange outpourings of the Spirit and gave me a tender regard for con artists and voices in the wilderness, no matter how odd or suspicious their message might be. I believe it also put me in touch with a rough-cut and reckless side of myself that I otherwise might never have recognized, locked way back somewhere in cell memory, a cultural legacy I would have otherwise known nothing about" (*SSM* 10).

In documenting the troubling subject matter of snake handling and poverty, which intermingles aspects of the grotesque and religious, Covington invokes his sense of kinship with Flannery O'Connor. Like O'Connor, Covington earned his MFA from the Iowa Writer's Workshop. The epigraph for *Salvation on Sand Mountain* comes appropriately from O'Connor's essay, "Some Aspects of the Grotesque in Southern Fiction," in which she insinuates that artistic vision occurs through a process of descent into the depths of writer and region: "This descent into himself will, at the same time, be a descent into his region. It will be a descent through the darkness of the familiar into a world where, like the blind man cured in the gospels, he sees men as if they were trees, but walking." O'Connor originally wrote her essay in response to complaints that her fiction was full of freaks and not inspirational enough for the weary reader. She felt the need to explain the orientation of not only her fiction, but also other Southern writers who were similarly criticized for being obsessed with the grotesque. O'Connor laments a public that demands "a literature which is balanced and which will somehow heal the ravages of our times." This self-help inclination amounts to the reader expecting the writer to be "the handmaid of his age" by encouraging social order and well-being. According to O'Connor, much of the public craves fiction where "novels are considered entirely concerned with the social or economic or psychological forces that they will by necessity exhibit," making the current demand for "realism" a litmus test for "orthodoxy." This emphasis, according to O'Connor, serves to limit rather than broaden the novel's scope.[11] O'Connor contends that a writer who embraces mystery, rather than the typical social patterns mandated to the public through social sciences, will write from a subjective sense of clarity. Writing from inner vision, she asserts, involves distorting reality by decentering the reader: "Instead of reflecting a balance from the world around him, the novelist now has to achieve [a world] from a felt balance inside himself." Covington later echoes O'Connor by claiming that the artist writes not with the literal eye but "an eye on the inside of his head" (*SSM* 175). It is only from the inner eye of the writer's imagination that he "beholds the connectedness of things, of past, present, and future" (*SSM* 175).

Yet this search for artistic vision within the self must not be performed in isolation, as O'Connor warns, for creative acts of self-descent can pose a particular problem: How far can the writer distort without destroying? O'Connor's solution suggests that descent into the self involves a simultaneous descent into the region. In "The Catholic Novelist in the Protestant South," O'Connor commends the benefits of living intimately among "backwoods prophets and shouting fundamentalists" in the Southern region, arguing that the writer should generate a greater interest and sympathy with these grotesque religious characters "because descending within himself to find his region, he discovers that it is with these aspects of southern life that he has a feeling of kinship strong enough to spur him to write."[12]

Following O'Connor, Covington anticipates his audience's repulsion toward snake-handling churches; therefore, like O'Connor, it is important for Covington to present the handlers seriously and remain sympathetic to their earnest faith and strong sense of spiritual purpose. Covington discovers how these aspects of the grotesque and evangelical reveal a rural South marginalized and "under assault" by the mainstream. As a result, the handlers' peculiarities and extremes are often an inverted vision of what Covington describes as "a violent reaction to a modern world who is hostile to them and spiritually dead" (*SSM* xvii–xviii). In the following passage, Covington contends that snake handling— or any other grotesque practices deemed unsuitable by modern culture— embodies an averse reaction to the very culture it offends:

> Snake handling, for instance, didn't originate back in the hills somewhere. It started when people came down from the hills to discover they were surrounded by a hostile and spiritually dead culture. All along their border with the modern world—in places like Newport, Tennessee, and Sand Mountain, Alabama—they recoiled. They threw up defenses. When their own resources failed, they called down the Holy Ghost. They put their hands through fire.

They drank poison. They took up serpents. They still do. The South hasn't disappeared. If anything it's become more Southern in a last-ditch effort to save itself. (*SSM* xvii–xviii)

With a tone of hostility in his prologue, Covington complains about the "scorn and ridicule the nation has heaped upon poor southern whites, the only ethnic group in America not permitted to have a history" (*SSM* xviii).

Covington expresses discomfort with the "skewed priorities" of the media who treat the Summerford trial as an exhibition for the amusement of their more educated readership (*SSM* 39). The Summerfords are dehumanized even by their own lawyers who characterize their clients as dysfunctional and unreasonable; Darlene's own attorney emphasizes her seventh-grade education, resulting in a "poverty of imagination" that would be incapable of the defense attorney's counterclaim that she was, in fact, trying to murder her own husband (*SSM* 40). Covington's sensitivity enables him to see beyond the awkward ducktails and outdated fashions that others might characterize as "white trash." Covington elaborates in the following description: "What might have been nothing more than ordinary decorum in a different social context appeared in this one to be wariness and suspicion. Their glances toward the journalists were thick-lidded and vaguely menacing [. . .] I saw now that the unnerving cast to the men's faces was probably just inflexibility, an unwillingness to give themselves up to public emotion. It had to do not so much with their religion, I reasoned, as with their poverty" (*SSM* 36). In his view, the handlers are "refugees from a culture on the ropes," who filled the spiritual vacuum left by the failed promises of modernity (*SSM* 24).

Covington resists references to the Civil War in order to disarm generalizations or sociological templates traditionally employed for understanding white Southern identity. This is illustrated in his discussion of Scottsboro, Alabama, the location of the Summerford trial. Covington teases out three versions of Southern identity from the Summerford case. The first is the city's historical identity, which proves troubling because of the 1931 Scottsboro Boys trial that wrongly framed and convicted nine Black youths for raping two white women—one of the grossest miscarriages of justice in the region's history that keyed an eventual cessation of all-white juries in the South.[13] Covington expresses fascination with how Scottsboro residents refer to the ordeal as one of the "accidents of history [. . .] that have marked the town unjustly for life" (*SSM* 22). The second identity he adduces from the Summerford case is the contemporary identity of the New South that the town's leaders want to accentuate through its business and commerce. The third is the religious identity that reveals the frustrations of poor white people who have not achieved the promises of economic prosperity. Covington explains that the New South "progress since World War II has been double-edged: it has meant higher wages, better health, and less isolation from the rest of the world, but it has also meant the loss of a traditional way of life" (*SSM* 23).

The families of snake-handling churches originally came down from the Appalachian Mountains after World War II, Covington explains, "trying to eke out a living and a sense of dignity," and Scottsboro, in particular, represented "an island of possibility in the midst of a southern culture in crisis" (*SSM* 23). Covington provides the same analysis of the snake handlers in Jolo, West Virginia, where hopeful citizens relocated from the mountains only to participate in an industrialized society that eroded purposeful labor, fractured families, and obliterated any sense of the sacred (*SSM* 88). The alluring promise of economic prosperity forced them into contact with the dominant secular culture, resulting in an inevitable compromise of traditional values and religious identity.

When promises of prosperity failed to materialize, the subsequent reaction of poor Southern white people swung them back into a fanatical spirituality as a violent means of reclamation. The resulting isolation from broader secular culture marks the snake handlers, in their own minds, as being in the world but not of the world. Reclaiming the eroded sense of spiritual identity, which they believed had been compromised in the pursuit of economic prosperity, the handlers enact an evangelical drama with their very lives that consists of never "backing up on the Lord," an expression also characterized as "backsliding" in one's religious faith (*SSM* 25). Covington wryly observes how backsliding actually became the crux of Reverend Summerford's trial, as both the prosecuting and defending attorneys refer to their clients as backslidden when recalling the events in question between Glenn and Darlene Summerford: "The only sure thing was that backsliding was serious business in this part of the state" (*SSM* 38).

Rather than casting himself as an evolved journalist-critic altering the perception of South as "other," Covington's investigations of these "others" ground his own evolving, personal quest of reclamation and renewal. In the first chapter, "Following Signs," Covington seems keenly aware that he is on the brink of a new experience through which a single choice will have life-changing consequences.[14]Attending his first snake-handling service at The Church of Jesus with Signs Following of the recently convicted Reverend Summerford, Covington feels a sense of kinship with the congregation. Covington's use of imagery

Descent and Vision *111*

proves symbolic for both the church and his own personal journey: "The snake appeared to be in the process of reinventing itself, forging a new self out of the old" (*SSM* 19). Covington is reinventing himself by participating in the snake-handling church, and Brother Carl Porter proves crucial as the interim pastor in facilitating that reinvention.

Early in the narrative, Covington indicates that Summerford's church is fractured and lost without a pastor to lead it. His curiosity and sympathy for the remaining flock becomes the basis for his participation and subsequent memoir of the account. Similarly, Covington's own sense of selfhood becomes fractured as he straddles the fence between his Methodist church in Birmingham and the snake-handling culture of the southern Appalachians: "But something was missing. I had reached that point in the middle of looking for something when you have forgotten what it is you have lost" (*SSM* 55). Covington's spiritual experience among the snake handlers decenters him in a way that makes him uncomfortable worshiping back home in his Birmingham church. Fittingly, Brother Carl becomes a spiritual mentor and father figure to Covington in his spiritual journey of descent.

Shortly after, Covington recounts his first authentic taste of Pentecostalism in the Holiness tradition. Covington discusses the characteristics of Pentecostalism and highlights a theological framework full of tension regarding intellectualism, tradition, and lay participation. For example, a strong suspicion of academic learning and intelligence coexists with esoteric emphases given privately by the Holy Spirit (e.g., a twelve-hour message is given on the word "polluted"); moreover, hostility exists toward religious tradition and liturgy ("snake handlers don't stand on ceremony") among many Pentecostals, yet their own litmus test for authentic worship in the Spirit accompanied by speaking in tongues betrays their own brand of ceremony. To further illustrate such disharmony, Covington analyzes the etymological tension in the phrase "brush-arbor," the outdoor worship site atop Sand Mountain. While "arbor" connotes what Covington describes as "civilized restraint," "brush" suggests wildness (*SSM* 67). This verbal irony captures Covington's own experience in a worship service where he unconsciously plays the tambourine, accompanying Aline McGlocklin, a traveling evangelist's wife, in the Spirit as she speaks in tongues. Rather than perceiving it as chaotic, Covington considers his experience of harmonic abandonment as an authentic religious experience that functions as his own rite of passage into the snake-handling community: "Through the tambourine, I was occurring with her in the Spirit, and it was not of my own will [...] It was after that brush-arbor meeting on Sand Mountain that they started to call me Brother Dennis"

(*SSM* 80). Covington contrasts his comfort among the handlers with the dull, restless feeling at his home church back in Birmingham, where he would long to put his hands in the air during service yet refrained from embarrassment (*SSM* 81).

Covington's metamorphosis continues as he travels to Jolo, plunging into a "chaos of intersecting planes" as he drives through the East Tennessee Appalachians, a place wild and formidable "to become lost in," where the awaited destination involves strangers handling rattlesnakes and drinking poison (*SSM* 83, 89). Covington's worshipful experience at Jolo fills him with a sense of destiny and reinforces the memoir's message concerning identity—that a loss of self precedes vision: "In both sexual and religious ecstasy, the first thing that goes is self. The entrance into ecstasy is surrender. Handlers talk about receiving the Holy Ghost. But when the Holy Ghost is fully come upon someone like Gracie McAllister, the expression on her face reads exactly the opposite—as though someone, or something, were being violently taken away from her. The paradox of Christianity, one of many of which Jesus speaks, is that only in losing ourselves do we find ourselves, and perhaps that's why photos of the handlers so often seem to be portraits of loss" (*SSM* 99). Covington compares this loss of self to a near death experience he had while freelance reporting in a combat zone in El Salvador; the adrenaline rush and invulnerability that accompanies combat provides him with the only other available analogue among all his previous experiences in which to express the newfound sense of illumination he claims to have possessed.

Anticipating his readers' skepticism concerning his religious experience, Covington makes it a point to detail that while he is typically a person "excessively calculating," who can feign spontaneity, his spiritual experience was authentic: "But what happened that Friday night in Jolo wasn't calculated. I had experienced something genuine, and I was awed by what I had seen. I might as well have been watching people defy the law of gravity or breathe underwater. It was that startling, that inexplicable" (*SSM* 103). Covington recalls a conversation with his friends, Jim and Melissa, who function as stand-in skeptics for the reader; they advance alternative theories—balanced handling in the middle of the snake, group hypnosis, manipulation, hysteria, and so on—to explain the chaos of serpent handling and ecstatic experience that Covington narrates. Covington claims he was surprised by his own thinking and answer to his friends' (and readers' by proxy) skeptical theories: "the presence of the Holy Ghost" (*SSM* 104). After his ecstatic religious experience, he emerges with a homesick feeling for a place he had never been—a motif he appropriates throughout the memoir until the very end (*SSM* 108).

Covington submerges himself into the Holiness roots of his own Methodist church and family history to achieve a more authentic sense of self: "My journey with the snake handlers had become not so much a linear progression through time as a falling through levels of platitude toward some hard understanding of who I was" (*SSM* 132). His descent into the lower recesses is signified by the image of the snake, its uncoiling skin embodying Covington's superficial Southern identity being pared away. In chapter 6, appropriately titled "Roots," Covington begins to mix his own personal search through his family's genealogy with the historical tracing of the Holiness-Pentecostal church. The history of American Methodism holds a special significance, for it mirrors Covington's own religious heritage. John Wesley, the founder of Methodism, planted the beginnings of the Holiness movement with its emphasis on a baptism in the Holy Spirit separate from conversion, a doctrine further developed by Pentecostalism that required corresponding signs (snake handling eventually being one of them in some sects). The Methodist church would eventually split from the Holiness movement along economic lines, the middle class remaining within the more "respectable" traditional denomination and the lower class following the Holiness thread to live more radically separated lives in devotion to their religion.

Originating at the beginning of the twentieth century in the ministry of Charles Fox Parham and the Azusa Street revivals in Los Angeles, Pentecostalism emerged out of the Wesleyan-Holiness movement. The Pentecostal movement received its name from the biblical account of Acts 2:1–4, where Christians first received the Holy Spirit, marked by the ability to speak in tongues and other outward signs. The dynamic essence of Pentecostalism lies in stressing what God is doing now. Cecil Robeck claims that Pentecostals actively rediscover the human psyche by fully integrating the conscious and the subconscious through a "radical decentering of the self, including tears, groanings, apparent babel," and other "phenomena such as visions, dreams, speaking in tongues, miracles, and revelation." Pentecostalism's positive legacy, according to Robeck, lies in its democratization of Christianity—both in church government and in stressing equality of members regardless of race, gender, age, or any other forms of classification; thus, from its beginnings at Azusa Street from 1906–1909, led by William Joseph Seymour, a Black man, Pentecostals are the most racially diverse denomination in America. Robeck further praises Pentecostalism's democratization as embodied in the personal testimony, a "people's theology," which is just as important as the pastor's sermon.[15]

Uncovering the Holiness roots in his own family, Covington discovers that his great-great-grandfather was a circuit-riding Methodist evangelist who frequented Sand Mountain and might have planted seeds from the Holiness tradition that later emerged into the snake-handling culture of Scottsboro. In addition, Covington discovers another set of Covingtons, who were snake handlers in Tennessee and who may or may not be related to him. Covington embraces a Southern past in his ongoing quest to uncover his present spiritual identity by participating in unsettling practices that prove revelatory in understanding the South's troubling legacy. At the climax of his memoir, Covington again inverts the conventional pattern of the Southern memoirist who transcends the Southern past through critical distance. This becomes clear when, near the end of his memoir, he reveals his own history and fascination with snakes—a puzzling rhetorical shift clearly meant to come as a surprise. By revealing his long-time obsession with snakes *after* documenting his religious experiences with snake-handling culture, Covington uncoils his own identity and past to the reader, thus further inverting the conventional pattern and approach of memoir writing. Not only has the snake served as an object of affection for Covington since boyhood but also it now serves as a sacramental object that represents the mysterious and unpredictable past that we all must handle if we desire to understand ourselves: "All of us were handling one kind of snake or another" (*SSM* 151).

In another sense for Covington, snakes function metaphorically for the South's dangerous legacy of racial strife, an "uncertain past" that was "problematic and embarrassing because it contained poverty, ignorance, racism, and defeat." As Covington keenly remarks, "No one wanted to claim it. No one wanted to take it out of the box" (*SSM* 151). The snakes of the South's cultural legacy embody a past that might seem preferable to ignore. To be conquered, however, "snakes" must be handled and taken up. Covington takes up his own legacy by handling a poisonous snake in a frenzied worship service in Sand Mountain. During the service, Covington describes himself engaged in a semiconscious, out-of-body experience, as he suddenly realizes he is shouting and holding a rattlesnake. This victory of self-loss proves to be personally empowering for Covington because he takes up not only the literal snake but also the suppressed snakes of his past.

After this pivotal experience, Covington informs the reader of a story he had written at the age of nineteen entitled, "Salvation on Sand Mountain" (the title of the memoir and the climactic chapter where he takes up the snake). Much like his own personal history with snakes, which he withholds from the reader, the Holiness church on Sand Mountain of his teenage story turns out to be the very

Descent and Vision   *115*

church where he takes up the snake in real life as an adult. Covington claims he never even visited Sand Mountain when he wrote the story, and that his own experience at the Old Rock House Holiness Church in real life charts a mystery. Crucial at this juncture is Covington's description of mystery and vision for the artist to tell stories. It is here that Covington echoes the pivotal epigraph of O'Connor by claiming that the artist writes not with the literal eye, but "an eye on the inside of his head" (*SSM* 175). By becoming his own subject for a memoir along with the snake handlers, Covington reflects upon the mystery of motivation that he suggests we all possess—that is, to seek knowledge about our world and, more importantly, about ourselves.

Covington's metamorphosis continues when he realizes soon after his first handling that "madness and religion were a hair's breadth away" (*SSM* 177). Here, the journalist in Covington resurfaces; he sends mixed signals of believing in the validity of these spiritual experiences by injecting skeptical sarcasm. In documenting what he calls the "War Stories" of snake handlers, Covington seems intent on overwhelming the reader with sensational stories of violence and death. Throughout these stories, he portrays the handlers who suffer casualties as heroic, like soldiers dying for a transcendent cause. Their war is a spiritual one, as Covington makes clear, and the "tragedy is not the death of a particular snake handler but the failure of the world to accept the gospel that the handler risked his life to confirm" (*SSM* 184). Yet much of this warfare he depicts is rooted in class and economics as much as it is religion. The cultural clash between rural and urban cultures in the South is crystallized when snake handlers defend their way of life by stating they would rather die by snakes than in the mines or from drugs. Covington sees the absurdity of this fundamentalist imperative (God or the devil), and this recognition proves to be a turning point when he realizes that his desire to be sympathetic to the snake handlers has clouded his judgment.[16]

A noticeable shift in tone occurs over the course of the memoir: The narrative shifts from curiosity, fascination, and admiration to shock and disillusionment. A character introduced late in the memoir, Elvis Presley Saylor, embodies Covington's own dissatisfaction and movement away from the handlers. Saylor uses Scripture and logic to debunk the irrationality of the handlers. Saylor becomes a centering point in Covington's own melding of religious experience and exploration. Covington reflects: "I thought about Elvis, and the way he had been ostracized. What I didn't know was that what had happened to him was about to happen to me. At the time, I just turned the radio off when I got to the interstate that would take me to Akron, the same one that would eventually lead me home" (*SSM* 212). As this passage makes clear, Pentecostals operate according to a zero-sum logic: A person is either hot or cold—in the Lord or in the devil. Those who are moderate, like Saylor, become suspicious to partisans and fanatics. Covington turns the tables and inverts the snake handlers' logic through the story of Saylor: The snake handlers have now become the establishment, akin to the legalistic Pharisees found in the New Testament, while Saylor has become the visionary outcast because of his compassionate and intellectual moderation.

In the final chapter, Covington provides a sober reflection that reveals a more objective distance from his experiences. In particular, he informs his readers that his "career as a snake-handling preacher was a brief one" (*SSM* 213). Covington closes the memoir with a call to home by his father. As he returns home to Birmingham with his family, he recalls how his father differed from other parents who simply yelled from the door (or garage) for their kids to come home for dinner; instead, his father would approach to where his son was before calling him home. The curiosity and active participation of his father inspires Covington's reconstruction of his own spiritual journey that connects him to his past and leads him back home. The story of his father signifies for Covington the narrative strategy he employs in writing *Salvation on Sand Mountain*. It seems crucial that Covington's vision is achieved by coming to the place that connected him to his past. While it is not required that he remain in the depths of his Southern roots, coming to this place of vision required descent and participation to achieve such clarity.

Rather than depicting Southern evangelical culture as an oppressive antagonist, Covington's memoir casts Pentecostal snake handling as an earnest and authentic community filled with excitement, danger, ecstasy, and complexity. *Salvation on Sand Mountain* is a memoir that engages in a sympathetic yet sorrowful look at the South's troubled past and casts a courageous glance into its future. Covington submerges himself in a marginalized section of Southern culture where most would never dare to venture—a dual descent into the Southern region and the artist's soul. It is through intimacy with the handlers that Covington can see his own faults, and it is thus through incorporating rather than leaving the South that he achieves clarity and vision. Covington finds his people and himself in the rural South, and his memoir thus emerges as a rhetorical integration of subject and object. By presenting the evangelical South as a complex region that can yield an authentic sense of selfhood, Covington advances the genre of Southern memoirs by expanding our appreciation of a region deeply concerned with redemption and reclamation.

Chapter 6

Evangelical Whispers in Doris Betts's
The Sharp Teeth of Love

American identity has long been constructed by hopeful visions of a prosperous future—a dream ingrained into the psyche by stories of American pioneers and entrepreneurs. This dream, so often driven by marketing, leads Americans to see beyond the present and pull up the stakes of communities, relationships, and other commitments, as they look toward a hopeful yet unrealized future. As C. Vann Woodward explains, "It is not the concrete but the abstract that captures the imagination of the American and gives him identity, not the here-and-now but the future." Woodward heralds the South and its literature as a corrective exception to these abstract tendencies that so often generate the physical mobility and general feeling of superiority and indifference to place that characterizes American identity. Southern writers have often fixated upon the adverse consequences of looking beyond the concrete present, associating the American tendency to abstraction (to "draw away") with a disembodied sense of space and freedom that sheds the embodied sense of place and community. Robert Penn Warren describes this Southern concern as an "instinctive fear, on the part of Black or white, that the massiveness of experience, the concreteness of life, will be violated; the fear of abstraction."[1]

Abstractionism has also been a concern in theological discourse over the nature of spirituality. As a disembodied epistemology that divorces ideas and thoughts from concrete contexts, abstractionism privileges the mind (or spirit) over matter.[2] Focusing largely on passages in the Bible (mostly extracted from Pauline epistles) that lend themselves toward a spirit-body dualism and a subsequent stratification of each, theological debates after the Protestant Reformation moved well beyond the reforms of Martin Luther to take on a more disembodied orientation. Reformed theologians particularly in Switzerland (e.g., John Calvin and Ulrich Zwingli) championed the biblical precept found in John 4:24 that Christians must worship God in spirit and truth. Developing a regulative principle that entails worship practices follow only what is prescribed in Scripture, Reformed theologians gradually detached the spiritual from the material. As the Reformation progressed in the sixteenth century, evangelicals ramped up iconoclastic "purifications" of what they viewed as Catholic heresies; as a result, evangelical Protestant churches were largely purged of images, liturgies, and doctrines that were believed to confuse the spiritual hierarchy by making the divine too earthly.

Raised in the ultraconservative Associate Reformed Presbyterian denomination in the North Carolina Piedmont, Doris Betts was familiar with the abstract tendencies of evangelical Protestants to emphasize the written word of Scripture. Betts would address these concerns in her final novel, *The Sharp Teeth of Love*, which takes a decidedly theological approach to examining the abstract violation of the physical body. In *The Sharp Teeth of Love*, both protagonists, Luna and Paul, George Hovis observes, "share the southern unease with abstraction."[3] Luna's abstract issues are manifested in her anorexia—a psychological identity disorder with physiological consequences. Paul, on the other hand, is plagued by an abstracted mind that leads him to multiple crises with his religious faith, resulting in a disconnection of his spiritual identity from the body of his familial and church communities in Wisconsin. In these two characters, Betts examines the problems of abstractionism and ultimately affirms a distinctly evangelical Lutheran sacramentalism that reorders the characters' relationship to materiality and redefines their understanding of spirituality.

In the previous chapter, narrative negotiation was introduced as a hybrid strategy that transgresses boundaries through cultural borrowings and subjective participation. Characterized as a borderland strategy, narrative negotiation fashions identity and meaning by redefining and repurposing cultural materials within existing zones. My analysis of Covington demonstrated how his memoir inverts the strategies of resistance covered in part one through subjective participation and ecstatic experience. By speaking in tongues and taking up snakes, Covington trespasses congealed boundaries of class and culture to translate subjective experience into a complex, sympathetic portrayal of marginalized evangelical communities.

In this final chapter, I examine how negotiation manifests in fiction by complicating theological categories and denominational boundaries. Whereas Covington stresses ecstatic experience among Pentecostals to highlight spiritual components of community and identity, Betts emphasizes theological nuance among Lutherans to heal the abstract violations of the human body. Employing geographic mobility as her borderland strategy, Betts's negotiation entails a sophisticated theological translation that blurs the boundaries separating regions, communities, and denominations; moreover, her hybrid strategy contrasts with the dialogic parody of narrative satire covered in part two. Just as Covington expands our understanding and appreciation of evangelical religion by treating a marginalized spiritual subset, Betts does the same by repurposing sacramental theology to promote a sense of embodiment and community. By highlighting the theological nuances of Betts's novel, the chapter demonstrates how sacramentalism does not preclude evangelicalism. In order to make this argument, it is important to distinguish Betts from Flannery O'Connor and to correct misreadings that equate sacramentalism only with Catholicism.

An avid reader from an early age, Betts was given an illustrated volume on her fifth birthday, "Story of the Bible for Young and Old," which retold 168 biblical stories in 757 pages. Spending her childhood reading these stories, Elizabeth Evans asserts, "prepared Betts for the biblical allusions threading their way throughout Western literature, resonating connections and levels of meaning, and for a lifelong association with the King James Bible and the church." With a denomination that was committed to an educated clergy that stressed a robust knowledge of the Bible and theology, Betts memorized Scripture and the Reformed catechisms and spent countless hours in church services each week. The strict Calvinist upbringing—particularly its doctrines of predestination and views concerning women and homosexuals—began to trouble Betts when she became an adult, and she abandoned the church to become what she characterized as an "unaffiliated theist" and at times, an agnostic. However, Betts eventually returned to Presbyterianism (what she described as a long and private story) and pursued many of the church's theological paradoxes in her fiction.[4]

Betts discussed the tendency of Presbyterianism to elevate the written word over material elements in her essay, "The Fingerprint of Style" (1985). Claiming that words functioned as Reformed substitutes for the elements found in Catholicism, Betts attributes sacramental properties to the way language functioned in her Presbyterian church, where "words and The Word were almost sub-sacraments themselves, could work wonders, could transubstantiate any old thing by the side of a red-clay road."[5] Certainly, as Betts illustrates, the Bible foregrounds the power of words when God creates the universe through spoken imperatives, burns the Ten Commandments into tablets of stone with a finger, and even refers to Jesus in the New Testament simply as the Word in John's Gospel. However, in an interview with Marti Greene, Betts lamented the evangelical tendency to purge its churches of the symbols and rituals of sacramental liturgy which encourages "a way of making the body do what the heart is inclined to do."[6]

Betts's interests in recovering sacramentalism have led to comparisons with O'Connor, as well as readings that argue for a Catholic vision in her fiction. However, Betts differentiated herself from O'Connor repeatedly in interviews and essays. O'Connor's narrative strategy can be best summarized in her famous essay "The Fiction Writer and His Country," where she prescribes the following approach: When a Christian writer determines—by assumption—that her audience does not share the same beliefs, she must make her "vision apparent by shock—to the hard of hearing you shout, and for the almost blind you draw large and startling figures."[7] Betts's strategy is advanced in her essay, "Everything I Know about Writing I Learned in Sunday School," where she affirms many of O'Connor's theological convictions yet distances herself in how to communicate with her audience: "Like mothers and kindergarten teachers, I find that whispering is also sometimes effective, and even with the volume turned down I hope my theology can be heard in my stories." Contending that there are far too many shouters when it comes to communicating religious themes in fiction, Betts repeats the word "whisper" throughout the article to suggest the artistic importance of theological nuance in her literature; she seemed content to respect her reading audience and their ability to listen, trusting and hoping that her whispers advance the faith as "one more mustard seed, one more widow's mite."[8] To illustrate their contrasting strategies, Betts uses O'Connor's short story, "The River," which ends with a young boy who accidentally drowns in a river while attempting to baptize himself. While O'Connor suggests this outcome is an act of grace that achieves eternal life, Betts takes a more concrete approach, as she remarks that she would prefer "to pull that boy out of the river and go give him a haircut and something to eat and leave the rest to the Father . . . Maybe that's a difference between Catholicism and Protestantism."[9]

Betts also distinguishes herself from O'Connor in her sacramental views of fiction. In an interview with Susan Ketchin, Betts observes that O'Connor "wrote about incarnation, or immanence, in a whole different way. She would have the red sun seem to be God peeping over the pines. I don't go that far. I don't trust God as magic. It's not something I see everyday." Pressing the sacramental distinction between O'Connor and Betts, Evans notes how Betts's characters "do not experience dramatic confrontations with the moment of grace," so much as they "struggle through the mundane, if perilous, ups and downs of their lives." Betts's sacramentalism affirms the quotidian, perceiving divine grace as a gift that imbues our day-to-day interactions. Her fiction affirms the diurnal, where "the value of life is in the process of living."[10] Betts's social emphasis differs from O'Connor's sacramentalism by contrasting their respective Protestant and Catholic faiths, according to Hovis: "Unlike O'Connor's characters, who are capable of finding grace only in the most violent, often fatal events, Betts's characters undergo gradual conversions; her stories and novels typically depict pilgrims whose journeys remain far from complete."[11]

In *The Sharp Teeth of Love*, Betts explores such conversions by having her female protagonist, Luna Stone, undergo physical, emotional, and spiritual transformations. Similar to her previous novel, *Heading West* (1981), Betts interrogates female autonomy by extricating her protagonists from the cultural and geographic confines of the American South, according to Ashley Robinson, to achieve self-actualization by traveling west—a symbolic site for absolute freedom and transformation.[12] The connection Luna makes from mind to body reinforces the novel's concerns with abstraction—specifically her father's idea (or at least what Luna perceives to be his idea) of a perfect body—as a threat to Luna's well-being and sense of selfhood. Betts depicts a deconversion experience that Luna undergoes to unlearn and discard the dangerous abstractions rooted in her family and Roman Catholic doctrine. Consequently her recovery involves healthy physical intimacy and a sacramental faith that reorders her relationship between the spiritual and the material.

The novel opens by following the twenty-eight-year-old aspiring artist who is uprooted from her home in Chapel Hill, North Carolina, to move westward with her fiancé, Steven, who has just accepted a position at the University of California Riverside. Along the way, the couple plans to marry in Reno, Nevada. The first chapter reveals, however, that Luna is trapped in a carnivorous relationship with Steven, who selfishly feeds off her generosity; plagued by an eating disorder, Luna notices after sex that Steven "had been gaining weight this spring while she got thinner" (*STL* 11).[13] The novel makes it abundantly clear from the outset that Steven's academic career takes precedent in their relationship, and Luna has taken on the domestic role of nourishing him professionally and personally, while her own desires and needs (both professionally and physically) are secondary. Luna's anorexia, however, did not begin with Steven. Luna's father, a retired military officer aptly referred to as Major Stone, made her conscious of her body and weight as a young girl, warning her of the dangers of ice cream and eventually placing her in a fat girl's camp at the age of eleven. In an eye-opening passage, Luna highlights the physiological damages enacted by psychological violence: "After a while I got so thin I didn't have enough body to cover my mind decently" (*STL* 250).

While traveling west and visiting tourist attractions with Steven, Luna remarks, "We're on a trip into somebody's mind, some effect that's been thought up and prepared especially for tourists before they come. Something unnatural. Invented. They've set traps for the eyes of tourists" (*STL* 46). Luna's keen observations about the abstract commodification of tourism echo the concerns found in Walker Percy's "The Loss of the Creature." Imagining a Spaniard visiting the Grand Canyon for the first time on a trip to America, Percy illustrates how humans transfer their sovereignty to so-called experts, whose preformulations dictate what we see, hear, read, and experience: "The thing is no longer the thing as it confronted the Spaniard; it is rather that which has already been formulated—by picture postcard, geography book, tourist folders, and the words *Grand Canyon*." Toward the end of the essay, Percy connects this creaturely loss with abstractionism:

> The dogfish, the tree, the seashell, the American Negro, the dream, are rendered invisible by a shift of reality from concrete thing to theory, which Whitehead has called the fallacy of misplaced concreteness. It is the mistaking of an idea, a principle, an abstraction, for the real. As a consequence of the shift, the "specimen" is seen as less real than the theory of the specimen. As Kierkegaard said, once a person is seen as a specimen of a race or a species, at that very moment he ceases to be an individual. Then there are no more individuals but only specimen.[14]

Percy believed that the abstract theories of science appropriated in an American marketplace culture relegate humans to mere consumers, thus robbing them of their dignity as sovereign creatures. Hovis reinforces this abstract orientation in his reading of *The Sharp Teeth of Love*, noting "the modern world produces an epistemological crisis for Luna that she can resolve only by escaping that world of abstractions and fleeing to the wilderness, where she hopes to make contact with the concrete world of nature."[15]

Luna is also haunted by two historic specters of Western myth turned nightmare. During her westward travels with Steven, she is inundated and sickened by the news coverage of David Koresh and the Branch Davidians, who, after the raid and shootout with the ATF, set their compound aflame, killing families (including twenty-one children) in the destruction of the compound outside of Waco, Texas, in 1993. Luna also fixates on the pioneering Donner party who resorted to cannibalism for survival in their 1847 pioneer trip westward in pursuit of the manifest destiny of economic promise. Luna is particularly unsettled when she considers that Tamsen Donner remained behind in a camp with her dying husband, essentially forfeiting her freedom out of love and service, only to be eventually eaten herself. Both events haunt Luna's psyche by dramatizing the tensions of freedom within communities and how dreams turn into nightmares. In both the Donner party and the Branch Davidians, women subjugated themselves in religious and domestic devotion to patriarchal ideals of community; these selfless acts of love given to male religious leaders proved destructive for women, who were consumed by cannibalism and the flames of the Waco compound. Luna wonders whether her devotion to Steven will lead to her own destruction.

As the narrative continues westward, we learn more about Luna's unease with the abstractionism she encountered previously in the life she is leaving behind in Chapel Hill. At the university, Luna's art history professors, "mostly abstractionists, had treated her realistic freshman drawings as a naiveté to be outgrown" (*STL* 15). Luna uses her artistic talents to become a copyist for the university's medical school, drawing lab illustrations at first and then graduating on to realistic and detailed drawings of human anatomy. Luna becomes increasingly suspicious of abstract art as "a willful avoidance of the world" that "threw its stormy tantrums against the slightest constraint of reality" (*STL* 16). Changing majors from literature to art had marked an important shift for Luna from "verbal to pictorial," as she settled into her new life "like a brush into paint, a pen point wet with its true element" (*STL* 18). Luna's brief recovery from her mental and physical breakdown after her parents' divorce was intimately connected to this movement away from the abstract, toward a stronger sense of materiality that rooted her in the physical world.

Betts's depictions of Luna's breakdown prove crucial in detailing the worst moments of her past manic depression and eating disorder triggered by her parents' dissolving marriage when Major Stone abandons her mother, Priscilla, for a younger woman. These depictions highlight Betts's unique sacramental vision that first exposes the dangers of the Catholic tendency to stratify the spirit over the body so that she can advance a Lutheran reappraisal of materiality. In Luna's most dangerous state of starvation and mental collapse at Chapel Hill, she hangs outside of her dorm window teetering on the edge of suicide. Her neighbor hangs out a nearby window to help coax Luna back inside by talking to her in order to take her mind off of what ails her. Connecting her anorexia and Catholicism, Luna asks the woman, "if she knew about Anela of Fogliano, who dined solely on roses and tulips and took her only fluid when nuns would brush water on her lips with a feather" (*STL* 88). In the third chapter, Luna similarly discusses the fasting of Catherine of Siena, "who yearned to live off the Host alone and would thrust twigs down her throat to make herself vomit" (*STL* 137). Also, when Luna is hospitalized for her disorder, she tells the doctor "that when Saint Veronica fasted she would stop on Fridays and eat five orange seeds for the five wounds of Jesus" (*STL* 185–186).

Martha Green Eads interprets these passages as Betts's attempt to draw links between Luna and ascetic Catholic saints, pulling heavily from Caroline Walker Bynum's *Holy Feast and Holy Fast*, a study that explores food asceticism found among holy women in medieval Catholicism.[16] Eads asserts that Betts uses sex, money, and food as spiritual signposts, which function as "outward and visible signs of inward and spiritual grace" to serve as sites of redemption; Luna's changing sexual, financial, and dietary habits, according to Eads, signify a "budding faith" at the end of the novel. In a surprising reading, Eads seems to suggest that Luna's misuse or lack of appreciation for material things stems from being a lapsed Catholic—as though Catholic orthodoxy and orthopraxy would not lead to eating disorders or unhealthy abstractions that demonize materiality. Observing how Catholics historically have affirmed the material world in ways that most Protestants have not, Eads contends that the carnality in Betts's novel "exhibits a sacramental 'Catholic' sensibility that takes some readers by surprise." Despite clear distinctions from her medieval counterparts, Luna's fasting, according to Eads, prepares her for a "remarkable visionary experience," as she feeds an abused child and eventually feeds on Christ in the sacrament at the novel's close.[17]

Eads's assertion that Catholic sacramentalism functions as a cure for the ills of Luna's abstractionism is deeply problematic. In fact, the novel strongly indicates that Catholic theology poses a serious threat to Luna's well-being. Luna's mother, Priscilla, assists in unmasking the destructive Catholic tendencies that pose harm to her daughter, affording the reader another perspective of Luna's disorder. Priscilla serves as a corrective to misreading a wholesale affirmation of Catholicism as Luna's panacea, for she was once a novitiate at a convent training to be a nun. Priscilla left the convent because of the diminution of physical pleasures found in the Catholic faith: "I never got over the tables where we nuns were granted such rare and tiny amounts of mustard, pepper, vinegar, and spices—inflammatory foods that might cause lonely women to masturbate" (*STL* 325). The physical pleasures attributed to food and sex here are treated cautiously, or strictly forbidden, as worldly pleasures that novices are taught to approach with fear and trembling, lest they lose any sense of self-control.

Essential to Priscilla's rejection of the novitiate was the unhealthy Catholic ascetic theology that diminishes the inherent goodness of consumption and enjoyment of physical pleasures. Furthermore, Priscilla denies any religious significance to Luna's fasting by differentiating between the saint and the anorexic: "Good people fasted in the Bible, she thought, but toward some purpose and with a specific duration. The fasts of modern Trappists had no similarity to Jane Fonda's vomiting her meals at Vassar or singer Karen Carpenter's heaving her food out an upstairs window until she finally died of hunger" (*STL* 325). True spiritual nourishment for Luna, according to Priscilla, requires physical love and intimate sex to "anchor her to the earth" (*STL* 321). Priscilla does not stop with physical intimacy, as she also wants Luna "to love food, to love life" (*STL* 325). As these passages on sex, food, and the guilt associated with physical appetites indicate, Luna's Catholicism actually exacerbates her fragile condition. Despite Betts's own insistence (which I have noted) that her fiction does not promote the Catholic sacramentalism found in O'Connor's fiction, Eads's article misses some of the more important theological nuances by virtually ignoring the Lutheran theology that abounds in the text.[18]

Betts continually pinpoints Luna's body as the site that will ultimately determine her sense of selfhood. As Luna considers copying a vagina in her book of medical illustrations, she observes her own with a handheld mirror in a passage that contains profound implications concerning the Catholic degradation of the human body:

> She told herself that alone was not lonely, though she was surely the oldest living virgin in the southeastern United States, but it seemed to her then that she was content to be so; she envisioned her female organs nestled inviolate above her intact hymen. Untroubled, easy to draw. She got a hand mirror and held it between her legs. Instantly though she could remember only fragments of Catholic liturgy, there flashed into Luna's mind: *Inter faeces et urinem hascinur.* That's what we're born between, all right. And next came a great longing that someone would love her body someday soon, that very part of her body, love also her should, that she would be able to act out the first Latin verb she ever conjugated: I love, you love, he loves. (*STL* 18)

Here, Luna's latent Catholicism is conjured up negatively. The Augustinian quote, translated "we are born between shit and piss," assigns a sense of degradation to the female body as the filthy source of human life. Such degraded views of human anatomy induce Luna to engage in neurotic appropriations of Catholic fasting and saints that justify her self-destructive anorexia. Only an affirmative estimation and sensual nourishing of Luna's body can alleviate such degradation.

Betts begins constructing her Lutheran sacramental vision through a would-be-seminarian, Paul Cowan, who has fled from religious abstractionism to embrace the rugged physicality of the Sierra Nevada wilderness. Paul originally left his home and Lutheran faith behind in Wisconsin to pursue a freer spirituality out west in California, where religion is reduced to a "mood, an attitude" (*STL* 193). Paul's mother, Erika, alludes to his tendency to conceptualize life rather than live it in an embodied state later in the novel when she suggests that given the choice, Paul would rather discuss heaven than actually dwell there (*STL* 245). Yet Paul soon realizes that California preaching commodifies abstracted brands of spirituality that appeal not only to the innate narcissistic tendencies of humans, but also their proclivity to assert independence by separating from orthodox traditions in favor of less restrictive theologies (*STL* 140).

In an interview with Dale Brown, Betts elaborates on this suspicious view of "California religion," as seen in Paul's rants. Betts quips that the decline of the church and its diminished relevance in mainstream American culture is typified by its mixture with what Betts calls "various California religions": "After a while, I can't sit through any more about my child within, or about my anima and animus [. . .] That is not what I come to church for. I come to church to learn whether this thing is really true and what difference it really makes to me [. . .] We've (the church) tried to be all things to all people so that anybody can come in. Just believe any little ol' thing, you just come right in and smile, have a little sunshine."[19] As Hovis observes, Betts "traces the decline of religion to the rise of a fragmented, pleasure-driven commercial culture" throughout the novel.[20]

Paul contends that it is the Californians who love abstraction or any other form of esoteric initiation that puffs them up with a sense of assurance (*STL* 140–41). According to Paul, Californian spiritualists are marked by asceticism, "so it seems anybody who's sensitive ought to reject these worldly pleasures and rise to some higher spiritual plane" (*STL* 141). For Paul, it makes sense that these New Age Californians would love Buddhism, which privileges the spirit over the body. As he attempted to study theology out west, Paul discovered that California seminaries seemed to offer a choice between Gnosticism and "redneck fundamentalism" (*STL* 142). Paul discerns how evangelicals ironically share the Gnostic degradation of flesh, as both theological poles view the material body as sinful, leading to either asceticism or legalism.

Emerging from his most recent crisis of faith, Paul wanders into the western wilderness of the Sierra Nevada to seek enlightenment—suggesting his desire to connect with an empirically affirming theology—when he meets Luna and Sam. In one of their early conversations, Paul takes exception to Luna's simplistic characterization of Luther's *sola scripture,* claiming that she confuses the declaration with a strictly verbal, abstracted faith of mere spoken words. "If Scripture alone was all there was to Luther," Paul asserts, "he could have been right at home in California, making bumper stickers" (*STL* 140). Obsessed with religious inquiry, Paul explains how Lutheran sacramentalism serves as a corrective to not only the abstractions he encountered in California, but also an unhealthy Catholic asceticism—both of which diminish the value of the human body: "But Luther—no—Luther thought God started us off with a good world and a good body to move around in it. You know where he was when he got this big revelation about God? He was in a privy in a tower at Wittenberg monastery, so high that gravity took everything down and out better than any flush toilet. Sure, he was a raunchy, crude man, but he was healthier than one of your monk nuts that would scald himself for God" (*STL* 141).

Betts's theological sophistication is revealed through Paul, as he references Luther's "tower experience," the birth of the Protestant Reformation, as taking place in a monastery latrine. Luther's "momentous discovery that inspired his rebellion against Rome, his understanding of the term 'the righteousness of God'" was inspired by a passage he read in Romans 1:17, according to Erik Erikson's provocative psychoanalytical biography, while defecating. According to Erikson, Luther's relief from constipation corresponded with the relief from the abstract fears that held him in bondage to a Catholic faith of self-hatred and guilt.[21] In a book on Francois Rabelais, Mikhail Bakhtin makes an important observation about the material significance of excrement in Luther's time: "Excrement was conceived as an essential element in this life of the body and of the earth in the struggle against death. It was part of man's vivid awareness of his materiality, of his bodily nature, closely related to the life of the earth."[22]

With the aim of reforming doctrines that he believed unscriptural, abusive, and dangerously abstract, Luther placed the humanity of Christ at the center of his evangelical theology, declaring "there is no God apart from Christ." Luther believed that God is revealed to people only through the humanity of Christ, and that anything said about the divine should be viewed through the lens of the Incarnation: "The glory of our God is precisely that for our sakes he comes down to the very depths, into human flesh, into the bread, into our mouth, our heart, our body; moreover, for our sakes he allows himself to be treated ingloriously both on the cross and on the altar." Gerhard Forde, one of the most prominent Lutheran theologians of the twentieth century, asserts that Luther's central theological theme is that God is "down to earth" in his approach to humanity. Forde maintains that Christians "should be seeking like our Lord to come down to earth, to learn what it means to be a Christian here on this earth."[23]

For evangelical Lutherans, the sacrament models this down-to-earth approach most clearly, Forde describes, as "an event in which God breaks through to us in a particular and concrete manner." Lutherans believe in the "real presence" of Christ in the sacrament of the Eucharist, meaning that Christ is physically present with the sacrament of bread and wine. Lutheran sacramentalism is actually more affirming of materiality when it comes to the Eucharist, believing that the elements are already good as God's creation; therefore, Christ is present *with* the bread and wine. Catholic transubstantiation requires a transformation of elemental matter into something more spiritual—namely, the bodily presence of Christ. This Catholic doctrine betrays an assumption that the material world is somehow lesser than the spiritual, for the elements are not worthy for the presence of Christ on their own. Eads misses this nuance in her analysis when she asserts that the Catholic doctrine of transubstantiation "yields a distinctive appreciation of matter." It is rather the Lutheran view that affirms the value of physical elements not found in either the abstracted, Reformed doctrine of "spiritual presence" or the Catholic view of transubstantiation—both of which set up a hierarchy that privileges the spiritual world "up there" over the material world "down here." Both the Catholic and Reformed doctrines privilege the spiritual over the material.[24]

Lutherans contend that the "Lord's Supper is not merely a kind of earthly mimicry of a vague spiritual generality [found in Reformed theology]," nor does Christ "have to be made present by some magical kind of formula [found in Catholic theology], [for] he is present throughout creation already—even in his human, bodily form," thus Christ is present "in, with, and under" the elements of the Lord's Supper to affirm the goodness of materiality. Lutheran sacramental theology, in this sense, negotiates a via media, a middle way that affirms the goodness of matter as God's creation. Forde asserts that Lutheran sacramentalism affirms materiality and redefines the meaning of the term *spiritual*:

> Luther's insistence, however, is that our understanding of good and bad, material and spiritual needs to be overhauled. This is what the sacrament does. The "spiritual" in Luther's view is not to be understood as a different level of being or a different "place" from the material. "Spiritual" has to do with how things are used, what our relationship to a thing is. "Spiritual" is what is done in us by the Spirit and by faith, says Luther. That is to say that we cannot look down on

things like bread and wine because they are "material" and then go off elsewhere looking for something more "spiritual." Through the Word they become truly spiritual because they are put to a spiritual use.[25]

Luther's understanding of spirituality wrested terminology away from the metaphysical baggage of dualism. German Lutheran theologian, Paul Althaus, notes the penetrating insight Luther possessed in debating his opponents who "understand spirit as the opposite of flesh in the sense of bodiliness." Rather than employing a Hellenistic duality that stratifies spiritual as "up there" or "out there," Luther contended that spirituality refers to our usage and relationship to physical things. Luther, according to Althaus, considered "spiritual" to be a life of faith where people appreciate physical pleasures as a gift from God who created them. Acting in the flesh, therefore, is sinful when we misuse those physical things, not because they are simply material and, therefore, inherently bad. As Althaus states, "it is meaningless to consider the bodiliness in the sacrament unimportant and unworthy of God in order to assess the Spirit's interests. Bodily eating is itself a 'spiritual' eating when it takes place in faith. For everything which is done in faith is spiritual." The Lord's Supper proves prominent in Lutheran faith because it involves eating in faith to reorder humanity's proper relationship to physical things.[26]

In *The Sharp Teeth of Love*, Betts employs a distinctly Lutheran sacramentalism to reorder both Luna and Paul's relationship to the material world they have lost touch with. After a long day of hunting down Sam who has been re-kidnapped by a child prostitution ring in Reno, Luna and Paul check in to a hotel room. While watching Luna sleep in her bed, Paul's dormant sexual desire is reawakened as he admires her breasts. As this sudden surge of sexuality induces an erection, Paul declares to himself, "*Sweet Jesus*" (*STL* 170). This ironic and instinctive connection between sex and religion leads Paul to a reaffirmation of Lutheran theology: "The fullness of the reaction made me grin, proud of myself, even of the one-way trip from passion to whatever; also tickled at the link between sex and religion because both carry us outside ourselves, which Luther knew" (*STL* 170). The act of sex is linked with religion in its potential to take humans outside of themselves, a physical and embodied remedy for the abstractions that cut humans off from nourishing and intimate relationships.

Paul invokes Jesus's name again when he makes love to Luna in the mountains after nearly escaping death while searching for Sam, whom they helped escape from the kidnappers after creating a diversion. When Luna touches his erection, Paul simply says, "'Jesus.' I believe it was a reverent word; it was certainly awed" (*STL* 210). Physical contact proves significant for both characters in reorienting them to live their lives affirmatively. After their adventures in the mountains, Paul's mother, Erika, arrives at the hospital to see her son and his newfound love. Erika notices "that Paul could not keep his hands off" Luna as she is recovering in the hospital (*STL* 250). The sensual emphasis suggests how the physical touch will help both characters to heal from the psychological damage, thus hearkening back to Luna's wish at the start of the novel for "someone to love her body" (*STL* 18).

In the concluding passage of *The Sharp Teeth of Love*, Luna and Paul are traveling east toward a new life with Sam and Erika on the Cowan farm in Wisconsin. When Luna mentions that her mother asked whether Lutherans light candles and take the Eucharist from a priest, Paul answers affirmatively, "From the pastor. There are parallels" (*STL* 335). The parallels of Lutheran liturgy to Catholicism consist of moderate reform, not separation or replacement of those significant empirical practices, which according to Betts, feed "that longing in human beings for music, for kneeling, for chanting, for lighting candles."[27] Liturgy and sacraments aid the body to perform what is in the heart, and thus align body and spirit in a healthy manner that does not privilege one over the other. Paul's mention of the Lutheran pastor as the one who serves the Lord's Supper becomes an important qualification in distinguishing Lutheranism from Catholicism, for it provides yet another more down to earth emphasis on the one who performs the office of administering the sacrament. This distinction is significant when we consider the closing imagery of the wedding and Eucharist that Luna envisions: "She fixed the picture in her mind: she, Paul, and Sam at the altar rail, kneeling—she in lace scarf, maybe a mantilla in honor of Sam's heritage; then Erika kneeling next, and then Priscilla Stone beside her but slightly turned away from Martin and mouse-brain Corinne and above them with the sacrament the pastor in . . . in what kind of vestment? Luna made his suit satin and blue, with gold embroidery. *Take, eat. This is my body*" (*STL* 336). While the passage certainly embodies an interfaith emphasis with the mantilla and multicolored vestments associated with Catholicism, it is noteworthy that a pastor, not priest, is administering the Eucharist to the family, signifying the embrace of the Lutheran church as a via media for Luna and Paul, a religious settlement suitable to nourish and affirm their physical bodies.

Rather than shouting her Christian message like O'Connor, Betts turns down the volume in The Sharp Teeth of Love to whisper a Lutheran sacramental vision that celebrates the goodness of materiality and reveals how the sensual pleasures of life are no less spiritual than reading Scripture, meditation, or prayer. The symbolic move to the Midwest of Wisconsin at the novel's end parallels the embrace of Lutheran sacramentalism: Luna and Paul have found a middle way to center their identities between community and individuality, body and spirit, place and space. While Luna's and Paul's reasons for going West may differ, both discover a spiritual and communal significance that has been malnourished by abstract tendencies. The path to recovery for both is found in an evangelical sacramentalism that affirms the value of materiality in restoring each character's humanity; this path sets them in a healthy and intimate relationship with one another that enables them to embrace the present world of community.

Coda

Narrative Reckoning

The current conservative climate in the United States puts the concerns of my study into sharp relief. As my title suggests, *Southern Strategies* examines the essential role evangelical religion plays in shaping many of the manifestations we come to regard as Southern culture by tracing not only the political engagement of white evangelicals, but also the narrative strategies of writers who take measure and navigate that influence. Interrogating the interplay of religion and politics, I argue that white evangelicals engage culture with what they consider theological conviction, and in doing so misinterpret the nature and meaning of their faith. An institution that claims to be "in the world but not of the world" reveals itself to be susceptible as any to compromise in pursuit of power and influence. The presidency of Donald Trump provided the ultimate stress test for evangelicals and other so-called "family-values" conservatives in the Republican Party by placing their convictions and support in public view. Despite the political gains achieved in supporting Trump, evangelicals failed to live up to their own theological convictions. The consequences of this alliance resulted not only in many defections from evangelical communities but also a reckoning among historians to reexamine the foundations of white evangelical political engagement.

In the years leading up to his foray into politics, Donald Trump challenged the legitimacy of Barack Obama's presidency with the "birther conspiracy," insinuating that his predecessor was born in Kenya and secretly a Muslim. During the 2016 Republican primary, Trump employed racist tropes by suggesting that Mexican immigrants were criminals, drug dealers, and rapists who posed threats to national security; he promised to build a wall along the southern border and force Mexico to pay for it. Only a month before the general election, an audio tape leaked with Trump lewdly bragging about sexual assault while preparing for a 2005 promotional interview for his reality show. In the immediate aftermath, twenty-six women alleged sexual assault and misconduct against Trump. Trump paid hush money to numerous women, including a porn star with whom he had an affair a few months after his wife gave birth to their son. While in office, Trump referred to white nationalists marching with torches in Charlottesville to preserve a Confederate monument as "very fine people," drawing a moral equivalence between white supremacists and those who oppose them.

The final year of Trump's presidency fully exposed his incompetence and poor leadership. At the onset of a global pandemic, Trump likened COVID-19 to a flu that would magically disappear by Easter, flouting masks and social-distancing measures put in place to stop the spread of a deadly virus. During a coronavirus task force press conference in April 2020, Trump suggested a "cleaning" therapy by injecting disinfectant and ultraviolet rays into the body to eliminate the virus; both Lysol and the CDC released statements warning people not to ingest bleach. The shock and dismay by medical experts and journalists proved so baffling that the daily task force meetings were disbanded, and Trump's pandemic response became hands-off for the remainder of his tenure (a strategy emulated by many Republican governors). The murder of George Floyd in Minneapolis by a police officer sparked waves of protests and riots engulfing many cities throughout the summer of 2020, as well as antiracist activism that led to collective discussions of systemic racism across institutions and corporations. In response, Trump employed alarmist rhetoric and "law and order" tactics (echoing Richard Nixon's 1968 campaign mantra) that were epitomized on 1 June 2020 in Washington, DC, at St. John's Episcopal Church in Lafayette Square, in which peaceful protestors were tear-gassed shortly before the president's photo op holding a Bible in front of the church. The juxtaposition of these images crystallized his presidency like no other. After losing the 2020 election in November, Trump propagated the "big lie" that the election was stolen, culminating in a riot on 6 January 2021, in which a mob of supporters, incited by the president himself during a rally, stormed the capital in an attempt to stop the certification of the electoral college results. Trump was impeached for the second time, putting an exclamation point on a dark and disgraceful presidency. Despite all these degradations, Trump enjoyed overwhelming majority support among white evangelicals (81%) that had barely wavered from 2016 to 2020.

Many scholars and journalists were mystified as to how evangelicals, the core constituency of the Republican Party, could support a leader so antithetical to their family values. Evangelicals rationalize their support by telling themselves a story about the origins of their political engagement with American culture. Constructing a narrative that inscribes their experience within a political context, white evangelicals cast themselves as defenders of traditional family values under attack in an increasingly secular culture. When asked why they support Trump, most evangelicals cite abortion as their central concern, noting how Trump appointed three "pro-life" justices to shift the judicial balance in favor of criminalizing abortion and protecting religious liberty. Indeed, on 24 June 2022 the Supreme Court voted 5–4 in *Dobbs v. Jackson Women's Health Organization* to rule that the US Constitution does not confer the right to an abortion, overturning fifty years of federal protection. According to evangelical discourse, modern political engagement commenced as a response to the fateful 1973 *Roe v. Wade* Supreme Court decision legalizing abortion; consequently, the *Dobbs* ruling epitomized a crowning achievement produced by four decades of resolute evangelical activism. This representative narrative draws meaningful connections to historic events in order to make sense of political motives subjected to scrutiny; however, this narrative misrepresents the actual history.

Many recent historical works emerged in the wake of the Trump presidency, which interrogate this conventional narrative concerning evangelical engagement with American culture. These narrative reckonings, written largely by evangelicals or former evangelicals, deconstruct foundational discourse in a way that uncovers a much darker history to illuminate the paradox of evangelical support for Trump. Similar to the narratives of resistance in part one of my study, these writers confront the racist and misogynistic roots of white evangelical culture to challenge long-held origin myths concerning political support and activism. In corresponding fashion, their experience and participation in evangelical communities authorizes their critique, enabling the research to resonate beyond what typical histories can achieve. What is common in these studies is an inside, informed critique of evangelical complicity in constructing a culture of white supremacy.

In *Unholy: How White Christian Nationalists Powered the Trump Presidency, and the Devastating Legacy They Left Behind* (2021), Sarah Posner confronts the confounding alliance between Donald Trump and evangelicals by tracing the lineage of the religious right's political engagement. Going back to the 1970s, Posner reveals how resentment and grievance over lost dominance animates the political activism of white evangelicals. Posner deconstructs the origin myth of the modern Christian right, which casts Jerry Falwell and other evangelical leaders as heroes "roused to action as a direct result of the Supreme Court's 1973 *Roe v. Wade* decision legalizing abortion, driving previously apolitical evangelicals out of the pews with a moral imperative to protect babies from slaughter."[1] However, this evangelical abortion myth collapses under scrutiny.

Upon closer inspection, the actual history of the 1970s reveals a different story with different priorities. In *Bad Faith: Race and the Rise of the Religious Right* (2021), evangelical historian Randall Balmer highlights the evangelical silence on abortion in the aftermath of *Roe V. Wade,* noting how Falwell himself did not preach on abortion until 1978. The Southern Baptist Convention in 1971, 1974, and 1976, actually supported abortion "under such conditions as rape, incest, clear evidence of severe fetal deformity, and carefully ascertained evidence of the likelihood of damage to the emotional, mental, and physical health of the mother." One of the most prominent evangelical leaders during the 1970s, W. A. Criswell, president of the Southern Baptist Convention and pastor of First Baptist Church in Dallas, affirmed the *Roe* decision: "I have always felt that it was only after a child was born and had a life separate from its mother that it became an individual person."[2] It's astonishing to observe how such pro-choice language defining human life *after* birth comprised an evangelical consensus in the aftermath of *Roe,* exposing how much evangelicals shifted on their so-called primary political issue. In reality, evangelicals considered abortion to be a "Catholic issue" until the end of the 1970s.

The true catalyst for modern evangelical political engagement, according to Posner, was a "racist backlash against school desegregation and other civil rights advances, all cloaked in the language of freedom and religion."[3] As previously discussed in the introduction, evangelicals were galvanized by government intervention when the IRS began enforcing a policy that would deny tax exemptions to private schools that discriminated on the basis of race.[4] In 1979, journalist and activist Paul Weyrich, cofounder of the conservative Heritage Foundation, forged an alliance with Falwell to rouse white evangelicals in resistance to unwelcome cultural and social changes; their moral majority coalesced around the notion of white grievance by casting elite liberal government as a threat to religious liberty. Balmer explains the strategy:

> Weyrich and other founders of the Religious Right cannily sought to shift the justification for their political activism away from a defense of racial segregation and toward a putative defense of religious freedom, all the while ignoring the fact that religious institutions were free to pursue whatever racial policies they chose—so long as they surrendered their tax exemptions. Indeed, the most obvious, commonsense reading of the Religious Right is that conservative evangelicals were mobilizing in defense of racial segregation. Weyrich's sleight of hand brilliantly shifted perceptions of the movement away from racism

toward a more high-minded defense of religious freedom. (The Religious Right's later opposition to abortion further burnished its image as a movement crusading against moral evil.)[5]

Weyrich and Falwell's deception exemplifies the Southern Strategy by using abortion, religious liberty, and family values to conceal their true aims of preserving white dominance. By casting progressive government as an authoritarian oppressor, white evangelicals could lay claim to victimhood status. Posner contends that this embattlement framework best explains evangelical affinity for Trump.[6]

The Southern Strategy's legerdemain pivots on notions of religious liberty. In *The End of White Christian America* (2017), evangelical historian Robert P. Jones observes how religious liberty was traditionally understood by evangelicals as a constitutional protection that secures freedom of worship; however, with the rise of civil rights, evangelicals refashioned religious liberty, wielding it as "a rearguard insurgency," to assert "that individuals should be able to carry religious objections from their private life into their public roles as service providers, business owners, and even elected officials."[7] Such a weaponized interpretation of religious freedom centers evangelical activism on the judicial branch of government. This notion explains why evangelical activism focuses so much on the Supreme Court: The ultimate goal is to pass Christian laws that require everyone to submit.[8]

In *Believe Me: The Evangelical Road to Donald Trump* (2018), evangelical historian John Fea argues that fear, power, and nostalgia are the ideas that best explain the evangelical embrace of Trump, who tapped into these with his campaign to "make America great again." Echoing Jones's assessment on the alteration of religious freedom, Fea argues that in the aftermath of civil rights, "white evangelicals have waged a desperate and largely failing war against the thickening walls of separation between church and state, the removal of Christianity from public schools, the growing ethnic and religious diversity of the country, the intrusion of the federal government into their everyday lives (especially as it pertains to desegregation and civil rights), and legalized abortion."[9] Fea describes what he calls "the playbook" of modern evangelical activism, exhibited by the moral majority, to win America for their Christian agenda. The moral majority exhorted evangelicals to vote not only for conservative policies, but more important, for the moral character of politicians who seek office. Implicit in this belief is the notion that character arises from personal belief and morality. In 1998, this notion was fully displayed when Bill Clinton was impeached for lying under oath about a sexual relationship with an intern. Among the likes of Jerry Falwell and James Dobson, white evangelicals condemned Clinton in unison, charging that he was morally unfit to hold the highest office of the presidency.

Twenty years later, white evangelicals were conspicuously silent on the moral fitness of Donald Trump, claiming that policy, not character, was what truly counted. Evangelicals justified this shift by claiming American culture became increasingly progressive and hostile toward them during the two terms of Obama's presidency. Citing the legalization of gay marriage, many claimed their religious liberties were threatened. The playbook shifted, so to speak, so evangelicals could no longer rely on lip service paid to them by career politicians and insiders. What they needed was a strongman unconcerned with diplomatic norms or notions of political correctness. Policy and expediency now took precedence; moral character no longer mattered. But was this really a new wrinkle in the playbook?

In fact, Southern evangelicals once occupied the White House when Jimmy Carter was elected president in 1976. Carter was a Southern Baptist who taught Sunday school and claimed to be a born-again Christian. Because of Carter, the term evangelical was introduced to most Americans when *Newsweek* christened 1976 "the year of the evangelical." However, Carter's evangelical faith proved too progressive in his concerns for the poor, commitment to peace, and pursuit of racial justice by enforcing the removal of tax-exempt status among discriminatory private schools. Ironically, the Southern Strategy was deployed most effectively in the 1980 election, according to Fea, when Southern evangelicals overwhelmingly "rejected the first United States presidential candidate to identify himself as a 'born-again Christian' and had thrown their support behind a formerly pro-choice California governor. From this point forward, conservative evangelicals would see the Republican Party as their vehicle to achieve political change."[10]

Reagan's election served as the watershed moment of the Southern Strategy, revealing a permanent realignment of white evangelicals to the Republican Party. In observing how the Republican Party made inroads to secure their full support, we must not deny evangelical agency. It's all too common to frame this discussion as if Republicans misled or exploited white evangelicals by pandering to their anxieties around race, gender, and sexuality. In fact, renowned evangelist Billy Graham proved indispensable in abetting the Southern Strategy through his relationship with Richard Nixon, advising the president on how to influence Southern evangelicals. Moreover, Southern Baptist leaders were early adopters of the Republican Party, coinciding with the conservative resurgence within the denomination that purged liberals and moderates from leadership and seminary positions.[11]

Politics, in many respects, supplanted religion in the United States over the past twenty years, serving as a quasi-religion that offers a systematic worldview, orthodox ideology, partisan saints, Manichean dualism, and proselytizing engagement with opposition. A 2019 Gallup poll reveals that church membership precipitously declined more than twenty points over the past twenty years, from 70% in 2000 to 47% in 2020. While Southern evangelicals still comprise the highest church membership and attendance, these declining trends exist across every subgroup and generation. It's becoming increasingly clear that political and cultural alliances are fueling precipitous declines in those who once identified as evangelical. Sociologist James Davison Hunter concedes that "the dominant public witness of the Christian churches in America since the early 1980s has been a political witness."[12] In today's hyper-partisan landscape fueled by online discourse, many white evangelicals embrace politics as an immediate source of spiritual and cultural warfare. As Fea rightly contends, "Instead of doing the hard work necessary for engaging a more diverse society with the claims of Christian orthodoxy, evangelicals have become intellectually lazy, preferring to respond to cultural change by trying to reclaim a world that is rapidly disappearing and has little chance of ever coming back."[13]

Surveying the damage of their political engagement in American culture, historian Kristin Kobes Du Mez published one of the most impactful studies on white evangelicals in many years. In *Jesus and John Wayne: How White Evangelicals Corrupted a Faith and Fractured a Nation* (2020), Du Mez documents the cultural entanglements of evangelicals that consummated their fateful embrace of Trump. Similar to other evangelical historians under discussion, Du Mez contends that the Trump-evangelical alliance was no aberration or pragmatic choice, but "rather, the culmination of evangelicals' embrace of militant masculinity, an ideology that enshrines patriarchal authority and condones the callous display of power, at home and abroad."[14] *Jesus and John Wayne* resonates because of the author's intimate knowledge and experience with major evangelical leaders, conferences, institutions, and books. Because evangelicalism permeates so much of American culture due to its many parachurch organizations, Du Mez gives considerable attention to cultural consumption as a definitive marker of evangelical identity. By deftly threading history, theology, and culture together to trace this culmination through the twentieth century, Du Mez concludes that evangelicalism must be defined as a cultural and political movement rather than a community living out the teachings of Scripture. In other words, American evangelicals comprise a particular interpretation of Christian faith, and their fallibility manifests in the interplay between culture and theology.

On the other hand, claiming that white evangelicals are a product of American culture might be letting them off too easily. In reality, white evangelicals were chiefly responsible for cultivating a closed society of white supremacy in the South. The Southern Baptist Church, the largest denomination not only in the region but also the entire United States, was born out of the belief in white supremacy and the enslavement of Black people. It's a cold historical fact to assert that white evangelicals in the South used what they considered an inerrant Bible to sacralize white supremacy and Black inferiority through slavery and segregation (and their perpetuating legacies); yet, when confronted with this history, evangelicals blame culture and context as corrupting a faith situated in a shameful past.

Many white evangelicals possess a willful ignorance concerning the evangelical roots of white supremacy, which flourishes in their forgetfulness. In *White Evangelical Racism* (2021), Anthea Butler confronts this notion by delineating the term evangelical beyond the connotations of theology. Having once identified as evangelical, Butler makes it clear why many Black Americans like herself feel excluded from the designation. Exposing cultural, political, racial, and nationalistic alliances, Butler centers her definition on the more empirical manner in which evangelicalism has been transmitted to the American public as a white nationalistic movement. Evangelicals, Butler argues, have historically revealed themselves to be "concerned with keeping the status quo of patriarchy, cultural hegemony, and nationalism." According to Butler, evangelical "support for current-day policies that seem draconian and unchristian is linked inescapably to a foundational history" that she uncovers in her study.[15] Southern evangelicalism manifests itself to be a white nationalistic movement through its initial support of slavery and subsequent complicity in segregation; therefore, Butler rightly concludes that racism is a core feature (not a bug) of white evangelicalism.

Perhaps the most powerful reckoning of these recent works is Robert P. Jones's *White Too Long: The Legacy of White Supremacy in American Christianity* (2020). Blending history, theology, sociology, and autobiography, Jones's narrative comprises a powerful deconstruction of American evangelicalism. As a white evangelical, Jones definitively argues that "the historical record of lived Christianity in America reveals that Christian theology and institutions have been the central cultural tent pole holding up the very idea of white supremacy";

Coda *141*

moreover, Jones contends that the "genetic imprint of this legacy" remains present and measurable in evangelical culture.[16] According to Jones, Trump's presidential campaign reactivated that genetic imprint. Augmenting historical deconstruction with personal memoir, Jones inserts his own experience as a Southern white evangelical who grew up in the Southern Baptist church. Recalling childhood memories in Jackson, Mississippi, during the desegregation of public schools in the 1970s and 1980s, Jones remembers an education that minimized white supremacy, revised histories of the Civil War and Reconstruction, and couched racism in the rhetoric of heritage and tradition. Jones confesses that he never fully realized the racist foundations of his own denomination until graduate school at Emory University. Ultimately, Jones argues that white evangelicals must undergo the same narrative reckoning that confronts the shameful role their tradition asserted in constructing a culture of white supremacy; this reckoning, Jones asserts, is "the only path that can salvage the integrity of our faith, psyches, and legacies," for evangelical identity is at stake.[17]

Evangelicals believe in original sin: that Adam's sin is imputed to the entire human race, making them guilty before God. Evangelicals believe in the substitutionary atonement of Christ: that Jesus's death on the cross vicariously covers the sins of all who believe, making them righteous before God. In other words, the most cherished beliefs of evangelicals assign complicity based on past actions in which they played no role. Yet when confronted with the historical legacy of white supremacy, evangelicals claim minimal responsibility for the past. There's an old cliché that Sunday morning worship is the most segregated hour of the week; this segregation is not a manifestation of cultural differences or worship styles, but rather the direct legacy of evangelicals sanctioning white supremacy. White evangelicals must confront this history to deconstruct the foundations of their political and cultural engagement. For too long, willful ignorance has been a shield for white people; for everyone else, ignorance is a liability.

Evangelicals compromised biblical principles in pursuit of political power and cultural influence—the ramifications of which will be felt for many generations to come. All these narrative reckonings under discussion have unearthed buried histories to best explain the Trump-evangelical alliance that mystifies so many. In doing so, these works decisively frame modern evangelical engagement in American politics. It's striking to observe the similarities of these contemporary works with the Southern writers of narrative resistance covered in part one, as many of the same concerns about authoritarianism and white supremacy are echoed in these critiques of evangelical complicity. Evangelical support for Trump makes better sense when we understand white grievance as the core animating principle and dispense with the fiction of family values. Seen in this light, Trump's birther claims and racist outbursts attracted white evangelicals more than repelling them. Evangelical support for Trump is not an aberration; on the contrary, the Trump-evangelical alliance is the embodiment of the Southern Strategy.

NOTES

Introduction: Southern Strategies

1. Frances Fitzgerald, *The Evangelicals: The Struggle to Shape America* (New York: Simon & Schuster, 2017), 2, 637; Mark Noll, *The Scandal of the Evangelical Mind* (Grand Rapids, MI: William B. Eerdmans, 1994), 7–10; Noll attributes these key impulses to David Bebbington's *Evangelicalism in Modern Britain: A History from the 1730s to the 1980s;* also see Noll's *Evangelicalism and Modern America* and *American Evangelical Christianity.*

2. Richard Hofstadter, *Anti-intellectualism in American Life* (New York: Alfred A. Knopf, 1963), 74–75.

3. Randall Balmer, *Bad Faith: Race and the Rise of the Christian Right* (Grand Rapids, MI: William B. Eerdmans, 2021), 4–5; Harold Bloom, *The American Religion* (New York: Chu Hartley, 2006), 47–53.

4. Noll, *Scandal of the Evangelical Mind,* 157; Samuel Hill, *Southern Churches in Crisis Revisited* (Tuscaloosa: University of Alabama Press, 1999), xii; also see Samuel Hill, Introduction in *Religion and Politics in the South: Mass and Elite Perspectives,* eds. Todd A. Baker, Robert P. Steed, and Laurence W. Moreland (New York: Praeger, 1983), ix–xiv.

5. Fitzgerald, *The Evangelicals,* 52–54; Balmer, *Bad Faith,* 6–8.

6. Charles Reagan Wilson, *Baptized in Blood: The Religion of the Lost Cause, 1865–1920* (Athens: University of Georgia Press, 1980), 5, 9. Fitzgerald, *The Evangelicals,* 4–6.

7. Balmer, *Bad Faith,* 17–18; see George M. Marsden, *Fundamentalism and American Culture: The Shaping of Twentieth-Century Evangelicalism, 1870-1925* (New York: Oxford University Press, 1980).

8. Edwin McNeill Poteat, "Religion in the South," in *Culture in the South,* ed. W. T. Couch (Chapel Hill: University of North Carolina Press, 1935), 253; Francis Simkins, *The Everlasting South* (Baton Rouge: Louisiana State University Press, 1963), 79.

9. Kristin Kobes Du Mez, *Jesus and John Wayne: How White Evangelicals Corrupted a Faith and Fractured a Nation* (New York: W. W. Norton, 2020), 11.

10. John G. Turner, *Bill Bright & Campus Crusade for Christ: The Renewal of Evangelicalism in Postwar America* (Chapel Hill: University of North Carolina Press, 2008), 3, 6.

11. Randall Balmer, *Thy Kingdom Come: An Evangelical's Lament* (New York: Basic Books, 2006), 13–15.

12. See Peter Applebome, *Dixie Rising* (New York: Random House, 1996) and John Egerton, *The Americanization of Dixie: The Southernization of America* (New York: Harper's Magazine Press, 1974).

Chapter 1: Evangelical Authoritarianism in W. J. Cash's *The Mind of the South*

1. Louis D. Rubin, Jr., "W. J. Cash After Fifty Years," *Virginia Quarterly Review* 67.2 (1991): 215–16; In *The Sacred Circle: The Dilemma of the Intellectual in the Old South* (Philadelphia:

University of Pennsylvania Press, 1977), Drew Faust notes that as far back as the antebellum period, Southern thinkers have carried a heavy burden in solitude because a life of the mind aroused public suspicions among the general public in the South that regarded such people as subversive.

2. W. J. Cash, "The Mind of the South," *American Mercury* 18 (October 1929): 193.

3. Robert H. Brinkmeyer, *The Fourth Ghost: White Southern Writers and European Fascism, 1930-1950,* Southern Literary Studies Series (Baton Rouge: Louisiana State University Press, 2009), 73. "What would be central in the book—an analysis of the authoritarian forces under which southerners lived—is almost entirely absent in the essay," Brinkmeyer notes as he observes that the 1929 published essay, "The Mind of the South," posits Southerners who are "prisoners of their own thoughtlessness and their determination not to analyze," while the 1941 published book, *The Mind of the South,* presents Southerners as "prisoners of authoritarian forces" (73).

4. Hannah Arendt, *The Origins of Totalitarianism* (New York: Harcourt, 1951), 353.

5. Anne Goodwyn Jones, "The Cash Nexus," *The Mind of the South: Fifty Years Later*, ed. Charles W. Eagles (Jackson and London: University Press of Mississippi, 1992), 32–33.

6. Kent Puckett, *Narrative Theory: A Critical Introduction* (Cambridge: Cambridge University Press, 2016), 2.

7. H. Porter Abbott, *The Cambridge Introduction to Narrative Theory* (Cambridge: Cambridge University Press, 2020), 15.

8. Linda Myrsiades. "Constituting Resistance: Narrative Construction and the Social Theory of Resistance." *symploke* 1.2 (Summer 1993): 103.

9. David L. Moore, "Decolonializing Criticism: Reading Dialectics and Dialogics in Native American Literatures," *Studies in American Indian Literatures* 6.4 (Winter 1994): 7–35

10. Bruce Clayton, *W. J. Cash: A Life* (Baton Rouge: Louisiana State University Press, 1991), 12.

11. Joseph L. Morrison, *W. J. Cash: Southern Prophet; A Biography and Reader* (New York: Alfred A. Knopf, 1967), 17–20.

12. Clayton, *W. J. Cash*, 24.

13. Ibid., 36.

14. Fred Hobson, *Serpent in Eden: H. L. Mencken and the South* (Chapel Hill: University of North Carolina Press, 1974), 112.

15. Morrison, *W. J. Cash*, 26–27.

16. Quoted in Clayton, *W. J. Cash*, 36–37.

17. Morrison, *W. J. Cash*, 33, 35.

18. Ibid., 37–39.

19. Clayton, *W. J. Cash*, 53.

20. Morrison, *W. J. Cash*, 42–44; Clayton, *W. J. Cash*, 57.

21. Clayton, *W. J. Cash*, 54; Morrison, *W. J. Cash*, 13.

22. W. J. Cash, "What Constitutes Decency?" *Charlotte News,* March 25, 1928.

23. Clayton, *W. J. Cash*, 57–61, 64.

24. Ibid., 78.

25. Ibid.

26. Ibid., 112.

Notes to Pages 25–35   *145*

27. W. J. Cash, "Close View of a Calvinist Lhasa," *American Mercury* 28 (April 1933): 446, 449.

28. Ibid., 449–50; Brinkmeyer notes how in this pivotal essay "Cash goes on to make it clear that Charlotte's citizens live imprisoned not in ignorance but in fear; or as Cash puts it, "they submit to authority," never daring to confront or rise above it (75).

29. Clayton, *W. J. Cash*, 162, 114, 109; Clayton, "A Mind of the South," in *W. J. Cash and the Minds of the South*, ed. Paul D. Escott (Baton Rouge: Louisiana State University Press, 1992), 10.

30. W. J. Cash, *The Mind of the South* (New York: Vintage Books, 1941), 56. All parenthetical citations henceforth in my discussion of this primary text are labeled as "*MS*" followed by the page number.

31. Noll, *Scandal of the Evangelical Mind*, 157.

32. Clayton, *W. J. Cash*, 53–54.

33. Wilson, *Baptized in Blood*, 9.

34. Clarence Cason, *Ninety Degrees in the Shade* (Chapel Hill: University of North Carolina Press, 1935) 65.

35. Cason, *Ninety Degrees*, 63.

36. Ibid., 89. Cason's discussion extends in a chapter titled, "Fascism: Southern Style," where he contextualizes the Southern political orientation in Mississippi between the years 1890 and 1934 to extrapolate the following conclusion about politics in the entire region: "If one must seek a classification for the Heflins, Bilbos, and Longs, it would not be too wide of the mark to term them American Fascists (southern style). Their political victories have been won through the mass force of machines built upon every conceivable form of racial, sectional, class, and religious prejudice; these they have been able to fan into furies sufficient to consume their opponents. But, as for actually accomplishing anything to assist their deluded followers, they seem able to operate successfully on the theory that most campaign promises are forgotten between elections" (106).

37. V. O. Key Jr., *Southern Politics in State and Nation* (New York: Vintage Books, 1947), 664.

38. Bertram Wyatt-Brown, "W. J. Cash: Creativity and Suffering in a Southern Writer," in *W. J. Cash and the Minds of the South,* ed. Paul D. Escott (Baton Rouge: Louisiana State University Press, 1992), 39, 55.

39. Fred Hobson, *Tell About the South: The Southern Rage to Explain* (Baton Rouge: Louisiana State University Press, 1983), 8.

40. Rubin, "W. J. Cash After Fifty Years," 216.

Chapter 2: Deconversion and Redemption in Lillian Smith's *Killers of the Dream*

1. Charles K. Piehl, "Telling About the South on Paper and Canvas," Reviews in American History XII (December 1984): 544. For critical assessments of Smith's place in Southern intellectual life, see Morton Sosna's *In Search of the Silent South: Southern Liberals and the Race Issue* (New York: Columbia University Press, 1977), chapter 9; Richard King's *A Southern Renaissance: The Cultural Awakening of the American South, 1930-1955* (New York: Oxford University Press, 1980), chapter 8; Hobson's *Tell About the South*, pp. 307–23; Daniel Joseph Singal's *The War Within: From Victorian to Modernist Thought in the South, 1919–1945* (Chapel Hill: University of North Carolina Press, 1982), 374–75. Among these works, Sosna

146 Notes to Pages 35–41

and Hobson treat the influence of Southern evangelical religion as crucial to their thinking, while King emphasizes Freudianism and Singal focuses more on Modernism in the South.

2. Erik M. Bachman, "Sin, Sex, and Segregation in Lillian Smith's Silent South," in *Literary Obscenities: U.S. Case Law and Naturalism after Modernism* (University Park: Penn State University Press, 2018), 160.

3. See Robert Brinkmeyer, *Fourth Ghost*, 120. Brinkmeyer frames Smith's work as a forceful expansion of Cash's project: "Even more so than Cash, Smith focused her analysis on the crippling effects of segregation, exploring the damaging neuroses besetting southern children and the destructive manifestations these neuroses later took in adulthood. Her 'mind of the South' was thus even more frightening than Cash's folk mind."

4. Fred Hobson, *Tell About the South*.

5. John P. Hussey, "Agee's Famous Men and American Non-Fiction," *College English* 40.6 (1979): 680, 682.

6. Lillian Smith, "Autobiography as a Dialogue Between King and Corpse," in *The Winner Names the Age*, ed. Michelle Cliff (New York: W. W. Norton, 1978), 197.

7. See Fred Hobson, *But Now I See: The White Southern Racial Conversion Narrative* (Baton Rouge: Louisiana State University Press, 1999), 160. Included among these white racial converts in Hobson's estimation are Lillian Smith, Katharine Du Pre Lumpkin, James McBride Dabbs, Sarah Patton Boyle, Will Campbell, Willie Morris, Larry L. King, and Pat Watters.

8. For full-length studies of conversion narratives, see Patricia Caldwell, *The Puritan Conversion Narrative: The Beginnings of American Expression* (New York: Cambridge University Press, 1983); Charles Lloyd Cohen, *God's Caress: The Psychology of Puritan Religious Experience* (New York: Oxford University Press, 1986); Peter A. Dorsey, *Sacred Estrangement: The Rhetoric of Conversion in Modern American Autobiography* (University Park: Penn State University Press, 1993); C. C. Goen, Introduction to *The Great Awakening* by Jonathan Edwards (New Haven: Yale University Press, 1972); and Philip F. Gura, *A Glimpse of Sion's Glory: Puritan Radicalism in New England, 1620-1660* (Middletown, CT: Wesleyan University Press, 1984).

9. Hobson, *But Now I See*, 4.

10. See James Cox, "Between Defiance and Defense: Owning Up to the South," in *Located Lives: Place and Idea in Southern Autobiography*, ed. J. Bill Berry (Athens, GA: University of Georgia Press, 1990), 121.

11. Hobson, *But Now I See*, 5.

12. The passages from this section about Lillian Smith's family and childhood are taken from her memoir, *Killers of the Dream* (New York: W. W. Norton, 1994), the primary text under consideration in this chapter. All parenthetical citations from the text are labeled "*KD*."

13. Kathleen Miller's dissertation, "Out of the Chrysalis: Lillian Smith and the Transformation of the South" (Emory University, 1984), examines Smith's childhood and early family relationship, based in part from her interviews with her younger sister, Esther Smith. Miller speculates that Smith's feelings of childhood rejection stemmed from her doubts about her own personal salvation.

14. Anne C. Loveland, *Lillian Smith: A Southerner Confronting the South: A Biography* (Baton Rouge: Louisiana State University Press, 1986), 19. See Lillian Smith to Robert Coles,

September 28, 1961, Lillian Smith Collection, Special Collections, University of Georgia Libraries.

15. For a more in-depth discussion, see Loveland, *Lillian Smith*, 9–16.

16. Loveland, *Lillian Smith*, 20–21. See Lillian Smith to Wilma Dykeman Stokely, February 24, 1965, Lillian Smith Collection, Special Collections, University of Georgia Libraries.

17. Loveland, *Lillian Smith*, 23.

18. Lillian Smith and Paula Snelling, "Across the South Today," *North Georgia Review* 6 (Winter 1941): 58–59, 66–67, 100; Lillian Smith, "Personal History of 'Strange Fruit': A Statement of Purposes and Intentions," *Saturday Review of Literature*, (February 17, 1945): 10; see Loveland, *Lillian Smith*, 49, for a more in-depth discussion.

19. Lillian Smith, "Putting Away Childish Things," *South Today*, (Spring–Summer 1944): in *From the Mountain*, 137; Lillian Smith, "Growing Into Freedom," *Common Ground* 4(Autumn 1943): 50–51.

20. Loveland, *Lillian Smith*, 62.

21. All parenthetical citations in this section from Smith's novel *Strange Fruit* (New York: Reynal & Hitchcock, 1944) are labeled "*SF*," followed by the page number.

22. Loveland, *Lillian Smith*, 66.

23. Lillian Smith, "A Trembling Earth," in *The Winner Names the Age: A Collection of Writings*, ed. Michelle Cliff (New York, 1978), 123; Lillian Smith to Lawrence Kubi, June 2, 1955, Lillian Smith Collection, Special Collections, University of Georgia Libraries, Athens, Georgia.

24. Lillian Smith, "Personal History of 'Strange Fruit,'" 10; "Miss Smith: Speaking from New York," *Northwestern University on the Air: Of Men and Books*, Radio program, March 4, 1941, 5–6.

25. Cash, *Mind of the South*, 59–60.

26. Scott Romine, "Framing Southern Rhetoric: Lillian Smith's Narrative Persona in *Killers of the Dream*," *South Atlantic Review* 59.2 (1994): 96.

27. Ibid., 97, 107.

28. Martin E. Marty, "The Revival of Evangelicalism and Southern Religion," *Varieties of Southern Evangelicalism*, ed. David Edwin Harrell (Macon, GA: Mercer University Press, 1981), 9–10, 12.

29. Marty, "The Revival of Evangelicalism and Southern Religion," 13, 15–18, 19. The ensuing chapters show how evangelicalism's cultural adaptability troubled Southern writers who otherwise shared its redemptive vision.

30. Singal, *War Within*, 374.

31. See Loveland, *Lillian Smith*, 102–104.

32. Lillian Smith, *The Winner Names the Age*, 217–18.

33. Margaret Rose Gladney, Preface to *How Am I To Be Heard?: Letters of Lillian Smith* (Chapel Hill: University of North Carolina Press, 1993), xvi; Hobson, *But Now I See*, 22.

34. Lillian Smith to George Reynolds, August 7, 1939, in Morton Philip Sosna, *In Search of the Silent South: White Southern Racial Liberalism, 1920-1950* (Madison: University of Wisconsin–Madison, 1972), 327.

35. Lillian Smith, *The Journey* (New York: World Publishing, 1954). All parenthetical citations from Smith's memoir, *The Journey*, in this section are labeled "*J*," followed by the page number.

148 Notes to Pages 57–66

36. Lillian Smith to Donald Seawell, November 14, 1959, Lillian Smith Collection, Special Collections, University of Georgia Libraries.

37. Quoted in Loveland, *Lillian Smith*, 109.

38. Lillian Smith, "The South Reacts to Segregation," *New Leader* (September 3, 1951): 4–5.

Chapter 3: Evangelical Sales Culture in Flannery O'Connor's *Wise Blood*

1. Mikhail Bakhtin, "Discourse in the Novel," in *The Dialogic Imagination: Four Essays*, ed. Michael Holquist, trans. Caryl Emerson and Michael Holquist (Austin: University of Texas Press, 1984), 51–82, 259–422.

2. Frank Palmeri, *Satire in Narrative: Petronius, Swift, Gibbon, Melville, and Pynchon* (Austin: University of Texas Press, 1990).

3. Flannery O'Connor, "The Fiction Writer and His Country," in *Flannery O'Connor: Collected Works*, ed. Sally Fitzgerald (New York: Library of America, 1988), 805–6.

4. Walker Percy, *The Second Coming* (New York: Picador, 1980), 156–88.

5. Throughout the essay, I refer to the character exclusively as Onnie Jay Holy, the fictional persona portrayed by Hoover Shoats, who embodies the performance, charm, and influence necessary to be a successful minister-salesman.

6. Flannery O'Connor, *Wise Blood*, in *Flannery O'Connor: Collected Works*, ed. Sally Fitzgerald (New York: Library of America, 1988), 84. All citations from *Wise Blood* are from the Library of America edition and cited parenthetically with "*WB*" and the page number.

7. Flannery O'Connor, unpublished manuscripts, Flannery O'Connor Collection, Georgia College Library.

8. Turner, *Bill Bright & Campus Crusade*, 3.

9. Turner, *Bill Bright & Campus Crusade*, 6, 8; Martin E. Marty, "The Revival of Evangelicalism and Southern Religion," 8.

10. R. Laurence Moore, *Selling God: American Religion in the Marketplace of Culture* (New York: Oxford University Press, 1995), 272–76; Turner, *Bill Bright & Campus Crusade*, 7; D. G. Hart, *Deconstructing Evangelicalism: Conservative Protestantism in the Age of Billy Graham* (Grand Rapids, 2004), 185.

11. Robert H. Brinkmeyer, "A Closer Walk with Thee: Flannery O'Connor and Southern Fundamentalists," *Southern Literary Journal* 18.2 (1986): 3–13. Brinkmeyer discusses the early misreadings of *Wise Blood* that frustrated the author: "Interestingly, a number of early reviews asserted that O'Connor's work revealed the evils and the fraudulence of evangelists; they failed to note the great respect and concern that O'Connor felt for her characters. In the introduction to the 1959 French edition of *Wise Blood*, Maurice-Edgar Coindreau devoted a good deal of space to a discussion of some of America's more notorious evangelists; O'Connor's Catholicism, he asserted, gave her the perspective to recognize the terrors of evangelism. Such misreadings in turn intensified both her scorn for modernity and her doubts that as a writer of fiction she could communicate with an overwhelmingly hostile audience" (11).

12. Flannery O'Connor, "The Catholic Novelist in the Protestant South," in *Mystery and Manners: Occasional Prose*, ed. Sally Fitzgerald and Robert Fitzgerald (New York: Farrar, Straus, and Giroux, 1961), 204, 207, 859. I am not arguing that O'Connor herself was an evangelical. Her fiction and nonfiction, however, made it very clear that she was sympathetic to the evangelical imperative to confront secular culture with the Gospel.

Notes to Pages 66–77   *149*

13. Michael Kreyling, Introduction to *New Essays on* Wise Blood, American Novel Series (Cambridge: Cambridge University Press, 1995), 3, 10.

14. Christopher Owen Lynch, *Selling Catholicism: Bishop Sheen and the Power of Television* (Lexington: University Press of Kentucky, 1998), ix, 6–7.

15. Flannery O'Connor, *Flannery O'Connor: Collected Works*, ed. by Sally Fitzgerald (New York: Library of America, 1988), 934.

16. George W. Crane, "The Worry Clinic," *Atlanta Constitution,* Jan. 18, 1954–Jan. 7, 1957; O'Connor, *Collected Works*, 958.

17. O'Connor, *Collected Works*, 935; Loxley Nichols, "Keeping Up with Dr. Crane," *Flannery O'Connor Bulletin* 20 (1991): 23.

18. Flannery O'Connor, *The Violent Bear It Away*, in *Flannery O'Connor: Collected Works*, ed. Sally Fitzgerald (New York: Library of America, 1988), 362; Crane, "The Worry Clinic," April 23, 1954; Nichols, "Keeping Up with Dr. Crane," 23, 29.

19. Dale Carnegie, *How to Win Friends and Influence People* (New York: Simon & Schuster, 1990), 33–34; O'Connor, *Collected Works*, 958.

20. O'Connor, unpublished manuscripts; also see Stephen G. Driggers and Robert J. Dunn, *The Manuscripts of Flannery O'Connor at Georgia College* (Athens: University of Georgia Press, 1989). All early, unpublished versions of *Wise Blood* from the Flannery O'Connor Collection are referenced in this chapter parenthetically according to manuscript entries.

21. Jon Lance Bacon, "A Fondness for Supermarkets: *Wise Blood* and Consumer Culture," in *New Essays on Wise Blood*, ed. Michael Kreyling (New York: Cambridge University Press, 1995), 26–27, 39.

22. Bacon, "A Fondness for Supermarkets," 43.

23. Flannery O'Connor, *The Habit of Being: Letters*, ed. Sally Fitzgerald (New York: Farrar, Straus, and Giroux, 1988), 354.

24. Norman Vincent Peale, *The Power of Positive Thinking* (New York: Simon & Schuster, 2008); William James, *The Varieties of Religious Experience: A Study in Human Nature* (New York: Crowell-Collier, 1902), 105.

25. Brinkmeyer, "A Closer Walk with Thee," 7.

26. Joel Osteen, *Your Best Life Now: 7 Steps to Living at Your Full Potential* (Boston: Faith Words, 2007); O'Connor, *Collected Works*, 958.

27. O'Connor, *The Habit of Being*, 516.

28. O'Connor, "The Fiction Writer and His Country," 806; Lewis Lawson and Victoria A. Kramer, eds., Walker Percy, *More Conversations with Walker Percy* (Jackson: University Press of Mississippi, 1993), 112.

Chapter 4: Diagnostic Satire in Walker Percy's Fiction

1. Several critics do not agree with Percy's self-assessment. See Harold Bloom, ed., *Modern Critical Views: Walker Percy* (New York: Chu Hartley, 1986); Michael Kobre, *Walker Percy's Voices* (Athens: University of Georgia Press, 2000); Keiran Quinlan, *Walker Percy: The Last Catholic Novelist* (Baton Rouge: Louisiana State University Press, 1996). Bloom contends that *The Moviegoer* is Percy's greatest achievement, "a permanent American book" that never yields to the temptation to moralize. Bloom is not so sympathetic to Percy's subsequent novels (sans *The Last Gentleman*), stating that his latter works reveal a "waste of Percy's authentic

talents"; furthermore, Bloom claims that Percy's work can be characterized as a "lamentable instance of art yielding to moralism, of storytelling subverted by religious nostalgias" (3). To illustrate, Bloom examines each novel's concluding lines to reveal a progression (or digression) "from narrative poignance to a theocentric anxiety" (2). Quinlan regards Percy's latter development as a writer to be that of a reactionary religious conservative. Kobre also expresses a sense of disappointment in Percy's third and fourth novels, *Love in the Ruins* and *Lancelot*, which seem to establish a moralist's voice in the narrative structure. Kobre agrees with Quinlan's by assertion that Percy's fiction turns out to have as much of an agenda as his philosophical essays (120).

2. See Jay Tolson, *Pilgrim in the Ruins: A Life of Walker Percy* (Chapel Hill: University of North Carolina Press, 1992); Robert Brinkmeyer, "Percy's Bludgeon: Message and Narrative Strategy," in *Walker Percy: Art and Ethics*, ed. Jac Tharpe (Jackson: University Press of Mississippi, 1980). Writing to Caroline Gordon on 6 April 1962, Percy confided that he was more a moralist than a novelist: "My spiritual father is Pascal (and/or Kierkegaard). And if I also kneel before the altar of Lawrence and Joyce and Flaubert, it is not because I wish to do what they did, even if I could. What I really want to do is tell people what they must do and what they must believe if they want to live." Percy noted the difficulty of using religious terminology in fiction; in particular, he observed how God's "name is used in vain so often that there remains only one way to speak of him: in silence. Perhaps the craft of the religious novelist nowadays consists mainly in learning how to shout in silence." Percy's intentions suggest a desire to preach the Gospel in his fiction, a move inconsistent with many statements he made publicly in interviews to the contrary. Percy echoed Kierkegaard's sentiment that he was not authorized as an apostle to preach Christianity. His private correspondence with Gordon, on the other hand, indicates his private struggles as a writer desirous to advance a Christian message. As Tolson points out, the challenge for Percy was how to be "a moralist without moralizing" (301). Tolson highlights this particular struggle within the writer by framing it as a tension between the artist and philosopher. These two poles have been suggested by other scholars like Robert Brinkmeyer, who divides Percy's narrative strategies into the roles of diagnostician and prophet. Whichever strategy Percy used, the mode of satire abides through all his novels.

3. Peter Prescott, "The Big Breakdown," *Newsweek* 77 (1971), 106; Lawson and Kramer, *More Conversations*, 141, 147; the most common approaches to Percy criticism characterize him as existentialist, physician, autobiographer, and semiotician. William Rodney Allen asserts that the lack of diverse criticism in Percy's fiction is largely due to Martin Luschei's *The Sovereign Wayfarer*, the first published monograph of Percy, which cast the writer as chiefly concerned with the issues of European existentialism rather than Southern (much less American) regional writing. Consequently, Luschei's study dissuaded many future critics from seeing Percy as a Southern writer in the vein of Faulkner, O'Connor, and others, which explains why so much Percy scholarship has been conversant with Sartre, Kierkegaard, Camus, and Dostoevsky. Allen's monograph of Percy, *The Southern Wayfarer*, has resituated the writer among the greats of twentieth-century Southern literature. To this point, most religious criticism of Percy has treated the Catholic and apocalyptic characteristics of his fiction (Robert Brinkmeyer's *Three Catholic Novelists of the Modern South*, Gary Ciuba's *Walker Percy: Books of Revelations*, and Keiran Quinlan's *Walker Percy: The Last Catholic Novelist*).

Notes to Pages 77–86   *151*

John Desmond's study, *Walker Percy's Search for Community* (Athens: University of Georgia, 2004), has provided a nice model for how Percy's fiction can be studied for its commentary on contemporary religious culture and the writer's theological vision of community.

4. Brinkmeyer, "Percy's Bludgeon: Message and Narrative Strategy," 82–83.

5. Walker Percy, "Notes for a Novel About the End of the World," *The Message in the Bottle: How Queer Man Is, How Queer Language Is, and What One Has to Do with the Other* (New York: Farrar, Straus and Giroux, 1975), 101.

6. Brinkmeyer contends that in *The Moviegoer* and *The Last Gentleman*, Percy "has merely suggested, in a quiet voice," that Catholicism provides the way out of the modern malaise by using his first two novels "to diagnose the dilemmas facing those readers conscious of their alienation from their own deeper selves and from the center of life" (145–47). That fates of Binx Bolling and Will Barrett, Brinkmeyer asserts, represent the fate of the modern Southerner: "Both groups are cut off from the tradition by which they had been raised, since both traditions (Stoicism for the southerner, scientific humanism for the modern man) fail to account for what is happening in the modern world" (146).

7. Lawson and Kramer, *More Conversations*, 112; Linda Whitney Hobson, *Understanding Walker Percy* (Columbia: University of South Carolina Press, 1988), 139, 134; Doreen A Fowler, "Answers and Ambiguity in Percy's *The Second Coming*," *Modern Critical Views: Walker Percy*, ed. Harold Blood (New York: Chelsea House, 1986), 119. Dating back to ancient Greek and Roman traditions, satire has often been classified into three categories: Horatian satire, a more gentle and humorous mode that uses comedy to reveal folly; Juvenalian satire, a biting attack that exposes evil and corruption in society; and Menippean satire, a ridicule of particular cultural beliefs or attitudes rather than individuals or institutions. Percy employs the latter two categories in his fictional prose.

8. Walker Percy, "A 'Cranky Novelist' Reflects on the Church," in *Signposts in a Strange Land*, ed. Patrick Samway (New York: Farrar, Straus and Giroux, 1991), 322–23.

9. Percy uses "fundamentalist" and "evangelical" interchangeably. I realize some evangelicals take exception to the equivalence, yet the criticisms offered here by Percy, as well as in this essay, are relevant to both groups.

10. Percy, "A 'Cranky Novelist' Reflects on the Church," 323–24.

11. Hart, *Deconstructing Evangelicalism*, 196; Percy, "A 'Cranky Novelist' Reflects on the Church," 324; Lawson and Kramer, *More Conversations*, 120; Christopher Ellison and Eric McDaniel, "God's Party? Race, Religion, and Partisanship over Time," *Political Research Quarterly* 61.2 (2008): 182; Percy, "A 'Cranky Novelist' Reflects on the Church," 325.

12. Tolson, *Pilgrim in the Ruins*, 38-39; Patrick Samway, *Walker Percy: A Life* (New York: Farrar, Straus and Giroux, 1997), 20.

13. Samway, *Walker Percy*, 49.

14. Samway, *Walker Percy*, 83; Tolson, *Pilgrim in the Ruins*, 96.

15. Samway, *Walker Percy*, 68, 81–82; Tolson, *Pilgrim in the Ruins*, 121.

16. Tolson, *Pilgrim in the Ruins*, 156, 168.

17. Samway, *Walker Percy*, 127.

18. Tolson, *Pilgrim in the Ruins*, 177.

19. Ibid., 193–93.

20. Ibid., 200.

152 Notes to Pages 87–95

21. Samway, *Walker Percy*, 150.

22. Ann Waldron, *Close Connections: Caroline Gordon and the Southern Renaissance* (New York: G. P. Putnam's Sons, 1987), 257–58.

23. Tolson, *Pilgrim in the Ruins*, 198; Robert Brinkmeyer, *Three Catholic Writers of the Modern South* (Jackson: University Press of Mississippi, 1985), xvi.

24. Walker Percy, *The Moviegoer* (New York: Vintage Books, 1960). All citations from *The Moviegoer* are cited parenthetically with "*MG*" and the page number.

25. Samway, *Walker Percy*, 220–21; Judith Serebnick, "First Novelists—Spring 1961," *Library Journal* 86 (February 1, 1961): 597.

26. Soren Kierkegaard, *The Point of View*, eds. and trans. Howard V. Hong and Edna H. Hong (Princeton, NJ: Princeton University Press, 1998).

27. Kierkegaard, *The Point of View*, 41, 42–43, 53, 54–55, 56.

28. Vernon J. Bourke, Introduction to *City of God* by St. Augustine (New York: Image Books, 1958), 9–10.

29. Walker Percy, *The Last Gentleman* (New York: Picador, 1966). All citations from *The Last Gentleman* are cited parenthetically with "*LG*" and the page number.

30. Martin Luschei, *Sovereign Wayfarer: Walker Percy's Diagnosis of the Malaise* (Baton Rouge: Louisiana State University Press, 1972), 144–45; Desmond, *Walker Percy's Search*, 117; Lawson and Kramer, *More Conversations*, 14; Walker Percy, "Stoicism in the South" *Commonweal* 64 (1956): 343; Walker Percy, "The Failure and the Hope," *Katallagete*, Journal of the Committee of Southern Churchmen Winter 1967–68): 16–21.

31. Desmond, *Walker Percy's Search*, 94; Daniel Schenker, "Walker Percy and the Problem of Cultural Criticism," *South Atlantic Review* 53.1 (1988): 89; Fred Hobson, *The Southern Writer in the Post-Modern World* (Athens: University of Georgia Press, 1991), 8. Schenker problematizes the task of reading Percy as a cultural critic, contending that while most great works of Southern fiction have engaged in criticism of Southern culture, "it is more difficult for Percy than it was for his predecessors in the [Southern] region to find the Archimedean point upon which to lever his critique" (88). Schenker's crucial point lies in his argument that culture is a human enterprise, which makes Percy skeptical of engaging in culture as another abstraction that scientific humanism would employ. Scheker argues that cultural criticism, for Percy, strikes of "a kind of vampirism that ultimately throws us back upon ourselves and into despair; only religion can bring us into revivying contact with the mysterious reality around us" (91). Schenker's argument seems far too simplistic, for Percy clearly engages in cultural criticism by satirizing different social and politically partisan groups responsible for dehumanization in his novels. Desmond, on the other hand, situates Percy as a cultural critic who unites the diagnostic and satiric qualities: "As befitting one deeply interested in diagnosing the immediate state of things, Percy focused his search on America and its various forms of social community. In his novels he explored and satirized what he saw as the debilitated state of modern American culture, trapped in its self-absorbed individualism, consumerism, violence, racism, and general spiritual anomie" (6).

32. James C Cobb, *Away Down South: A History of Southern Identity* (Oxford: Oxford University Press, 2005), 248, 250; Lawson and Kramer, *More Conversations*, 111; Malcolm Jones, "A Moralist of the South," *More Conversations with Walker Percy*, eds. Lewis A. Lawson and Victoria A. Kramer (Jackson: University Press of Mississippi, MS, 1993), 170.

Notes to Pages 95–110   *153*

33. Cobb, *Away Down South*, 76.

34. Desmond, *Walker Percy's Search*, 112–13.

Chapter 5: Descent and Vision in Dennis Covington's *Salvation on Sand Mountain*

1. Stephen Greenblatt, *Shakespearean Negotiations: The Circulation of Social Energy in Renaissance England* (Oxford: Clarendon Press, 1988), 7; Thomas West and Gary A. Olson, "Rethinking Negotiation in Composition Studies," *JAC* 19.2 (1999): 244; Gary A. Olson and Lynn Worsham, "Staging the Politics of Difference: Homi Bhabha's Critical Literacy." *Race, Rhetoric, and the Postcolonial*, eds. Gary A. Olson and Lynn Worsham (Albany: State University of New York Press, 1999), 28. Henry Giroux, *Border Crossings: Cultural Workers and the Politics of Education* (New York: Routledge, 1992), 28.

2. For example, corporations rhetorically appropriate the virtue phrase, "Go Green," an ethical imperative for environmental conservation in the service of cutting costs and services, thus increasing profits.

3. Olson and Worsham, "Homi Bhabha's Critical Literacy," 31; West and Olson, "Rethinking Negotiation," 243–44.

4. West and Olson, "Rethinking Negotiation," 247.

5. Dennis Covington, *Salvation on Sand Mountain: Snake Handling and Redemption in Southern Appalachia* (Philadelphia: Da Capo, 1995), 67. All references to this primary text under discussion are referred to as "SSM" with the page number in parenthetical citations for the remainder of this chapter.

6. Smith, *Killers of the Dream*, 25–26.

7. Jacquelyn Dowd Hall, "Open Secrets: Memory, Imagination, and the Refashioning of Southern Identity," *American Quarterly* 50.1 (1998): 110; Romine, "Framing Southern Rhetoric," 96–97.

8. Other Southern identity memoirs that follow the conventional pattern include Richard Wright's *Black Boy* and Zora Neale Hurston's *Dust Tracks on a Road*. I would also classify W. J. Cash's *The Mind of the South* as following this same pattern of the Southern memoir, even though it does not technically qualify as such; for example, Cash establishes his Southern credentials as a North Carolinian early on and continues to style himself as one having risen above the conditions that narrow the Southern mind.

9. John P. Hussey, "Agee's Famous Men and American Non-Fiction," *College English* 40.6 (1979): 680–81.

10. James Agee and Walker Evans, *Let Us Now Praise Famous Men*, (Boston: Houghton Mifflin Harcourt, 2001), 365.

11. Flannery O'Connor, "Some Aspects of the Grotesque in Southern Fiction," in *Mystery and Manners: Occasional Prose*, eds. Sally Fitzgerald and Robert Fitzgerald (New York: Farrar, Straus and Giroux, 1969), 38–39, 46, 50. *Mystery and Manners* is a collection of O'Connor's essays and lectures, mostly about fiction writing as a Catholic and a Southerner. Both essays referenced in this section can be found there.

12. O'Connor, "The Catholic Novelist in the Protestant South," 207.

13. The Scottsboro Boys were granted posthumous pardons by Alabama's parole board on 21 November 2013.

14. Covington uses the titles of each chapter to convey a double meaning. One sense refers

to the subject matter of his memoir found in the snake-handling culture, while another sense refers to himself as the narrator-subject enduring his own struggle for identity.

15. Cecil M. Robeck Jr., "Pentecostalism," *The Oxford Companion to Christian Thought*, eds. Adrian Hastings, Alistair Mason, and Hugh Pyper (Oxford: Oxford University Press, 2000), 530–32.

16. Here I would like to add another connection to Flannery O'Connor, as her sympathetic vision of evangelical characters seemed to cloud her judgment toward nonbelievers. In O'Connor's fiction, the most common antagonists are secular intellectuals.

Chapter 6: Evangelical Whispers in Doris Betts's *The Sharp Teeth of Love*

1. C. Vann Woodward, "The Search for Southern Identity," in *The Burden of Southern History* (Baton Rouge: Louisiana State University Press, 1960), 130–31. See Robert H. Brinkmeyer, *Remapping Southern Literature: Contemporary Southern Writers and the West* (Athens: University of Georgia Press, 2000). Brinkmeyer notes how Southern writers explore these concerns by setting their fiction in the West as a site beyond confining culture to interrogate the tension between individuality and community.

2. This approach can be traced back to ancient Greek philosophers like Plato, who viewed the body as a cage of the spirit. This privileging of the mind (or spirit) over the body was taken to its clearest differentiation by Rene Descartes who posited mental processes as magisterial in grounding human existence as well as proceeding with any form of knowledge. The implications of such an epistemology entail an ordering of mental processes as being in a superior and uncorrupted realm, whereas matter and bodily concerns become associated with worldliness, imperfection, and corruption. While the abstract approach can be traced through the history of Western thought, its crystallization occurred most profoundly in Christian theology.

3. George Hovis, "Doris Betts: Plain Folk in Mill Town," *Vale of Humility: Plain Folk in Contemporary North Carolina Fiction* (Columbia: University of South Carolina Press, 2007), 54.

4. Elizabeth Evans, *Doris Betts, Twayne's United States Authors Series No. 689*, ed. Frank Day (New York: Twayne, 1997), 3–5.

5. Doris Betts, "The Fingerprint of Style," *Voicelust*, eds. Allen Wier and Don Hendrie Jr. (Lincoln: University of Nebraska Press, 1985), 9.

6. Marti Greene, "A Conversation with Doris Betts," *Carolina Quarterly* 52.2 (Spring 2000): 65.

7. O'Connor, "The Fiction Writer and His Country," 805–6.

8. Doris Betts, "Everything I Know about Writing I Learned in Sunday School," *Christian Century* 115.28 (October 1998): 966–67.

9. Dale Brown, "Interview with Doris Betts," *Southern Quarterly* 34.2 (Winter 1996): 101.

10. Susan Ketchin, "Doris Betts: Resting on the Bedrock of Original Sin," in *The Christ-Haunted Landscape: Faith and Doubt in Southern Fiction* (Jackson: University Press of Mississippi, 1994), 248; Evans, *Doris Betts*, 28; Mary Anne Heyward Ferguson, "Doris Betts," *The History of Southern Women's Literature*, eds. Carolyn Perry and Mary Louise Weaks (Baton Rouge: Louisiana State University Press, 2002), 532.

11. Hovis, "Doris Betts," 33. Hovis concurs with Betts's distinction from O'Connor, noting

how "Betts tends to see evidence of God more in the lives of people, and, although she believes in the presence of evil—demonstrated by the abundance of villains in her fiction—she defines 'original sin' as a biographically programmed selfishness that humans can at least provisionally overcome by teaching one another to recognize this 'centering on self'" (33).

12. Ashley Robinson, "Go West, Young Woman: Transforming Southern Womanhood through the Myth of the American West in Doris Betts's *Heading West* and *The Sharp Teeth of Love*," *CEA Critic* 75.2 (July 2013): 109.

13. Doris Betts, *The Sharp Teeth of Love* (New York: Knopf, 1997), 11. All parenthetical citations henceforth in the discussion of this primary text are labeled as "*STL*" followed by the page number.

14. Walker Percy, "The Loss of the Creature," in *The Message in the Bottle* (New York: Farrar, Straus and Giroux, 1975), 47, 58, 63.

15. Hovis, "Doris Betts," 54.

16. See Martha Greene Eads, "Sex, Money, and Food as Spiritual Signposts in Doris Betts's 'Sharp Teeth of Love,'" *Christianity & Literature* 54.1 (September 2004). Eads notes that Bynum posits three food practices that were central components: "fasting, feeding others, and feeding on God in the Eucharist." Luna's relationship to food in *The Sharp Teeth of Love*, according to Eads, echoes this triad to reveal "a deeply religious sensibility" (40).

17. Eads, "Sex, Money, and Food as Spiritual Signposts," 32, 47, 33, 41. The recent Catholic priest sex scandals aside, Catholicism has not exactly possessed the most affirming history of situating its followers to a healthy sense of sexuality and the human body. Eads couches her language in a dualistic stratification even when she discusses the importance of materiality by merely assigning it "theological significance," which suggests materiality can be affirmed only to the extent that it signifies something spiritual (32).

18. At one point in the essay, Eads refers to Paul as the "via media" between the sterile abstracted Steven Grier (Calvinist) and the spiritually hungry Luna (Catholic) but then fails to flesh out the significance of Paul's Lutheran theology as a middle way between the sacramental and the abstracted orientations that Christians have argued over for centuries.

19. Dale Brown, "Interview with Doris Betts," 102.

20. Hovis, "Doris Betts," 35. In a 1993 talk delivered at the Institute for the Arts and Humanities at the University of North Carolina at Chapel Hill, Betts bemoans American culture for having a "support group for every ailment, a political committee for every cause, a childish public life demanding all rights, no obligations; in a culture which has selected for aristocracy its athletes and entertainers. Sometimes our American individualism has moved so far from our American sense of community that the secret national ethic seems to be 'Every man for himself.' Or every woman for hers" (quoted in Hovis 35).

21. Erik H. Erikson, *Young Man Luther: A Study in Psychoanalysis and History* (New York: W. W. Norton, 1958), 204–5.

22. Mikhail Bakhtin, *Rabelais and His World*, trans. Helene Iswolsky (Bloomington, IN: Indiana University Press, 1984), 192.

23. Paul Althaus, *The Theology of Martin Luther*, trans. Robert C. Schultz (Philadelphia: Fortress, 1966), 398; Gerhard Forde, *Where God Meets Man: Luther's Down-To-Earth Approach to the Gospel* (Minneapolis: Augsburg, 1972), 8.

24. Forde, *Where God Meets Man*, 68; Eads, "Sex, Money, and Food as Spiritual Signposts,"

33; see Flannery O'Connor, "Novelist and Believer," in *Mystery and Manners: Occasional Prose*, ed. Sally Fitzgerald and Robert Fitzgerald (New York: Farrar, Straus and Giroux, 1961), for her discussion on her own Catholic view of sacramental writing. O'Connor perceived the role of the Catholic novelist as rendering the presence of grace in nature: "As a novelist, the major part of my task is to make everything, even an ultimate concern, as solid, as concrete, as specific as possible. The novelist begins his work where human knowledge begins—with the senses; he works through the limitations of matter, and unless he is writing fantasy, he has to stay within the concrete possibilities of his culture" (155). Here and in "Catholic Novelists and Their Readers," O'Connor notes how her sacramental fiction follows the Catholic tradition of Aquinas, Maritain, and Teilhard, who all held an obligation to penetrate concrete reality. It is important to note that Catholic theology does not neglect the empirical, but rather stratifies its importance in relation to the infinite or spiritual. This can provide another explanation (other than the reason too often given that she wrote to unbelieving readers) as to why physical acts or rites in O'Connor's fiction, such as a baptism, are rendered through distortions and exaggerations; O'Connor's distortions, in her own words, "reveal," which in my view betrays a belief that not only are her reader's inadequate but so are the physical elements that serve as a means to illuminate spiritual realities (162).

25. Forde, *Where God Meets Man*, 81, 83, 86.

26. Althaus, *The Theology of Martin Luther*, 395. Lutheran theology of sacraments and liturgy can be found in *The Book of Concord: The Confessions of the Evangelical Lutheran Church* (1580), a collection of the most significant writings by Martin Luther and Phillip Melanchthon that outline orthodox Lutheran teaching to illustrate that their theology is a continuation from the earliest creeds of the fourth century that continued through to the sixteenth century. The *Apology of the Augsburg Confession*, Article XXIV.1, states, "We do not abolish the Mass but religiously keep and defend it. Among us the Mass is celebrated every Lord's Day and on other festivals, when the Sacrament is made available to those who wish to partake of it, after they have been examined and absolved. We also keep traditional liturgical forms, such as the order of readings, prayers, vestments, and other similar things" (258).

27. Greene, "A Conversation with Doris Betts," 65.

Coda: Narrative Reckoning

1. Sarah Posner, *Unholy: How White Christian Nationalists Powered the Trump Presidency, and the Devastating Legacy They Left Behind* (New York: Random House, 2021), xvii–iii, 100.

2. Randall Balmer, *Bad Faith: Race and the Rise of the Religious Right* (Grand Rapids, MI: William B. Eerdmans, 2021), 33–34, 37.

3. Posner, *Unholy*, 100.

4. Ibid., 109.

5. Balmer, *Bad Faith*, 44.

6. Ibid., 109.

7. Robert P. Jones, *The End of White Christian America* (New York: Simon & Schuster, 2017), 144–45.

8. John Fea, *Believe Me: The Evangelical Road to Donald Trump* (Grand Rapids, MI: William B. Eerdmans, 2018), 61.

9. Ibid., 8.

10. Ibid., 60.

11. Kristin Kobes Du Mez, *Jesus and John Wayne*, 107.

12. James Davison Hunter, *To Change the World: The Irony, Tragedy, and Possibility of Christianity in the Late Modern World* (New York: Oxford University Press, 2010), 12.

13. Fea, *Believe Me*, 9.

14. Du Mez, *Jesus and John Wayne*, 3.

15. Anthea Butler, *White Evangelical Racism: The Politics of Morality in America* (Chapel Hill: University of North Carolina Press, 2021), 4, 6.

16. Robert P. Jones, *White Too Long: The Legacy of White Supremacy in American Christianity* (New York: Simon & Schuster, 2020), 6.

17. Ibid., 23–24.

BIBLIOGRAPHY

Abbott, H. Porter. *The Cambridge Introduction to Narrative Theory.* Cambridge: Cambridge University Press, 2020.

Agee, James, and Walker Evans. *Let Us Now Praise Famous Men.* Boston: Houghton Mifflin Harcourt, 2001.

Allen, William Rodney. *Walker Percy, A Southern Wayfarer.* Jackson: University Press of Mississippi, 1986.

Althaus, Paul. *The Theology of Martin Luther.* Translated by Robert C. Schultz. Philadelphia: Fortress Press, 1966.

Applebome, Peter. *Dixie Rising.* New York: Random House, 1996.

Arendt, Hannah. *The Origins of Totalitarianism.* New York: Harcourt, 1951.

Asals, Frederick. *Flannery O'Connor: The Imagination of Extremity.* Athens: University of Georgia Press, 1982.

Bachman, Erik M. "Sin, Sex, and Segregation in Lillian Smith's Silent South." In *Literary Obscenities: U.S. Case Law and Naturalism after Modernism,* 137–64. University Park: Penn State University Press, 2018.

Bacon, Jon Lance. "A Fondness for Supermarkets: *Wise Blood* and Consumer Culture." In *New Essays on Wise Blood,* edited by Michael Kreyling, 25–49. New York: Cambridge University Press, 1995.

Bakhtin, Mikhail. "Discourse in the Novel." In *The Dialogic Imagination: Four Essays,* edited by Michael Holquist, translated by Caryl Emerson and Michael Holquist. Austin: University of Texas Press, 1984.

———. *Rabelais and His World.* Translated by Helene Iswolsky. Bloomington: Indiana University Press, 1984.

Balmer, Randall. *Bad Faith: Race and the Rise of the Religious Right.* Grand Rapids, MI: William B. Eerdmans, 2021.

Barbour, John D. *The Conscience of the Autobiographer: Ethical and Religious Dimensions of Autobiography.* London: Macmillan; New York: St. Martin's, 1992.

———. *Versions of Deconversion: Autobiography and the Loss of Faith.* Charlottesville and London: University Press of Virginia, 1994.

Beard, Laura. *Acts of Narrative Resistance: Women's Autobiographical Writings in the Americas.* Charlottesville: University of Virginia Press, 2009.

Berger, Peter. *The Sacred Canopy: Elements of a Sociological Theory of Religion.* New York: Doubleday, 1967.

Betts, Doris. "Everything I Know about Writing I Learned in Sunday School." *Christian Century,* October 21, 1998, 966–67.

———. "The Fingerprint of Style." In *Voicelust,* edited by Allen Wier and Don Hendrie Jr., 7–22. Lincoln: University of Nebraska Press, 1985.

———. "Opening Statement: The Arts, the Humanities, the University and Public Culture." Autumn Sunday Symposium, Institute for the Arts and Humanities, University of North Carolina at Chapel Hill, October 10, 1993.

———. *The Sharp Teeth of Love*. New York: Simon & Schuster, 1997.

Bloom, Harold. *The American Religion*. New York: Chu Hartley, 2006.

———, ed. *Modern Critical Views: Walker Percy*. New York: Chelsea House, 1986.

Bourke, Vernon J., ed. Introduction in *City of God* by St. Augustine. New York: Image Books, 1958.

Brinkmeyer, Robert H., Jr. *The Art and Vision of Flannery O'Connor*. Baton Rouge: Louisiana State University Press, 1993.

———. "A Closer Walk with Thee: Flannery O'Connor and Southern Fundamentalists." *Southern Literary Journal* 18.2 (1986): 3–13.

———. *The Fourth Ghost: White Southern Writers and European Fascism, 1930–1950*. Southern Literary Studies Series. Baton Rouge: Louisiana State University Press, 2009.

———. "Percy's Bludgeon: Message and Narrative Strategy." In *Walker Percy: Art and Ethics*, edited by Jac Tharpe, 80–90. Jackson: University Press of Mississippi, 1980.

———. *Remapping Southern Literature: Contemporary Southern Writers and the West*. Athens: University of Georgia Press, 2000.

———. *Three Catholic Writers of the Modern South*. Jackson: University Press of Mississippi, 1985.

Brown, Dale. "The Big Questions: An Interview with Doris Betts." *Christian Century* 114.27 (October 1997): 870–75.

———. "Interview with Doris Betts." *Southern Quarterly* 34.2 (Winter 1996): 91–104.

Butler, Anthea. *White Evangelical Racism: The Politics of Morality in America*. Chapel Hill: University of North Carolina Press, 2021.

Caldwell, Patricia. *The Puritan Conversion Narrative: The Beginnings of American Expression*. New York: Cambridge University Press, 1985.

Carnegie, Dale. *How to Win Friends and Influence People*. New York: Simon & Schuster, 1990.

Caron, Timothy P. *Struggles Over the Word: Race and Religion in O'Connor, Faulkner, Hurston, and Wright*. Macon, GA: Mercer University Press, 2000.

Cash, W. J. "Close View of a Calvinist Lhasa." *American Mercury* 28 (April 1933): 443–51.

———. "The Mind of the South." *American Mercury* 18 (October 1929): 185–92.

———. *The Mind of the South*. New York: Vintage Books, 1941.

———. "What Constitutes Decency?" *Charlotte News*, March 25, 1928.

Cason, Clarence. *Ninety Degrees in the Shade*. Chapel Hill: University of North Carolina Press, 1935.

Clayton, Bruce. "W. J. Cash: A Mind of the South" In *W. J. Cash and the Minds of the South*, edited by Paul D. Escott, 9–36. Baton Rouge: Louisiana State University Press, 1992.

———. *W. J. Cash: A Life*. Baton Rouge: Louisiana State University Press, 1991.

Clelland, Donald A., Thomas C. Hood, C. M. Lipsey, and Ronald Wimberley. "In the Company of the Converted: Characteristics of a Billy Graham Crusade Audience." *Sociological Analysis* 35.1 (1974): 45–56.

Cobb, James C. *Away Down South: A History of Southern Identity*. Oxford: Oxford University Press, 2005.

Cohen, Charles Lloyd. *God's Caress: The Psychology of Puritan Religious Experience.* New York: Oxford University Press, 1986.

Covington, Dennis. *Salvation on Sand Mountain: Snake Handling and Redemption in Southern Appalachia.* Philadelphia: Da Capo, 1995.

Cox, James. "Between Defiance and Defense: Owning Up to the South." In *Located Lives: Place and Idea in Southern Autobiography,* edited by J. Bill Berry. Athens: University of Georgia Press, 1990.

Crane, George W. "The Worry Clinic." *Atlanta Constitution,* January 18, 1954–January 7, 1957.

Desmond, John. *Walker Percy's Search for Community.* Athens: University of Georgia Press, 2004.

Dorsey, Peter A. *Sacred Estrangement: The Rhetoric of Conversion in Modern American Autobiography.* University Park: Penn State University Press, 1993.

Driggers, Stephen G., and Robert J. Dunn. *The Manuscripts of Flannery O'Connor at Georgia College.* Athens: University of Georgia Press, 1989.

Du Mez, Kristin Kobes. *Jesus and John Wayne: How White Evangelicals Corrupted a Faith and Fractured a Nation.* New York: W. W. Norton, 2020.

Eads, Martha Greene. "Sex, Money, and Food as Spiritual Signposts in Doris Betts's 'Sharp Teeth of Love.'" *Christianity & Literature* 54.1 (September 2004): 31–49.

Egerton, John. *The Americanization of Dixie: The Southernization of America.* New York: Harper's Magazine Press, 1974.

Ellison, Christopher, and Eric McDaniel. "God's Party? Race, Religion, and Partisanship over Time." *Political Research Quarterly* 61.2 (2008): 180–91.

Elwell, Walter A., ed. *Evangelical Dictionary of Theology.* Grand Rapids, MI: Baker, 2001. 405–9.

Erikson, Erik H. *Young Man Luther: A Study in Psychoanalysis and History.* New York: W. W. Norton, 1958.

Eskridge, Larry. "One Way: Billy Graham, the Jesus Generation, and the Idea of an Evangelical Youth Culture." *Church History* 67.1 (1998): 83–106.

Evans, Elizabeth. *Doris Betts. Twayne's United States Authors Series No. 689.* Edited by Frank Day. New York: Twayne, 1997.

Faust, Drew Gilpin. *The Sacred Circle: The Dilemma of the Intellectual in the Old South.* Philadelphia: University of Pennsylvania Press, 1977.

Fea, John. *Believe Me: The Evangelical Road to Donald Trump.* Grand Rapids, MI: William B. Eerdmans, 2018.

Ferguson, Mary Anne Heyward. "Doris Betts." In *The History of Southern Women's Literature,* edited by Carolyn Perry and Mary Louise Weaks, 530–40. Baton Rouge: Louisiana State University Press, 2002.

Fitzgerald, Frances. *The Evangelicals: The Struggle to Shape America.* New York: Simon & Schuster, 2017.

Flynt, Wayne. "One in the Spirit, Many in the Flesh: Southern Evangelicals." In *Varieties of Southern Evangelicalism,* edited by David Edwin Harrell, 23–44. Macon, GA: Mercer University Press, 1981.

Forde, Gerhard. *Where God Meets Man: Luther's Down-To-Earth Approach to the Gospel.* Minneapolis, MN: Augsburg, 1972.

162 Bibliography

Fowler, Doreen A. "Answers and Ambiguity in Percy's *The Second Coming*." In *Modern Critical Views: Walker Percy*, edited by Harold Blood. New York: Chelsea House, 1986.

Gibson, Mel, dir. *The Passion of the Christ*. Newmarket Films, 2004. Film.

Giroux, Henry A. *Border Crossings: Cultural Workers and the Politics of Education*. New York: Routledge, 1992.

Gladney, Margaret Rose. Preface to *How Am I To Be Heard?: Letters of Lillian Smith*. Chapel Hill: University of North Carolina Press, 1993.

Goen, C. C., ed. Introduction to *The Great Awakening* by Jonathan Edwards. The Works of Jonathan Edwards Series, vol. 4. New Haven, CT: Yale University Press, 1972.

Goldberg, Michelle. *Kingdom Coming: The Rise of Christian Nationalism*. New York: W. W. Norton, 2006.

Greenblatt, Stephen. *Shakespearean Negotiations: The Circulation of Social Energy in Renaissance England*. Oxford: Clarendon, 1988.

Greene, Marti. "A Conversation with Doris Betts." *Carolina Quarterly* 52.2 (Spring 2000): 59–73.

Gura, Philip F. *A Glimpse of Sion's Glory: Puritan Radicalism in New England, 1620–1660*. Middletown, CT: Wesleyan University Press, 1984.

Hall, Jacquelyn Dowd. "Open Secrets: Memory, Imagination, and the Refashioning of Southern Identity." *American Quarterly* 50.1 (1998): 109–24.

Hardy, John Edward. *The Fiction of Walker Percy*. Urbana: University of Illinois Press, 1987.

Harrell, David Edwin, ed. *Varieties of Southern Evangelicalism*. Macon, GA: Mercer University Press, 1981.

Hart, D. G. *Deconstructing Evangelicalism: Conservative Protestantism in the Age of Billy Graham*. Ada, MI: Baker Academic, 2005.

Hill, Samuel S. Introduction to *Religion and Politics in the South: Mass and Elite Perspectives*, edited by Tod A. Baker, Robert P. Steed, and Laurence W. Moreland, ix–xiv. New York: Praeger, 1983.

———. *Southern Churches in Crisis*. New York: Holt, Rinehart and Wilson, 1966.

———. *Southern Churches in Crisis Revisited*. Tuscaloosa: University of Alabama Press, 1999.

Hill, Samuel S., and Dennis E. Owen. *The New Religious Political Right in America*. Nashville, TN: Abingdon, 1982.

Hobson, Fred. *But Now I See: The White Southern Racial Conversion Narrative*. Baton Rouge: Louisiana State University Press, 1999.

———. *Serpent in Eden: H. L. Mencken and the South*. Chapel Hill: University of North Carolina Press, 1974.

———. *The Southern Writer in the Post-Modern World*. Athens: University of Georgia Press, 1991.

———. *Tell About the South: The Southern Rage to Explain*. Baton Rouge: Louisiana State University Press, 1983.

Hobson, Linda Whitney. *Understanding Walker Percy*. Columbia: University of South Carolina Press, 1988.

Hofstadter, Richard. *Anti-intellectualism in American Life*. New York: Alfred A. Knopf, 1963.

Hovis, George. "Doris Betts: Plain Folk in Mill Town." In *Vale of Humility: Plain Folk in Contemporary North Carolina Fiction*, 22–57. Columbia: University of South Carolina Press, 2007.

Bibliography   163

Hunter, James Davison. *To Change the World: The Irony, Tragedy, and Possibility of Christianity in the Late Modern World*. New York: Oxford University Press, 2010.

Hussey, John P. "Agee's Famous Men and American Non-Fiction." *College English* 40.6 (1979): 677–82.

James, William. *The Varieties of Religious Experience: A Study in Human Nature*. New York: Crowell-Collier, 1961.

Jones, Anne Goodwyn. "The Cash Nexus." In *The Mind of the South: Fifty Years Later*, edited by Charles W. Eagles, 23–51. Jackson and London: University Press of Mississippi, 1992.

Jones, Malcolm. "A Moralist of the South." In *More Conversations with Walker Percy*. Edited by Lewis A. Lawson and Victoria A. Kramer. Jackson: University Press of Mississippi, 1993.

Jones, Robert P. *The End of White Christian America*. New York: Simon & Schuster, 2017.

———. *White Too Long: The Legacy of White Supremacy in American Christianity*. New York: Simon & Schuster, 2020.

Ketchin, Susan. *The Christ-Haunted Landscape: Faith and Doubt in Southern Fiction*. Jackson: University Press of Mississippi, 1994.

Key, V. O., Jr. *Southern Politics in State and Nation*. New York: Vintage Books, 1947.

Kierkegaard, Soren. *The Point of View*. Edited and translated by Howard V. Hong and Edna H. Hong. Princeton, NJ: Princeton University Press, 1998.

King, Richard. *A Southern Renaissance: The Cultural Awakening of the American South, 1930–1955*. New York: Oxford University Press, 1980.

Kobre, Michael. *Walker Percy's Voices*. Athens: University of Georgia Press, 2000.

Kolb, Robert, and Timothy J. Wengert, eds. *The Book of Concord: The Confessions of the Evangelical Lutheran Church*. Translated by Charles Arand, Eric Gritsch, Robert Kolb, William Russell, James Schaaf, Jane Strohl, and Timoth Wengert. Minneapolis, MN: Fortress, 2000.

Kreyling, Michael. Introduction to *New Essays on* Wise Blood. American Novel Series, 1–24. Cambridge: Cambridge University Press, 1995.

LaHaye, Tim F. *Left Behind: A Novel of the Earth's Last Days*. Carol Stream, IL: Tyndale House, 1995.

Lawson, Lewis, and Victoria A. Kramer, eds. *More Conversations with Walker Percy*. Jackson: University Press of Mississippi, 1993.

Loveland, Anne. C. *Lillian Smith, A Southerner Confronting the South: A Biography*. Baton Rouge: Louisiana State University Press, 1986.

Lumpkin, Katherine Du Pre. *The Making of a Southerner*. Athens: University of Georgia Press, 1991.

Luschei, Martin. "The Ruins of Consensus: Love in the Ruins." In *Modern Critical Views: Walker Percy*, edited by Harold Blood, 25–51. New York: Chelsea House, 1986.

———. *The Sovereign Wayfarer: Walker Percy's Diagnosis of the Malaise*. Baton Rouge: Louisiana State University Press, 1972.

Lynch, Christopher Owen. *Selling Catholicism: Bishop Sheen and the Power of Television*. Lexington: University Press of Kentucky, 1998.

Marius, Richard. *Martin Luther: The Christian Between God and Death*. Cambridge: Belknap Press of Harvard University Press, 1999.

Marsden, George M. *Fundamentalism and American Culture.* New York: Oxford University Press, 2006.

Marty, Martin E. "The Revival of Evangelicalism and Southern Religion." In *Varieties of Southern Evangelicalism,* edited by David Edwin Harrell, 7–21. Macon, GA: Mercer University Press, 1981.

McLoughlin, William G. *Billy Graham: Revivalist in a Secular Age.* New York: Ronald Press, 1960.

Miller, Kathleen Atkinson. "Out of the Chrysalis: Lillian Smith and the Transformation of the South." PhD diss., Emory University, 1984.

Moore, David L. "Decolonializing Criticism: Reading Dialectics and Dialogics in Native American Literatures." *Studies in American Indian Literatures* 6.4 (Winter 1994).

Moore, R. Laurence. *Selling God: American Religion in the Marketplace of Culture.* New York: Oxford University Press, 1995.

Morrison, Joseph L. *W. J. Cash: Southern Prophet; A Biography and Reader.* New York: Alfred A. Knopf, 1967.

Myrsiades, Linda. "Constituting Resistance: Narrative Construction and the Social Theory of Resistance." *symploke* 1.2 (Summer 1993): 101–20.

Nichols, Loxley. "Keeping Up with Dr. Crane." *Flannery O'Connor Bulletin* 20 (1991): 22–32.

Noll, Mark A. *American Evangelical Christianity: An Introduction.* Oxford: Blackwell, 2001.

———. *The Scandal of the Evangelical Mind.* Grand Rapids, MI: William B. Eerdmans, 1994.

O'Connor, Flannery. "The Catholic Novelist in the Protestant South." In *Collected Works,* edited by Sally Fitzgerald. New York: Library of America, 1988. 853–64.

———. "The Catholic Novelist in the Protestant South." In *Mystery and Manners: Occasional Prose,* edited by Sally Fitzgerald and Robert Fitzgerald, 191–209. New York: Farrar, Straus, and Giroux, 1961.

———. "The Fiction Writer and His Country." In *Flannery O'Connor: Collected Works,* edited by Sally Fitzgerald. New York: Library of America, 1988. 801–6.

———. *Flannery O'Connor: Collected Works.* Edited by Sally Fitzgerald. New York: Library of America, 1988.

———. *The Habit of Being: Letters.* Edited by Sally Fitzgerald. New York: Farrar, Straus, and Giroux, 1988.

———. *Mystery and Manners: Occasional Prose.* Edited by Sally Fitzgerald and Robert Fitzgerald. New York: Farrar, Straus, and Giroux 1961.

———. Unpublished manuscripts. Flannery O'Connor Collection. Georgia College Library.

———. *The Violent Bear It Away.* In *Flannery O'Connor: Collected Works,* edited by Sally Fitzgerald. New York: Library of America, 1988. 329–479.

———. *Wise Blood.* In *Flannery O'Connor: Collected Works,* edited by Sally Fitzgerald, 3–131. New York: Library of America, 1988.

Olson, Gary A., and Lynn Worsham. "Staging the Politics of Difference: Homi Bhabha's Critical Literacy." In *Race, Rhetoric, and the Postcolonial,* edited by Gary A. Olson and Lynn Worsham, 3–39. Albany: State University of New York Press, 1999.

Osteen, Joel. *Your Best Life Now: 7 Steps to Living at Your Full Potential.* Boston: Faith Words, 2007.

Bibliography 165

Packer, George. "Southern Discomfort." *New Yorker,* January 15, 2013.

Palmeri, Frank. *Satire in Narrative: Petronius, Swift, Gibbon, Melville, and Pynchon.* Austin: University of Texas Press, 1990.

Peale, Norman Vincent. *The Power of Positive Thinking.* New York: Simon & Schuster, 2008.

Percy, Walker. "A 'Cranky Novelist' Reflects on the Church." In *Signposts in a Strange Land,* edited by Patrick Samway. New York: Farrar, Straus, and Giroux, 1991.

———. "The Failure and the Hope." *Kialegee,* Journal of the Committee of Southern Churchmen (Winter 1967–68): 16–21.

———. *Lancelot.* New York: Picador, 1977.

———. *The Last Gentleman.* New York: Picador, 1966.

———. *Love in the Ruins.* New York: Picador, 1971.

———. *The Message in the Bottle: How Queer Man Is, How Queer Language Is, and What One Has to Do with the Other.* New York: Farrar, Straus and Giroux, 1975.

———. *The Moviegoer.* New York: Vintage Books, 1960.

———. "Notes for a Novel About the End of the World." In *The Message in the Bottle: How Queer Man Is, How Queer Language Is, and What One Has to Do with the Other.* New York: Farrar, Straus and Giroux, 1975.

———. *The Second Coming.* New York: Picador, 1980.

———. "The State of the Novel: Dying Art or New Science?" *Michigan Quarterly Review 16* (1977).

———. "Stoicism in the South." *Commonweal 64* (1956).

———. *The Thanatos Syndrome.* New York: Picador, 1987.

Piehl, Charles K. "Telling About the South on Paper and Canvas." *Reviews in American History* 12 (December 1984).

Posner, Sarah. *Unholy: How White Christian Nationalists Powered the Trump Presidency, and the Devastating Legacy They Left Behind.* New York: Random House, 2021.

Poteat, Edwin McNeill. "Religion in the South." In *Culture in the South,* edited by W. T. Couch, 248–69. Chapel Hill: University of North Carolina Press, 1935.

Prescott, Peter. "The Big Breakdown." *Newsweek,* 77 1971, 106.

Puckett, Kent. *Narrative Theory: A Critical Introduction.* Cambridge: Cambridge University Press, 2016.

Ramsey, G. Lee. *Preachers and Misfits, Prophets and Thieves: The Minister in Southern Fiction.* Louisville, KY: Westminster John Knox, 2008.

Robeck, Cecil M., Jr. "Pentecostalism." In *The Oxford Companion to Christian Thought,* edited by Adrian Hastings, Alistair Mason, and Hugh Pyper, 530–32. Oxford University Press, 2000.

Robinson, Ashley. "Go West, Young Woman: Transforming Southern Womanhood through the Myth of the American West in Doris Betts's *Heading West* and *The Sharp Teeth of Love.*" *CEA Critic* 75.2 (July 2013): 109–28.

Romine, Scott. "Framing Southern Rhetoric: Lillian Smith's Narrative Persona in *Killers of the Dream.*" *South Atlantic Review* 59.2 (1994): 95–111.

———. *Narrative Forms of Southern Community.* Baton Rouge: Louisiana State University Press, 1999.

Rubin, Louis D., Jr. "W. J. Cash After Years." *Virginia Quarterly Review* 67.2 (1991): 214–28.

Samway, Patrick. *Walker Percy: A Life.* New York: Farrar, Straus and Giroux, 1997.

Schenker, Daniel. "Walker Percy and the Problem of Cultural Criticism." *South Atlantic Review* 53 (1988): 83–97.

Serebnick, Judith. "First Novelists—Spring 1961." *Library Journal* 86 (February 1, 1961): 597.

Simkins, Francis. *The Everlasting South.* Baton Rouge: Louisiana State University Press, 1963.

Singal, Daniel Joseph. *The War Within: From Victorian to Modernist Thought in the South, 1919–1945.* Chapel Hill: University of North Carolina Press, 1982.

Smith, Christian. *Christian America? What Evangelicals Really Want.* Berkeley: University of California Press, 2000.

Smith, Lillian. "Autobiography as a Dialogue between King and Corpse." In *The Winner Names the Age,* edited by Michelle Cliff. New York: W. W. Norton, 1978.

———. "Do You Know Your South?" *North Georgia Review* 6 (Winter 1941).

———. "Growing Into Freedom." *Common Ground* 4 (Autumn 1943).

———. *The Journey.* New York: World, 1954.

———. *Killers of the Dream.* New York: W. W. Norton, 1994.

———. Letters. Lillian Smith Collection. Special Collections. University of Georgia Libraries.

———. "Miss Smith: Speaking from New York." *Northwestern University on the Air: Of Men and Books.* Radio program. March 4, 1941.

———. "Personal History of 'Strange Fruit': A Statement of Purposes and Intentions." *Saturday Review of Literature* (February 17, 1945).

———. "Putting Away Childish Things." *South Today* (Spring–Summer, 1944).

———. "The South Reacts to Segregation." *New Leader* (September 3, 1951).

———. *Strange Fruit.* New York: Reynal & Hitchcock, 1944.

———. *The Winner Names the Age: A Collection of Writings.* Edited by Michelle Cliff. New York: W. W. Norton, 1978.

Smith, Lillian, and Paula Snelling. "Across the South Today." *North Georgia Review* 6 (Winter 1941).

Sosna, Morton. *In Search of the Silent South: Southern Liberals and the Race Issue.* New York: Columbia University Press, 1977.

Tolson, Jay. *Pilgrim in the Ruins: A Life of Walker Percy.* Chapel Hill: University of North Carolina Press, 1992.

Turner, John G. *Bill Bright & Campus Crusade for Christ: The Renewal of Evangelicalism in Postwar America.* Chapel Hill: University of North Carolina Press, 2008.

Waldron, Ann. *Close Connections: Caroline Gordon and the Southern Renaissance.* New York: G. P. Putnam's Sons, 1987.

Warren, Rick. *The Purpose Driven Life: What on Earth Am I Here For?* Grand Rapids, MI: Zondervan, 2002.

West, Thomas, and Gary A. Olson. "Rethinking Negotiation in Composition Studies," *JAC* 19.2 (1999): 241–51.

Whitehead, Andrew L., and Samuel L. Perry. *Taking America Back for God: Christian Nationalism in the United States.* Oxford: Oxford University Press, 2020.

Wilson, Charles Reagan. *Baptized in Blood: The Religion of the Lost Cause, 1865–1920.* Athens: University of Georgia Press, 1980.

Bibliography 167

Woodward, C. Vann. "The Search for Southern Identity." *The Burden of Southern History.* Baton Rouge: Louisiana State University Press, 1960.

Worth, Robert F. "From Bible-Belt Pastor to Atheist Leader." *New York Times,* August 22, 2012.

Wyatt-Brown, Bertram. "W. J. Cash: Creativity and Suffering in a Southern Writer." In *W. J. Cash and the Minds of the South,* edited by Paul D. Escott, 38–64. Baton Rouge: Louisiana State University Press, 1992.

INDEX

Abbott, H. Porter, 15

abortion, 82, 135–36, 137

abstractionism, 117, 118; and California spirituality, 126; in *The Sharp Teeth of Love* (Betts), 121–24; Walker Percy on, 122

activism, 2, 27, 56, 134, 135, 136–37

Acts of Narrative Resistance (Beard), 15

Agee, James, 105–6

Agrarians, 6, 42, 43

Althaus, Paul, 129

anti-intellectualism, 1–2, 6–7, 19–20, 68, 81

Applebome, Peter, 6

Arendt, Hannah, 14

Ashmore, Harry, 56

Augustine (Saint), 37; city of God/city of man, 69, 91

authoritarianism, 14, 25; resistance to, 16, 33

author's methodology, 7–10

autobiography as genre, 15. *See also* memoir as genre

back-yard/front-yard duality, 52–53

Bacon, Jon Lance, 72

Bad Faith (Balmer), 136

Bakhtin, Mikhail, 61–62, 127

Balmer, Randall, 4, 136

Baptist Church, 3; revivalism, 49–50. *See also* Southern Baptist Church

Beard, Laura, 15

Believe Me (Fea), 137–38

Betts, Doris: and abstractionism, 117–18; childhood Bible storybook, 119; religious influences, 119–21; *The Sharp Teeth of Love*, 118, 121–31

Bhabha, Homi, 101–2

Bible: Biblical literalism, 2, 82; children's stories, 119; Gospel of Luke, 35; King James Version, 16–17, 119

Bill Bright & Campus Crusade for Christ (Turner), 64

Billy Graham Crusades, 65

Bloom, Harold, 149–50n1

Bob Jones University, 6

Bright, Bill, 64

Brinkmeyer, Robert H., 13–14, 74, 78, 87, 148n11

The Brothers Karamazov (Dostoevsky), 92

Brown, Dale, 126

Brown v. Board of Education (1954), 5

Bryan, William Jennings, 4, 19, 27

Burke, Vernon, 91

business. *See* capitalism and consumer culture; sales culture

Butler, Anthea, 140

Butler Act, 4

Bynum, Caroline Walker, 124

Caldwell, Erskine, 43

Call to Home (Stack), 104–5

Calvin, John, 117

Calvinism, 25, 30, 43, 119

camp meetings (Cane Ridge, Kentucky), 2–3

capitalism and consumer culture, 28–29, 54, 64, 66–67, 72, 81, 95. *See also* sales culture

Carnegie, Dale, 68–69

Carter, Hodding, 56

Carter, Jimmy, 138

Cash, W. J., 8; alienation from religious South, 24–25; childhood and family background, 16–17; college education, 17–19; death of, 31–32; deconversion experience, 18, 21; European trip (1927), 20–21; journalism, 20–25; *The Mind of the South*, 13–14, 25–31; and narrative resistance, 8; writing process, 13–14

Cason, Clarence, 28, 31

169

Index

Catholic Church, 9, 23, 66–67; ascetic saints, 123–24; contrasted with Lutheranism, 130; conversion to, 87; Eucharist, 128; and outsider perspectives, 77–78; pro-life policies, 82; sacramentalism, 119; Walker Percy's conversion, 77, 84, 85–86

Charlotte News, 20, 21

Chartres Cathedral, 20–21

child-labor laws, 29

church affiliation and attendance, decline, 139

civil rights movement, 5–6

Clayton, Bruce, 16, 21, 23–24, 26, 27

Clinton, Bill, 137–38

Cobb, James C., 95

Coindreau, Maurice-Edgar, 148n11

Coles, Robert, 41

Columbia University, 41

community: conceptions of, 102–3; and conformity, 13; and individuality, 131, 154n1

"compliment club," 68

Confederacy, 95

confessional autobiographies, 37

Confessions (Augustine), 37–38

conformity: and authoritarianism, 13–14; clergy's role, 27–28; and homogeneity, 4, 33, 95

consumer culture. *See* capitalism and consumer culture; sales culture

conversion narratives, 37–38

COVID-19 pandemic, 134

Covington, Dennis, 9, 101–16

Cox, James, 38

Crane, George W., 67–68, 69

Criswell, W. A., 136

Cuddihy, John Murray, 54

Darrow, Clarence, 4

Deconstructing Evangelicalism (Hart), 65

deconversion narratives, 8; J. W. Cash, 18, 21; Lillian Smith, 38

Democratic Party, 4, 23

desegregation, 5–6, 136

Desmond, John, 94, 96

Dixie Dirt Dobbers, 43

Dobbs v. Jackson Women's Health Organization, 135

Dobson, James, 64, 82, 138

Donner, Tamsen (Donner Party), 122–23

Dostoevsky, Fyodor, 92

Douglass, Frederick, 38

dualism, 117–18, 129, 139, 154n2

Du Bois, W. E. B., 105

Du Mez, Kristin Kobes, 5, 139–40

Eads, Martha Green, 124–25, 128

eating disorders, 121–26

economics. *See* capitalism and consumer culture; sales culture

Edmonds, Henry M., 83

Edwards, Jonathan, 37

Egerton, John, 6

The End of White Christian America (Jones), 137

Erikson, Erik, 127

esthetic mode (Kierkegaard), 89–90

evangelical Protestantism: activism, 137–38; background and overview in American South, 1–7, 26–27; and conservative politics, 16; contradictory nature, 49, 52; culture wars, 5, 19, 82; engagement with secular culture, 6–7; fundamentalism, 81–82, 115; and modernity, 53–54; narcissism of, 50–51, 57; Old vs. New South, 93–95; pervasiveness in South, 20; political ties, 27, 31; preaching styles, 74–75; satire of, 96–97; support for Donald Trump, 134–35, 139–42; training of children, 47–48; white grievance/white supremacy, 136–37, 140–41

evangelists, circuit-riding, 49–51

Evans, Elizabeth, 119

Evans, Walker, 105

evolutionary science, 4, 19, 82

existentialism, 89

Falwell, Jerry, 82, 135, 136–37, 138

Faris, Ellsworth, 55

Fascism, 31, 145n36

Faulkner, William, 26

Fea, John, 137–38, 139

Index *171*

Finding Purple America (Smith), 1
Fitzgerald, Frances, 3–4
Floyd, George, 134
Focus on the Family, 64
Foote, Shelby, 86, 88
Forde, Gerhard, 127–29
Fortugno, Arthur, 85
The Fourth Ghost (Brinkmeyer), 13
Fowler, Doreen, 80
Freudianism, 41, 55

Gable, Sister Mariella, 75
Georgetown College, 20
Giroux, Henry, 101
Gladney, Margaret Rose, 56
Gordon, Caroline, 55, 87, 88
Graham, Billy, 5, 64, 65, 67, 69, 138
Great Awakening, 2, 64
Greene, Marti, 119
Green v. Connally (1972), 6

Hall, Jacquelyn Dowd, 104
Hardart, Frank, 84
Hart, D. G., 65
Hays, Charlotte, 82
Heading West (Betts), 121
Hegel, Georg Wilhelm Friedrich, 85
Heritage Foundation, 136
Hester, Betty, 67
heteroglossia, 61–62
Hill, Samuel S., 3
Hobson, Fred, 18, 32–33, 36, 37, 38, 56, 94
Hobson, Linda Whitney, 80
Hofstadter, Richard, 2
Holiness movement, 111, 113–15
Holy Feast and Holy Fast (Bynum), 124
Hoover, Herbert, 23
Hovis, George, 118, 121, 122, 126
How to Win Friends and Influence People (Carnegie), 68
Hunter, James Davison, 139
Hussey, John, 36–37, 105

individualism, 1, 2, 27, 78
In His Steps (Sheldon), 39
Iowa Writer's Workshop, 107

James, William, 74
Jekyll-Hyde motif, 30
Jesus and John Wayne (Du Mez), 139–40
Johnson, Walter Nathan, 17
Jones, Anne Goodwyn, 14–15
Jones, Malcolm, 95
Jones, Robert P., 137, 140–41
Jones, Sam, 39
The Journey (Smith), 56–57

Kemp, John, 94
Ketchin, Susan, 120
Key, V. O., 32
Kierkegaard, Soren, 85, 86, 89, 90–91
Killers of the Dream (Smith), 35–58, 104–5
Knopf, Alfred, 26, 27
Koresh, David, 122
Kreyling, Michael, 66
Ku Klux Klan, 23

Lakewood Church, Houston, Texas, 75
Lancelot (Percy), 78
The Last Gentleman (Percy), 78, 80, 93–97
The Law of Success (Hill), 95
Let Us Now Praise Famous Men (Agee & Evans), 105
Life is Worth Living (television program), 67
Lost Cause period (1865–1920), 4
Love in the Ruins (Percy), 78
Loveland, Anne, 41, 44
Luke, Gospel of, 35
Lumpkin, Katharine Du Pre, 36, 104–5
Luschei, Martin, 93, 150–51n3
Luther, Martin, 117
Lutheranism, 118–19, 125, 126–30
Lynch, Christopher Owen, 66–67

Macauley, Robie, 67
The Making of a Southerner (Lumpkin), 104
Marcel, Gabriel, 85
Marty, Martin, 53–54, 65
Mary and Martha (New Testament story), 35–36, 41–42
Mather, Cotton, 37
McAllister, Gracie, 112
McGill, Ralph, 55, 56

McGlocklin, Aline, 111
McGready, James, 2
McKelway, Alexander, 29
memoir as genre, 36–37, 103–4, 114
Mencken, H. L., 4, 13, 18
The Message in the Bottle (Percy), 78
Methodism, 3, 113; revivalism, 49–50
The Mind of the South (Cash), 13–33
mixed-race children, 53
Moody, Dwight L., 39
Moore, R. Laurence, 65
morality: contrasted with decency, 22; and
    religion in South, 3, 29; and women's roles,
    53
Morrison, Joseph L., 17, 18–19, 21, 23
Mouzon, Edwin, 23
The Moviegoer (Percy), 78, 80, 88–93, 97
Myrsiades, Linda, 15
mythmaking, 27

narcissism of evangelicalism, 50–51, 57
narrative negotiation, 101–2, 106, 118
narrative resistance, 8, 15–16, 36, 101
narrative satire, 9, 61–62, 80–81, 92, 95–96,
    101, 119, 151n7
narrative theory, 15
Nashville Agrarians, 6, 42, 43
New Birth movement, 2
New Essays on Wise Blood (Kreyling), 66
New South, 93–95, 110
Nichols, Loxley, 67–68
Ninety Degrees in the Shade (Cason), 31
Nixon, Richard, 6, 138
Noll, Mark, 3, 27
North Georgia Review (magazine), 42, 43

Obama, Barack, 133
occultism, 81
O'Connor, Flannery: Catholicism, 61;
    "The Fiction Writer and His Country," 62;
    influence of, 107–8; influence on Betts,
    120–21; on religion and sales culture,
    66–69; secular characters, 79; *The Violent
    Bear It Away*, 68; *Wise Blood*, 63–66,
    69–76
Odum, Howard, 20

Old South, 94–95
Olson, Gary, 101–2
The Ordeal of Civility (Cuddihy), 54
The Origins of Totalitarianism (Arendt), 14
Osteen, Joel, 75

Palmeri, Frank, 62
parachurch organizations, 5, 64–65
Parham, Charles Fox, 113
Paterna (Mather), 37
patriarchal ideals, 5, 91, 122–23, 139, 140
Peabody Conservatory, 41
Peale, Norman Vincent, 74
Pentecostalism, 103, 111, 113, 116
Percy, LeRoy, 82–83
Percy, Mattie Sue, 82–83
Percy, Walker: Catholicism, 79, 84, 85–88;
    childhood and family background, 82–84;
    early writing, 88; education, 84–85; *The
    Last Gentleman*, 78, 80, 93–97; "The Loss
    of the Creature," 122; *Love in the Ruins*,
    78; *The Message in the Bottle*, 78; *The
    Moviegoer*, 78, 80, 88–93, 97; prophetic
    literature, 79; satire and worldview, 80–82;
    The Second Coming, 62–63, 78; shock as
    strategy, 78–79; *The Thanatos Syndrome*,
    78; theology of, 77–79, 82, 150n2
Percy, William Alexander, 36, 83
Piehl, Charles K., 35
populism, 27
Porter, Carl, 106, 111
Porter, Katharine, 55
Posner, Sarah, 135–36, 137
Poteat, Edwin McNeill, 5
Poteat, William Louis, 18, 19
poverty, 40, 105–6, 108–9
The Power of Positive Thinking (Peale), 74
predestination, 25, 43, 119
Prejudices (Mencken), 18
Presbyterianism, 25, 118, 119
Prohibition, 29, 39
pro-life movement, 135–36
Pseudopodia (magazine), 42
public vs. private identities, compartmental-
    ization, 29–30, 37, 48–49
Puckett, Kent, 15

Index   173

Quinlan, Keiran, 149–50n1

Rabelais, Francois, 127
racism: and desegregation, 136–37; employed during 2016 presidential election, 133–34; and evangelical Protestantism, 140–41; racial strife, cultural legacy of, 114; systemic, 134; and white grievance, 136–37. *See also* white supremacy
Reagan, Ronald, 138
Reformation, 117–18, 127–28
religious liberty, 135, 136–37, 138
Republican Party, 6, 133, 134–35, 138–39
Restoration movements, 2
revivalism, 3, 27, 49–51, 107
Ridenour, Nina, 55
Robeck, Cecil, 113
Robertson, Ben, 36
Robertson, Pat, 64, 82
Robinson, Ashley, 121
Roe v. Wade, 135–36
Romine, Scott, 47, 105
Rubin, Louis, 13, 33

sacramentalism, 119–21, 124; Lutheran, 126, 128–29
sales culture, 51, 63, 66–67, 68, 71–72, 73–74. *See also* capitalism and consumer culture
salvation: cultural, 47; personal, 27, 50–51; and sales culture, 51; vocabulary of, 81
Salvation on Sand Mountain (Covington), 103–16, 118
Samway, Patrick, 86–87
satire, 9, 61–62, 80–81, 92, 95–96, 101, 119, 151n7
Saylor, Elvis Presley, 115–16
Schenker, Daniel, 152n31
Scopes, John, 4
Scopes Monkey Trial, 4, 19
Scottsboro, Alabama, 109–10
Seawell, Donald, 57
The Second Coming (Percy), 62–63, 78
Second Great Awakening, 3
segregation, 5–6; harms of, 43–44, 45–46
Selling Catholicism (Lynch), 66–67
Serebnick, Judith, 89

700 Club, 64
sexuality: homosexual, in *Wise Blood,* 69–70, 72; lesbianism, 56; and Lutheran theology, 129–30; racial patterns of, 49, 53
Seymour, William Joseph, 113
The Sharp Teeth of Love (Betts), 118, 121–31
Sheen, Bishop Fulton, 66–67, 69
Sheldon, Charles Monroe, 39
Simkins, Francis, 5
Singal, Daniel, 55
slavery, 3; slave narratives, 38
Smith, Al, 23
Smith, Calvin, 39–40
Smith, Jon, 1
Smith, Lillian: as bridge to Civil Rights era, 35–36; on child development, 33; critical reception and legacy, 55–58; deconversion, 41, 46–47, 57; education, 40–41; family background and early life, 38–39; *The Journey,* 56–57; *Killers of the Dream,* 35–38, 46–55, 104–5; Laurel Falls Camp, 41–42; lesbianism, 56; and narrative resistance, 8; *Strange Fruit,* 44–46; views of race, 43
snake handling, 103, 108–9, 110, 114. *See also Salvation on Sand Mountain* (Covington)
Snelling, Paula, 42, 56
socialism, 29
social justice, 29, 31
"Solid South," 4, 5
South: children raised by Black mammies, 53; internal splitting of Southern psyche, 49, 51; New South, 93–95, 110; Old South, 94–95; rural vs. urban culture, 115; "Solid South," 4, 5
Southern Baptist Church, 138–39, 140, 141; Southern Baptist Convention, 17, 136
Southern Politics in State and Nation (Key), 32
South Today (magazine), 42
Stack, Carol, 104–5
states' rights, 4, 6
Stevenson, Robert Louis, 30
Stoicism, 27, 83–84, 94
Stone, Barton, 2
Stovall, Harry, 84
Strange Fruit (Smith), 44–46

Strasbourg Cathedral, 21
suicide, 31–33, 83
Summerford, Glen/Summerford trial, 103, 109, 110
Supreme Court, 135–36, 137

Talmadge, DeWitt, 39
Tate, Allen, 87
Tell About the South: The Southern Rage to Explain (Hobson), 32–33, 36
The Thanatos Syndrome (Percy), 78
Thomas Aquinas, 77, 85
tolerance, conceptions of, 102
Tolson, Jay, 83–84, 85, 86, 87–88, 150n2
Townsend, Mary Bernice, 86
Trump, Donald, 133–34, 139; *Believe Me: The Evangelical Road to Donald Trump* (Fea), 137–38
Turner, John, 5, 64

Unholy (Posner), 135–36
United Writers of the Confederacy (UWC), 42

The Violent Bear It Away (O'Connor), 68
Voliva, Wilbur Glenn, 19
voluntarism, 3, 54

Wake Forest University, 17–19
Waldron, Ann, 87
Warren, Robert Penn, 117
Welty, Eudora, 55
Wesley, Charles, 50
Wesley, John, 50, 113
West, Anthony, 57
West, Thomas, 101–2
Weyrich, Paul, 136–37
White Evangelical Racism (Butler), 140
white supremacy, 3, 14, 26, 40, 43–44, 52–53, 134, 140. *See also* racism
White Too Long (Jones), 140–41
Whitfield, George, 50, 64
Wilson, Charles Reagan, 4, 28
Wise Blood (O'Connor), 63–66, 69–76, 148n11
Wolfe, Thomas, 26
womanhood, cult of, 52–53
Woodward, C. Vann, 6, 26, 117
Wright, Willard, 84
Wyatt-Brown, Bertram, 32

Your Best Life Now (Osteen), 75

Zwingli, Ulrich, 117